Resting Easy in the US

UNIQUE LODGING OPTIONS
FOR
WHEELERS
AND
SLOW WALKERS

Candy B. Harrington

PHOTOGRAPHS BY
Charles Pannell

Candy & Charles Creative Concepts

i

ISBN: 978-0-692430-57-6

Library of Congress Control Number: 2015939126

Candy & Charles Creative Concepts
PO Box 278
Ripon, CA 95366-0278

To Charles

Acknowledgements

A lot of people helped with the production of this book, from inception to completion. Some of them knowingly lent a hand, while others probably haven't a clue that they were helpful or inspirational to me. And although this isn't an exhaustive list, it's one that's offered up with heartfelt thanks.

To Roxanne Furlong, for suggesting that I include more photos with my property reviews. I listen to my critics.

To Beverly Blair Harzog for setting the bar high, with her 2,000-word per day goal to meet her deadline. It was truly the way I was able to push through and complete this title in a timely manner.

To Linda, Claire and Erin Wever for making sure the chickens and birdies were well cared for while Charles and I were away inspecting properties.

To Noreen Henson for her friendship, support and sarcastic sense of humor. They all helped me at one time or another during production.

To Sandra Beckwith, PR guru extraordinaire, for sharing her expertise with me, and for challenging me to get even more creative in my marketing endeavors.

To Laura Hershey who left this world far too soon, for enthusiastically sharing with me her favorite vacation property. I couldn't help but think of her (or her memory) when I wrote that chapter.

To Kimberley Barreda for constantly encouraging me to visit her neck of the woods. If I wouldn't have followed her advice I would have totally missed out on the perfect mountain lodge.

To all of my readers who offered property suggestions. Some of them worked out and some didn't, but I truly love getting reader feedback. Please keep those suggestions coming!

Last but certainly not least, to Charles Pannell for his never ending encouragement, love and support; and for his wonderful photos and awesome book design. And for not complaining when we still had "just one more" accessible room to shoot after a grueling nine-hour travel day. I couldn't have completed this project with you love!

Contents

Mountain States

Preface
Variety is the Spice of Life

When I first started covering accessible travel 19 years ago, accessible lodging options were pretty spotty. In most cases, if you wanted something that was truly accessible, you had to go to one of the big hotel chains. Don't get me wrong, I'm not dinging chain hotels, as I certainly spend my fair share of time in them; however they are far from unique. But again, they do serve a purpose.

As accessible travel gained popularity, more and more wheelchair-users and slow walkers ventured out and began exploring the world. And as their numbers increased so did the variety in accessible lodging. I first noticed this when I wrote *There is Room at the Inn: Inns and B&Bs for Slow Walkers and Wheelchair-Users*, as I looked at hundreds of properties during the research phase.

To be honest I was surprised at the number of accessible properties I found back then. After I finished that book I decided to actively seek out more unique accessible properties, and I've been collecting them every since. This book contains some of my favorites. Organized by time zones, there's a little bit of everything included in this book; from inns and B&Bs to guest ranches, cabins and even a yurt or two. I've also included some unique metropolitan hotels. The bottom line is, each property has something special about it, be it the owner, the room, the location or maybe even the whole lodging concept. Variety is the key word here.

Variety is also the key word for access — at least in this book. Although all the properties contained in this book have a minimum level of access, the access features from property to property vary. So for example, while some properties have bathrooms with roll-in showers, others have tub/shower combinations. I realize that my readers have a wide variety of access needs, and what works for one person may not exactly be ideal for another. So like in all my other work, I've described the access features in the properties contained in this book. That way readers can determine what will and what won't work for them.

And since this book is about unique properties, I've included a "Candy's Take" section with each property listing, which outlines why I like the property and what makes it unique. Also included with each property listing is a "Best Fit" section which explains what type of person would really like that property, and who it would work best for access-wise.

Of course it's also nice to know what there is to do in the area, so I've included some information about accessible sites and attractions in the "Nearby" section.

Last but not least, due to popular demand I've also included GPS coordinates with each property listing. A word of warning here though — be sure to check with the property owners or managers first (especially in rural properties), as GPS coordinates work better in some areas than others.

So dig in and enjoy. There's something for just about everyone in this book. And if you happen to come across a cool accessible property in your travels, let me know, as I'd love to check it out. Additionally, since things do change over time, I'll also be posting updates to this book on www.RestingEZ.com, so surf on by before you hit the road. And if you find some changes after you visit a listed property, let me know, so I can pass the information along.

Happy travels!

Candy B. Harrington
PO Box 278
Ripon, CA 95366
Facebook: Candy Harrington
www.RestingEZ.com
candy@EmergingHorizons.com

Pacific States

Hofsas House Hotel
Carmel-by-the-Sea, California

Located in the quaint village of Carmel-by-the-Sea, Hofsas House Hotel has been welcoming guests for over 60 years. From the Bavarian-themed welcome mural, to the Dutch doors on every room, this family-owned property simply oozes European charm. Service is first-rate too at Hofsas House Hotel, as everyone on staff is an expert on local attractions, restaurants and fun things to do. General Manager Carrie Theis is quick to pick up a map and point out the most accessible wine tasting room, or suggest the best restaurant for a romantic Sunday brunch. The hotel location is excellent too, as it's just a short walk to galleries, restaurants and shops.

Access Details

Although there are two steps up to the front office (and absolutely no room for a ramp), Carrie offers in-car registration for guests with mobility disabilities. After that, you can drive around and park right in front of accessible room 37. There are a few slight half-inch lips along the pathway to the room, but all in all it's pretty doable.

Access features in the room include wide doorways, good pathway access, and level access out to the spacious back balcony. Since the property is built into the hillside, this street level room is actually on the third floor, so the ocean view is awesome. There is wheelchair access on both sides of the 25-inch high king-sized bed, and the room is furnished with two easy chairs, a small table, a microwave and a refrigerator.

The bathroom has a full five-foot turning radius, and it's equipped with a roll-in shower with grab bars and a hand-held showerhead. The toilet has grab bars on the back and left walls (as seated), and a roll-under sink with a very spacious counter is located just outside the bathroom.

Although there's no ramp access to the lobby, Carrie is happy to deliver the daily Continental breakfast to guests who can't manage the stairs. Additionally, there is level access to the pool area and the pool has a lift; however it's best to drive down to the pool as the driveway is pretty steep.

Candy's Take

Carrie goes the extra mile for her guests, and because of her relationship with the Carmel Foundation (www.carmelfoundation.org), she can provide all sorts of medical equipment; from wheelchairs and shower chairs, to toilet risers and even walkers. She's also quite forthcoming about the access at her property, which is refreshing. Says Carrie, "If we can accommodate, we will; but I encourage people to call us and discuss their

Guestroom 37 at the Hofsas House Hotel

Bathroom in room 37 at the Hofsas House Hotel

access needs, so we can provide them with the right room. I know every property in town, and if our place won't work, I will suggest one that will." How can you go wrong with an honest manager who gives 110 percent?

Best Fit

Because of a few lips in the sidewalk on the way to the room, some folks may need a little assistance, so Hofsas House Hotel is probably not the ideal choice for manual wheelchair-users traveling alone. That said, it's the perfect location for exploring Carmel-by-the-Sea, as accessible parking is difficult to find in the village. Although there are some uneven patches of pavement on the way to the village center, it's doable for most power wheelchairs and scooters. Slow walkers who use canes or walkers should be mindful of the tripping hazards on the asphalt though; in fact high heels are not permitted in town because of these hazards.

Nearby

Shopping, dining and wine tasting are the main activities in Carmel-by-the-Sea. Interestingly enough, addresses are also prohibited (the founding fathers feared the village would become too citified if home mail delivery was allowed); however maps are available on every corner. The sidewalks are made of asphalt outside of the village center, and although there are bumps from the tree roots along the way, it's still fairly doable for most folks. Once you reach the village center, the sidewalks are paved with bricks and pavers, and there are curb-cuts at every corner. Most of the shops and galleries are located in the level section of the town center, and the majority of them have a level entrance .

The most accessible tasting rooms in the village are Scheid Vineyards (www.scheidvineyards.com), Wrath (www.wrathwines.com) and De Tierra Vineyards (www.detierra.com). They all have level access, and either a lowered tasting bar or tables.

A visit to the beach is in order too, but Ocean Avenue is pretty steep, so it's best to drive. There is accessible parking at the end of the road. From there you'll find a level path over to a short boardwalk that leads to a deck that overlooks the Pacific Ocean. Be forewarned though, it gets crowded later in the day, so try to visit in the morning. It's a great place to enjoy the sunrise.

Hofsas House Hotel
On San Carlos Street, between
Third Avenue and Fourth Avenue
Carmel-by-the-Sea, CA
(800) 221-2548
www.hofsashouse.com

GPS Coordinates
N 36.55812
W 121.92184

Mural by Maxine Albro greets guests at the Hofsas House Hotel

Creekside Inn

Guerneville, California

Nestled in the Northern California redwoods, the Creekside Inn is a great place to get away from it all. Whether it's a wine tasting weekend with the girls, or a romantic rendezvous with your sweetheart, this 28-room property offers something for just about everyone. Even better, owner Lynn Crescione puts a high priority on access, as she wants everyone to be able to enjoy her little piece of heaven.

Access Details

The inn is divided into two sections — the main house, where the office and six bed-and-breakfast rooms are located; and the surrounding buildings, which house a collection of second-floor cottages, suites and cabins. The accessible cabin is located in the latter section, with accessible parking near the office and elevator access up to the second floor. Accessible outdoor walkways and connecting decks wind through the elevated complex, to the accessible Lark Cabin.

The Lark Cabin boasts wide doorways and barrier-free pathways, and features a spacious bathroom with a roll-in shower and a fold-down shower seat. Other bathroom access features include a hand-held showerhead, shower grab bars, a roll-under sink and toilet grab bars on the back and both side walls.

The cabin is furnished with a 23-inch high queen-sized bed, and includes a roomy kitchen with a stove, sink, coffeemaker, refrigerator and even roll-out shelves. There's also a small accessible deck area outside.

Access to the public areas is good too at the Creekside Inn, with a lift available for the pool and hot tub. There's also a barbeque area with level access and an accessible picnic table. And with the Russian River flowing in the background it's the perfect place to sip a glass of wine and enjoy the natural beauty of Sonoma County.

Candy's Take

What's not to love about this property? The location is superb — smack in the middle of an old growth redwood forest, just a stones throw from the Russian River. Although trees tower around the buildings, being on the second floor puts you at eye level with Mother Nature. You never know what you'll see, and that's part of the fun of it all. Since you have everything you need in your cabin, you can cook your meals there, and enjoy them on the adjacent deck. Most of all, I love Lynn's proactive attitude about access. She had a pool lift long before it was required, and she really goes the extra mile to make things as accessible as possible.

Bedroom in the Lark Cabin at Creekside Inn

Kitchen in the Lark Cabin at Creekside Inn

Best Fit

Although the Lark Cabin is a great choice for full time wheelchair-users, one of the nature suites may also work for some slow walkers. Because of the elevator, there's access up to these second floor suites, however they don't have adapted bathrooms. So if you just can't do a whole flight of stairs, they might fill the bill.

Nearby

Ballooning is a very popular activity in Sonoma County, and Mike Kijak over at Up and Away Ballooning (www.up-away.com) offers wheelchair-accessible balloon excursions. His custom made gondola features a fold-down door, which allows for roll-on access. Because of weight restrictions, power wheelchair-users must transfer to a manual wheelchair — which Mike has on hand — for the hour-long flight; but that's really the only limitation.

Safety is a top concern too, and the gondola is equipped with tie-downs, a shoulder harness and even a safety cushion. And although the gondola was designed to be wheelchair-accessible, it's also great for slow walkers or others who are unable to climb aboard. After an early morning balloon ride over the rolling hills and colorful vineyards, passengers are treated to a champagne brunch. It's a great way to start the day.

If wine tasting is on your agenda, then check out Marimar Estate Vineyards & Winery (www.marimarestate.com), which is located just a few miles south of Guerneville in Sebastopol. The winery boasts level access to their hilltop tasting room, with barrier-free pathways to the public spaces. The tasting room, dining room and patio all reflect the Catalan style and tradition of the winery. Give the tapas and wine pairing a try. You won't be sorry!

And don't miss the majestic redwoods at Armstrong Redwoods State Natural Reserve (www.parks.ca.gov/?page_id=450). The Discovery Trail and the Armstrong Nature Trail are both wheelchair-accessible, and together they offer a good overview of the magnificent forest. Pack along a picnic lunch and enjoy it at one of the wheelchair-accessible picnic tables in the park.

Creekside Inn
6180 Neeley Road
Guerneville, CA 95446
(707) 869-3623
www.creeksideinn.com

GPS Coordinates
N 38.49932
W 122.99536

Bathroom in the Lark Cabin at Creekside Inn

Safari West

Santa Rosa, California

The brainchild of Peter Lang, Safari West is a wildlife sanctuary with a twist; it also boasts an African-style tent camp. This 400-acre game preserve is home to a bevy of exotic animals and birds, most of which roam free inside the gated compound. Visitors can take a safari tour or stay overnight in a luxury tent cabin; or both. It's almost like visiting Africa; except you don't get jet lag, you save about $4,000 and you can do it in a weekend.

Access Details

Accessible parking is located near the office. There is an accessible pathway to the office from the parking area, and a lowered check-in counter in the office. Safari West has two accessible tent cabins to accommodate overnight guests. Just like the upscale safari camps in Africa, they have hardwood floors, canvas sides and tops, indoor plumbing and electricity.

Cabin 1H is closest to the restaurant, primate enclosures and flamingo terrace. Access features include an accessible parking area just outside the cabin, a ramped entry, wide doorways and ample room to

11

maneuver a wheelchair. It is furnished with two 25-inch high double beds, with wheelchair access on both sides. The roomy bathroom is equipped with a roll-in shower with a fold-down shower seat, a hand-held showerhead and grab bars. The toilet grab bars are located on the back and right walls (as seated), and there is also a roll-under sink in the bathroom.

Cabin 2H is located directly above Cabin 1H. It has the same access features, but it is a little further from the public areas. An accessible pathway runs down to flamingo terrace from the cabin, so it's easy to roll down and enjoy a drink, or have a bite to eat in the nearby restaurant.

Both of the cabins have a roomy porch with great views of the compound. It's the ideal place to watch the sunset and enjoy a glass of wine. Plan ahead and bring the fixings for a picnic dinner. It's a fitting way to end your African safari day.

Candy's Take

There's nothing better than going to sleep listening to the sounds of the jungle. You'll hear rumblings all night, but that's the fun of it all. The tent cabins are very luxurious, but the bathrooms are vented to the outside, so those early morning showers can get chilly during the winter months. Fall and spring are ideal times to visit, but if the weather turns chilly, electric blankets are available.

Bedroom in Cabin 1H at Safari West

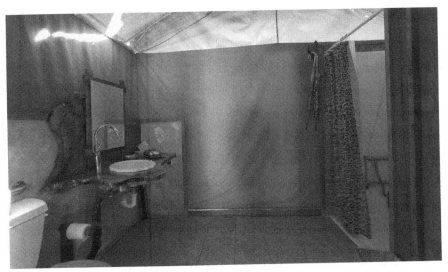

Bathroom in Cabin 1H at Safari West

Best Fit

Because of recent access improvements, Safari West is suitable for wheelchair-users as well as slow walkers. If you can't do distances, Cabin 1H is the better choice, as it's closer to the public areas. A loaner wheelchair is also available on a first-come basis. Safari West is a great choice for families, animal lovers and anybody who has ever wanted to visit the Dark Continent.

Nearby

To be honest, most people stay at Safari West to enjoy the animals in the compound, so in a sense the preserve is the main attraction. Although overnight guests are welcome to walk around the primate enclosures and check out lemur island, an accessible safari tour of the compound is available for an additional charge.

The one-and-a-half-hour-tour is conducted in a lift-equipped bus that can accommodate two wheelchair-users and three able-bodied passengers. The first part of the tour features a drive through the gated compound, where watusi cattle, cape buffalo, gazelles, zebras and giraffes roam free. The drivers are well versed about the habits of the animal residents and are happy to field questions, and stop for photos.

The walking part of the tour covers the primate enclosures near the tent cabins, in the main area of the preserve. The total distance covered is about a city block, and the pathways around the enclosures are paved and level. This part of the tour is excellent as it includes a look at the cheetahs and lemurs, and a stroll though the spectacular open-air aviary.

At least two weeks notice is required for an accessible safari tour, as it's conducted in a private vehicle, and an extra driver must be scheduled. The folks at Safari West have consistently worked to improve access since they first broke ground, so don't be afraid to let them know if you have any special access needs. This little piece of Africa really is accessible to everyone.

Safari West
3115 Porter Creek Road
Santa Rosa, CA 95404
(707) 579-2551
www.safariwest.com

GPS Coordinates
N 38.55820
W 122.70380

Shower in Cabin 1H at Safari West

Bothe-Napa Valley State Park Yurts — *Calistoga, California*

These bare bones yurts are located in the heart of California's Napa Valley, in the often overlooked Bothe-Napa Valley State Park. Filled with stands of coastal redwoods and dotted with forests of fir, oak and madrone trees, the park is usually pretty quiet — outside of the group camping area — and pleasantly devoid of crowds. And although they are very basic, the yurts provide an off-the-beaten-path accessible lodging option, in what can be a very over touristed area of the state.

Access Details

There's plenty of room to park on a level dirt pad in front of Yurt 26, with ramp access up to the front door. Access features in the yurt include a wide doorway, wooden floors and plenty of room to navigate a wheelchair inside. It's furnished with a 21-inch high queen-sized bed with wheelchair access on both sides, four folding cots, and a table with two benches.

You'll need to supply your own bedding, sleeping bags, pillows and towels; and since the yurt lacks electricity it's also a good idea to pack along a lantern, flashlights and a camp stove.

15

Outside, there is a short accessible path over to a picnic table and a storage locker. Yurt 26 is the closest yurt to the bathhouse, but Yurt 25 (which is located next door) also boasts the same access features.

The bathhouse is just a short walk away, but if you can't manage the distance, there is an accessible parking space in front of it. There is a paved level sidewalk up to the bathhouse, which features separate shower and toilet rooms.

A family restroom with a roll-under sink and toilet grab bars on the right and back walls (as seated), is located in the front, while the private pay showers are located on the side. One shower room is accessible with a wide doorway; and it includes a roll-in shower with grab bars and a built-in shower bench near the controls. Although there isn't a hand-held showerhead, a lowered showerhead has been added. There's plenty of room for an attendant, and the shower room also features a spacious changing area with lowered hooks.

The park also has a lift-equipped swimming pool near the group camping area. You will have to drive over to it, but there is accessible parking in front, and level access to the pool area.

Candy's Take

These yurts provide a very affordable lodging option in what can be an expensive neck of the woods. It's a great place to base yourself for a wine

Inside Yurt 26 at Bothe-Napa Valley State Park

Picnic area at Bothe-Napa Valley State Park

tasting weekend, if you don't require all the creature comforts of a five-star resort. As an added bonus, it's also very dark in the park, and with no ambient light you can really enjoy the night sky.

Best Fit

The yurts are a bit rustic, and to be honest, if you have back problems the mattresses won't do much for you. That said, they are accessible to both power and manual wheelchair-users as well as slow walkers, and it's a definite step up from pitching your own tent. It gives you a chance to enjoy the outdoors, sip some wine and relax as the sun sets. On the plus side, the yurts are located away from the highway, so it's very quiet.

Nearby

Unfortunately there aren't many accessible things to do in the park. The History Trail, which is located near the group campground, features a hard-packed surface, and it winds past a monument to an old church and out to the graveyard. As it gets closer to the graveyard, it gets bumpier, and although it's rated as accessible by many people, the bumps are problematic. Additionally, since it's right next to the highway, the traffic noise really takes away from the whole outdoor experience.

Wine tasting is probably the most popular activity in the area, and if you'd like to sample a number of wines in the same place, head down to

Cornerstone Sonoma (www.cornerstonesonoma.com). Located a half-hour south of Bothe-Napa Valley State Park, this unique complex is home to several tasting rooms, a few garden shops, and a quirky collection of gardens.

There's accessible parking in front, with level access to the gardens, shops and accessible restrooms. The gardens, which were crafted by a select group of landscape artists. are a creative marriage of art and horticulture. Best of all there's no admission charge.

There is level access to all the tasting rooms, and it's a pretty quiet and relaxed setting. Just down the road you'll also find Jacuzzi Family Vineyards (www.jacuzziwines.com) and Cline Cellars (www.clinecellars.com), both of which offer accessible parking and barrier-free access to their tasting rooms. And don't miss the olive oil tasting at Jacuzzi Family Vineyards. In the end, there's certainly no shortage of places to sample the local goodies, and even buy some to enjoy later.

Bothe-Napa Valley State Park Yurts
3801 St. Helena Highway
Calistoga, CA 94515
(707) 942-4575
www.parks.ca.gov/?page_id=477

GPS Coordinates
N 38.55370
W 122.52591

Asilomar Conference Center

Pacific Grove, CA

B uilt in 1913, Asilomar Conference Center was originally designed
to host YWCA leadership conferences. Today it's an architect's
dream, as 13 of the original Julia Morgan buildings still dot the
107-acre beachfront campus. Although the bulk of Asilomar's guests
are conference attendees and reunion groups, there's usually also space
available for leisure guests. And don't let the whole conference center label
dissuade you, as Asilomar is more of an oceanfront retreat, rather than
a city-center conference hotel. In fact, it's considered to be "Monterey
Peninsula's Refuge by the Sea". Additionally, as a state park, a good deal of
attention has been paid to access, and many of the historic buildings have
been remodeled to make them accessible to everyone.

Access Details

Named for a group of college women who thought the menial work they
were hired to do was well beneath them, the Stuck-Up Inn houses the
most accessible rooms in the historical section of the property. Accessible
parking is located near the front entrance and there is ramped access up

to the front door. The large public room features plenty of room to wheel around, and it has an accessible public restroom.

Rooms 401 and 413 both feature good pathway access, and bathrooms with a roll-in shower, a hand-held showerhead and a fold-down shower bench. A plastic shower bench, and a toilet seat riser with attached grab bars are also available for loan.

There is barrier-free access to other areas of the property, including Crocker Dining Hall, where communal meals are served. There is also an accessible picnic and campfire area, and a pool lift is available at the swimming pool. Additionally, a beach wheelchair is available for loan, to explore Asilomar State Beach.

Although the property is hilly in places, the management is working to make it more accessible for wheelchair-users and slow walkers. Alternatively, they have a ramp-equipped 24-hour jitney that transports guests anywhere on the property.

Candy's Take

This is definitely the place to reflect and commune with nature; in fact it's not unusual to look out your window and see deer grazing in the surrounding woodlands. I also like the communal dining arrangement, as it gives you a chance to meet other guests. It goes without saying that the old Julia Morgan buildings are a treasure, but I was also captivated by the

Room 401 in Stuck-Up Inn at Asilomar Conference Center

Boardwalk on the dunes at Asilomar Conference Center

stories of ghost sightings at Asilomar. The employees eagerly chatted about "The Lady by the Sea", who is sometimes seen walking along the coast, and the haunted banquet room which mysteriously lights up after all the guests are gone. Truth be told, I heard some strange voices one morning when I was alone in the Stuck-Up Inn public room, but it was probably just my overactive imagination. Then again, you never know.

Best Fit

The rooms are certainly accessible enough for wheelchair-users and slow walkers, but if you can't deal with taking a shuttle to some areas of the property, then you'd better pass on Asilomar. You also need to understand that this is a rustic place in the middle of nature, and sometimes a bit of Mother Nature creeps inside. If you don't like the outdoors, you absolutely won't like Asilomar. It's a great place for a family reunion or a girlfriends getaway, as the public spaces in the cabins are perfect for chats that last till the wee hours of the morning. It's also very family friendly, so if you don't like energetic kids of all ages running around and exploring the woods, then it's best to steer clear of this property.

Nearby

Of course the best thing to do at Asilomar is to enjoy the natural surroundings, and to that end there are two accessible trails on the property. Both of the trails are flat level boardwalks, that are suitable for wheelchair-users and slow walkers.

Just up the road, you'll find another must-see; Pebble Beach's famed 17 Mile Drive. Use the Pacific Grove entrance off of Sunset Drive and head over to Spanish Bay to enjoy a romantic picnic and a stroll along the beach. Spanish Bay features accessible picnic tables with great views of the bay, and a two-mile accessible boardwalk trail that follows the coastline to Bird Rock.

Littered with souvenir shops and chowder houses, Cannery Row is also worth a visit, especially if you are a John Steinbeck fan; as the as the author based many of his Cannery Row locations on the historic street. Access is good along the way, as the street is level with wide sidewalks and curb-cuts at every corner. Some of the historic buildings may have a step or two up to them, but for the most part the businesses along the way are also accessible.

Last but not least, don't forget to stop in at the Monterey Bay Aquarium (www.montereybayaquarium.org), which sits at the head of Cannery Row. There is level access to the world-class aquarium, with elevator access to all levels and barrier-free pathways to the exhibits. It's a must-do on any Monterey Peninsula itinerary.

Asilomar Conference Center

800 Asilomar Avenue
Pacific Grove, CA 93950
(888) 635-5310
www.visitasilomar.com

GPS Coordinates

N 36.61923
W 121.93573

Barretta Gardens Inn

Sonora, California

Located in the heart of California gold country, Barretta Gardens Inn is well known for its beautiful gardens and pleasant outdoor areas. This Sonora inn dates back to 1904, and quite frankly it just oozes Victorian charm. That said, innkeepers Astrid and Daniel Wasserman have added an accessible room, so this little piece of yesteryear is now accessible to everyone.

Access Details

Although there aren't any designated accessible parking spaces, there is a wide level area next to the Barretta Gardens sign, which works well for wheelchair-users and slow walkers. Take note that although there is a large "no parking" sign there, that doesn't apply to inn guests. From the parking area, just follow the path to the right, to the patio of the accessible Merlot Room. Since the historic farmhouse is not accessible, Astrid is happy to meet folks who can't negotiate steps at the Merlot Room, to complete the registration process. Just give her a call when you pull into the parking lot.

There's level access to the Merlot Room, which features good pathway access, wide doors and wood floors. The spacious room is furnished with a 31-inch high open-frame four-poster bed, with wheelchair access on both sides. It also includes an assortment of Victorian furniture and a quaint vintage soaking tub.

The nicely done bathroom has a roll-in shower with a hand-held showerhead, grab bars, a fold-down shower bench, and a very refreshing rainfall shower. The toilet grab bars are located on the left and back walls (as seated), and the bathroom also includes a roll-under sink. And with a full five-foot turning radius, there's plenty of room to roll around the bathroom.

There is also level access out to the balcony, which is a great place to enjoy the sunset. And of course the barrier-free front patio provides a nice place to relax any time of the day.

Candy's Take

This is the place to go for that romantic getaway with the one you love (or really like a whole lot). Bring along some wine and pick up some cheese and snacks in town and enjoy them on the balcony or on the private patio. Daniel also whips up a mean breakfast, which Astrid is happy to deliver to your room. There's no better way to start the day than with a long, leisurely, romantic breakfast, surrounded by a beautiful English garden.

The Merlot Room at Barretta Gardens Inn

Bathroom in the Merlot Room at Barretta Gardens Inn

Best Fit

Because of the open-frame bed and the spacious roll-in shower this property is a great choice for folks — both manual and power wheelchair-users — who travel with a portable hoyer lift. The suite has excellent pathway access, with plenty of room for scooters and large wheelchairs. It's also good for someone traveling with an extended family, group or an attendant, as the adjoining two-bedroom Sangiovese Suite can be opened up to accommodate larger parties. And of course, if you want a more intimate getaway, it's my top pick for a romantic retreat.

Nearby

Calaveras Big Trees State Park (www.parks.ca.gov/?page_id=551), located just outside of Arnold, tops the list of nearby attractions. It's just a short 45-minute drive to this off-the-beaten-track state park, which features two Giant Sequoia groves, with wheelchair access through both of them. The 600-foot Three Senses Trail offers a good introduction to the grove, while the one-and-a-half-mile North Grove Trail features hard-packed dirt paths and boardwalks around the massive trees and over damp areas of the forest.

After you've had your fill of hiking, head over to Ironstone Vineyards (www.ironstonevineyards.com) in nearby Murphys. With over 5,000 acres of vineyards, it's a great place to get a good overview of the winemaking process. Access is good in most areas of the winery, and free tours of the facility (including the wine-aging caverns) are offered daily. Although the walking tour covers a large area, golf cart transportation is available for slow walkers. Don't miss the 44-pound gold nugget in the Heritage Museum, and the 1,200-pipe organ in the Alhambra Music Room. And of course, save some time for some wine tasting before you head on your way.

Barretta Gardens Inn
700 South Barretta Street
Sonora, CA 95370
(209) 532-6039
www.barrettagardens.com

GPS Coordinates
N 37.97659
W 120.37814

Shower in the Merlot Room

Tallman Hotel

Upper Lake, CA

Constructed in 1890, the Tallman Hotel is truly a historic landmark. In the early days the property was frequented by gun-toting cowboys, and visitors who came to take the waters at the nearby hot springs. Over the years the hotel changed names and ownership a number of times, before it was abandoned and fell into disrepair. Enter Bernie and Lynne Butcher who bought the property, renovated it and welcomed their first guests in 2005. Today this boutique property boasts modern-day luxuries, but retains the charm of yesteryear.

Access Details

Located on Main Street, the Tallman Hotel features accessible parking in front, and access to the main lobby through the blue gate on the right. The accessible Farmhouse Suite (Room 13) is located behind the main building, and is connected to the rest of the complex by a level garden pathway. There is additional accessible parking in the lot behind the hotel, which is located just a few steps from the Farmhouse Suite.

The suite itself is very spacious with a bedroom, bathroom,

kitchenette and living area. There is barrier-free access throughout the suite and the vinyl floors and low pile carpeting make wheeling a snap. The bedroom includes a king-sized bed and there is also a fold-out sleeper sofa in the living room.

The bathroom features a full five-foot turning radius, a roll-under sink and a tub/shower combination with grab bars and a hand-held showerhead. Toilet grab bars are located on the back and left walls (as seated), and a portable shower bench is available upon request.

There is barrier-free access to the public areas of the hotel, including accessible pathways through the garden and level access to the pool and spa area. A pool lift is also available. A Continental breakfast is served in the dining room in the main building; however you can also request to have it delivered to your room. Even though the dining room is accessible, breakfast in your room is a more intimate and relaxing affair.

Candy's Take

Twenty years ago it was difficult to find a historic property that also had wheelchair access. Gladly that's not the case today, and the Tallman Hotel is a prime example of the changing tide. When the Butcher's made renovations to the property they planned for access, but they were also able to retain many historic features. For example, the front facade, with several steps up to the porch, was retained, while an alternate accessible

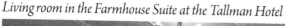

Living room in the Farmhouse Suite at the Tallman Hotel

Bedroom in the Farmhouse Suite at the Tallman Hotel

pathway was added. The result is the best of both worlds, and it's nice to do business with people who go the extra mile to make their property accessible to everyone.

Best Fit

There's plenty of space to maneuver a wheelchair in the Farmhouse Suite, so this property is a good choice for wheelchair-users and slow walkers who can use a an accessible tub/shower combination. Because of the sleeper-sofa, it's also suitable for a small family or someone traveling with an attendant. History buffs will simply love the property, and since it's just over two hours from San Francisco, it makes a good weekend getaway or an add-on to a west coast trip. Wine lovers will also enjoy the unpretentious tasting rooms that dot the county.

Nearby

The Blue Wing Saloon (which was also renovated by the Butcher's) is located next door, and is open for lunch and dinner. The menu features California comfort foods, microbrews and local wines. There is ramped access to the front entrance and plenty of room to maneuver inside. Save some time to meander along Main Street too. It's not very busy and there are curb-cuts on most corners and level access to most of the businesses. It's just a pleasant place to stroll.

If you like wine, then Lake County is the place for you. Billed as California's newest wine region, it's home to a plethora of small wineries, many of which are accessible. At the top of the list is the Wildhurst Vineyards (www.wildhurst.com) tasting room in the old IOOF hall in downtown Kelseyville. It has a ramped entrance with barrier-free pathways inside, and a very accommodating staff.

For a change of pace check out the Lakeport Historic Courthouse Museum (the first floor is accessible), or pack a picnic lunch and enjoy the accessible picnic area in Clear Lake State Park. Alternatively, you can always enjoy a scenic drive around the lake. Truly you can do as little or as much as you want to in Lake County, which makes for a very relaxing getaway.

Tallman Hotel
9550 Main Street
Upper Lake, CA 95485
(707) 275-2244
www.TallmanHotel.com

GPS Coordinates
N 39.16530
W 122.91067

Bathroom in the Farmhouse Suite at the Tallman Hotel

Manzanita Lake Camping Cabins

Lassen Volcanic National Park, CA

L ocated an hours drive from Redding, Manzanita Lake Camping Cabins are the newest lodging addition to Lassen Volcanic National Park. Built in 2011, they provide a very comfortable and accessible alternative to tent camping. They are located near the north park entrance, and although they lack electricity and bed linens, they make up for that in spades with acre after acre of magnificent scenery. And since you should allow at least two days to explore this Northern California national park, these cabins are the ideal home base for any Lassen visit.

Access Details

Although the cabins lack a traditional lobby, the camp store has a small registration desk. There's accessible parking in front of the camp store, level access to the entrance, and plenty of room to maneuver a wheelchair inside. From there it's just a short drive to Cabin 14, the most secluded accessible unit.

Reserved parking is available in back of the cabin on a level dirt pad, and although it's not striped, there's plenty of room for an accessible van and another vehicle. There's ramp access to back of the cabin via a wide ramp that winds around to the front porch. There are also steps up to the front porch, with handrails on both sides for slow walkers.

The cabin is furnished with a 19-inch high double bed (bedding not included), a dining table and two chairs. Although the pathway access is a bit tight as configured, if the bed is pushed all the way up against the far wall, there is a 36-inch access aisle on one side. The cabin comes equipped with a battery powered lantern and a propane heater, and it has a locking door, screened windows and a bare wood floor.

There are two chairs and a small table on the front porch, and an accessible picnic table and a fire grate in a dirt area in front of the cabin. There is also an accessible bear box nearby. Accessible pit toilets with grab bars, and potable water are located across the street from the cabin.

Men's and women's showers are located next to the camp store. They feature level access and each shower room has a private roll-in shower with a fold-down shower seat, grab bars and a hand-held showerhead. The adjacent changing areas have a fold-down seat, a lowered clothing hook and an accessible coin slot. Lowered mirrors are also located in both shower rooms. A restroom with a large accessible stall, grab bars and a roll-under sink is located next door.

Candy's Take

Although there are three other accessible cabins in the loop (1, 8 and 18), Cabin 14 is the most remote as it's located at the end of the road. Very few people wander down that way, so you'll pretty much have things to yourself. With a partial view of Manzanita Lake, it's the perfect place to just sit back on the porch and enjoy the scenery. It's also pretty dark at night, which makes for some great star gazing. Make sure and pack along a flashlight though, in case you have to make an after hours trek to the facilities.

Best Fit

Although the literature says that the cabin can accommodate three people, it would be very cozy if one of them was a wheelchair-user. It would also

Inside of Cabin 14 at Manzanita Lake in Lassen Volcanic National Park

not be a good choice for two wheelchair-users or anyone with a large power wheelchair. You can certainly make more room inside by moving the dining table out to the front porch, and realistically the only time you need to spend inside is when you turn in for the night. Because of its out-of-the-way location it's a great choice for a romantic getaway. It should be noted that the three-inch thick vinyl covered foam mattress is very firm, so it's best to pack along an egg crate or an air mattress if that's not your cup of tea.

Nearby

There are several accessible sites to explore in Lassen Volcanic National Park (www.nps.gov/lavo). The best place to begin your visit is at the Kohm Yah-mah-nee Visitor Center, located near the south entrance. Here you'll find accessible parking and level access to the building, which has a ranger on duty, interpretive exhibits and an orientation film. There's also level access to the cafe and picnic tables, as well as the paved Geological Timeline walk out back.

Sulphur Works, which is located just up the road, offers accessible parking and restrooms, with a paved pathway up to a collection of roadside sulphur pots, steam vents, mud pots and boiling springs.

The Devastated Area, located half-way to the north entrance, is also worth a stop. A half-mile hard-packed accessible trail leads through this area, which was obliterated by a mud flow after the 1915 Mt. Lassen eruption.

And don't miss the Loomis Museum, up near Manzanita Lake. This 1927 building features ramp access on the side, and it's filled with historic photos of the 1915 eruption.

Manzanita Lake Camping Cabins
39489 Highway 44 East
Singletown, CA 96088
(530) 335-7557
www.lassenrecreation.com

GPS Coordinates (Lassen Volcanic National Park)
N 40.49766
W 121.42066

Golden Eagle Vacation Rentals — *Trinidad, CA*

There's a certain ethereal quality to California's magnificent redwood coast; a quality that's echoed in a peaceful Trinidad property that's perched on a rocky bluff and surrounded by a stand of redwood and spruce trees. Golden Eagle Vacation Rentals features five secluded cabins that are located about 18 miles south of one of the most accessible groves of old growth coastal redwoods. Constructed in 2012, one of the cabins was built to be accessible; and proprietor Marke Matthews is very proud of that addition. Not only does he do everything in his powers to make all of his guests feel welcome, but he's also a veritable encyclopedia of knowledge on the local area.

Access Details

At first glance the property looks like a private home, and it is. Marke's house is located at the front of the property, and the cabins are down the road in the rear. The Orca Cabin features accessible parking on a cement pad, with ramp access to the front porch. From there, there's level access to the wide front door, and plenty of room to navigate a wheelchair inside.

The wood floors are also a plus for wheelchair-users.

The kitchen is equipped with a microwave, refrigerator, oven, dishwasher and coffee maker, and is nicely outfitted with a variety or dishes, pots, pans and utensils. The adjacent living area features a gas fireplace surrounded by a comfy love seat and an easy chair. And over in an alcove there's a 26-inch high queen-sized bed with wheelchair access on one side.

The bathroom has a full five-foot turning radius and is equipped with a tub/shower combination with a fold-down shower seat, a hand-held showerhead and grab bars. The toilet grab bars are located on the left and back walls (as seated), and the bathroom also has a roll-under sink.

Top it all off with a pair of rockers on the front porch, and a tranquil pond below, and you have a very comfortable and secluded cabin.

Candy's Take

The motto of Golden Eagle Vacation Rentals is "health, wellness and peaceful tranquility is our brand," and they certainly live up to their promise. This is the perfect place to unwind, de-stress and be at one with nature. I woke up one morning and found a doe and fawn grazing just below our deck; and the wood tones and furnishings of the cabin almost bring the outside in. It's a good choice for nature lovers, and although the

Kitchen in the Orca Cabin at Golden Eagle Vacation Rentals

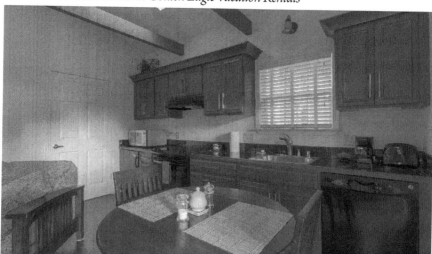

cabins are located close to one another, they are pretty private. Marke also respects his guests privacy.

Best Fit

Because of the size of the cabins, it's unlikely you'll find kids there, so it's a good choice for a couples getaway or a romantic retreat. That said, even though the bathroom is roomy enough to accommodate large power wheelchairs and scooters, if you absolutely need a roll-in shower, the Orca Cabin isn't for you. Additionally, depending on the size of your assistive device, you may need to rearrange some of the furniture for better pathway access. Still, because of the size of the place, that's totally doable.

Nearby

There's no shortage of natural sites in the area, but one of the closest ones is Prairie Creek Redwoods State Park (http://www.parks.ca.gov/?page_id=415). Located in nearby Orick, this stand of old growth coastal redwoods also boasts a number of accessible options.

The Newton B. Drury Parkway, which bisects the park, makes a very scenic drive. Although there are some nice windshield views along the 10-mile route, you'll definitely want to stop and get an up-close-and-personal look at the Big Tree, near the Visitor Center. There's accessible parking and restrooms near this wayside exhibit, and a 100-yard paved path to the tree. There's ramp access up to this 304-foot giant, which towers over the surrounding forest.

If you'd like to take a hike through the grove, the accessible Prairie Creek Foothill Trail is just up the road. The 2.3-mile loop combines portions of the Prairie Creek Trail and the Foothill Trail for an accessible hike through the virgin forest.

The loop starts just to the right of the Visitor Center and follows fern-lined Prairie Creek for 1.2 miles. The trail is hard-packed dirt, and although it's not totally level, the grade is up to code and there are level spots every 50 feet, with benches to rest along the way.

Bear right at the fork in the trail, and follow the signs to the parkway. After you cross the parkway, continue along to the Big Tree. From there it's another .9 miles back to the Visitor Center. It's a beautiful hike, which meanders through the old growth forest and even includes a tunnel through a downed redwood. Although there are no picnic areas along the way, there are benches and logs where you can enjoy your repast. Best of all, it's not a heavily trafficked route, so you'll probably have the forest to yourself.

Golden Eagle Vacation Rentals
3751 Patricks Point Drive
Trinidad, CA 95570   N 41.09814
(707) 677-9550   W 124.15750
www.goldeneaglevr.com

GPS Coordinates

Bathroom in the Orca Cabin at Golden Eagle Vacation Rentals

Yosemite Bug Rustic Mountain Resort — Midpines, CA

Yosemite Bug Rustic Mountain Resort began its life as a youth hostel. Over the years additions were made, and although dormitory rooms are still available, today the property has morphed into a full service mountain resort. Granted it still has an airy fairy feel to it all, but that's part of its charm. The property exudes a definite international ambiance, as backpackers and families from around the world flock to this very affordable lodging option near Yosemite National Park.

The cafe has a good selection of vegan and vegetarian dishes, while hostel guests share a communal kitchen. Everyone seems to exist in harmony at the Yosemite Bug. It doesn't feel crowded either, as the hotel rooms are housed in cabins perched on a tree covered hillside. And even though the property has some rustic touches, it also boasts a nicely accessible room.

Access Details
Accessible parking is available to the left of the office, with ramp access

up to the office in the back of the building. There is a wide doorway and plenty of room to navigate a wheelchair inside the office. From there, it's best to drive up to the accessible Sentinel A cabin, as it's located at the top of the property.

There is accessible parking in the lot adjacent to the Sentinel A cabin, with ramped access up to the shared front porch. The cabin features a wide doorway with good pathway access between two 24-inch high opened-framed queen-sized beds. A desk, two easy chairs and a dresser round out the furnishings.

The bathroom features a five-foot turning radius, and is equipped with a roll-in shower with grab bars and a fold-down shower seat. The shower controls are easily reachable from the shower seat, but there isn't a hand-held showerhead. The toilet grab bars are located on the left and back walls (as seated), and there is also a pedestal sink with a lowered mirror in the bathroom. It's a very spacious, accessible and well-designed bathroom

There is also good access to the public areas of the property, including the Yosemite Bug Cafe; which serves up a nice mixture of organic and sustainable menu items. Prices are reasonable, and they have a good selection of locally sourced dishes. Even if you don't stay there, it makes a nice lunch stop on the way to Yosemite National Park.

Inside Sentinel A Cabin at Yosemite Bug Rustic Mountain Resort

Candy's Take

One of the best things about this property is that it's close enough to Yosemite to visit it, but it's a world away from the hustle and bustle and the commercialism of Yosemite Valley. You can sit back on the porch and listen to sounds of the forest, smell the fragrant wildflowers and enjoy the peace and quiet. Although I love Yosemite National Park, the tourist aspect of the valley tends to take away from the beautiful natural surroundings. The Yosemite Bug is a great place to chill.

Best Fit

This property will work for both manual and power wheelchair-users and slow walkers, as the bathroom is large enough to accommodate large wheelchairs and scooters. The one caveat is that you really need a vehicle to stay here, as you have to drive from the office and cafe up to the accessible room. The pathway is pretty steep, and not wheelchair-accessible at all.

Nearby

Yosemite National Park (www.nps.gov/yose) is the big attraction in the area. It's just a 26-mile drive to the park, but if you'd like to leave the driving to someone else you can always take the Yosemite Area Regional Transit (YARTS) bus (www.yarts.com). The bus stop is located about a half-mile from the office, and since the road is far from level it's best to drive down to the bus stop and park in one of the pull-outs. The YARTS fleet has accessible buses, but 48-hours advance notice is required to secure a seat on one. The bus stops at the Yosemite Visitor Center, and from there you can catch an accessible shuttle bus, which stops at the major sites in Yosemite Valley.

Although there are a number of accessible sites in Yosemite Valley, the trails at Yosemite Falls and Happy Isles top the list. The paved loop trail at Yosemite Falls starts next to the shuttle stop and winds through the forest to the base of Yosemite Falls. The half-mile Happy Isles Nature trail is paved and level, with wooden bridges that cross over the Merced River. And don't miss the Happy Isles Nature Center, which has an interesting collection of interpretive exhibits and interactive displays about the area's natural history.

Yosemite Bug Rustic Mountain Resort
6979 Highway 140
Midpines, CA 95345
(866) 826-7108
www.yosemitebug.com

GPS Coordinates
N 37.57460
W 119.95132

Bathroom in Sentinel A Cabin at Yosemite Bug Rustic Mountain Resort

Orchard Hill Country Inn

Julian, CA

Perched on a hill on the outskirts of Julian, the Orchard Hill Country Inn is the perfect place to escape from the hustle and bustle of city life. This romantic inn features 22 cottages and guest rooms, but because of the placement of the cottages throughout the property, it also offers a high degree of privacy. Even when the property is sold-out, it never feels crowded. The grounds are dotted with gardens and nooks, which are perfect for some alone time; while the comfortable lobby is a great place to mingle with other guests and chat with the innkeepers about Julian's colorful past. The large patio, just off the lobby, offers sweeping views of the countryside, and it's a great place to enjoy a glass of wine and watch the sunset. Top it all off with some glorious star-gazing opportunities, and this luxurious country estate has everything you need to unwind, relax and recharge.

Access Details

Accessible parking is located near the entrance, with level access to the lobby. The accessible room (Room 2) is just around the corner, and it features a wide doorway with a lowered peephole. It's furnished with a 29-inch high queen-sized bed, adorned with a homey country quilt.

The spacious bathroom is outfitted with a roll-in shower with grab bars and a hand-held showerhead, toilet grab bars on the back and right walls (as seated) and a roll-under sink with a lowered mirror. The full five-foot turning radius makes it easy for everyone to navigate. A portable shower chair is also available upon request.

There's also barrier-free access through French doors out to a small private patio. And of course, they even remembered to lower the closet rod.

Guests are invited to enjoy afternoon wine and hors d'oeuvres in the lobby or on the adjacent patio, both of which feature barrier-free access. There's also level access to the dining room, where a full breakfast is served every morning.

Candy's Take

As an added bonus they also serve dinner at the inn on select nights. The view from the dining room is magnificent, and since there's only one dinner seating it's very relaxed. You set the pace, not the server. Suffice it to say, it's pretty exclusive, and reservations are required. Be sure and let them know if you are celebrating an anniversary, as they pull out all the stops with some special surprises. The menu features local produce, wines and specialties; and the presentation and the

Room 2 at the Orchard Hill Country Inn

Bathroom in room 2 at the Orchard Hill Country Inn

quality is top-drawer. The service just can't be beat either, but that's true in all areas of the inn.

Best Fit

The access at this property is first-rate, making it a good choice for wheelchair-users and slow walkers. That said, wheelchair-users will probably want at least one chair removed from the room, for better pathway access, but the innkeepers are very happy to do this. Since the property simply oozes romance, it's a great choice for a honeymoon, anniversary or a romantic getaway. Conversely, it's not a good choice for a family vacation; in fact children under four cannot be accommodated in the lodge rooms.

Nearby

The inn is within walking distance of downtown Julian; however it's best to drive because it's also on top of a steep hill. Accessible parking is available behind the Chamber of Commerce, on the corner of Washington and Main Streets.

From there, head down Washington Street to the Julian Pioneer Museum (www.julianpioneermuseum.org), on the corner of Washington and Fourth Streets. There's a barrier-free pathway to the museum, through the park next door. The bulk of the museum in housed in Joseph

Treshil's former blacksmith shop, which features level access and plenty of room to wheel around inside. It boasts a wide variety of artifacts, an impressive collection of mining equipment, an unusual lace collection, a plethora of taxidermy and a number of exhibits about the old gold rush days in the city.

Next door, the Grosskopf house is furnished as it would have been at the turn of the century. There's a one-inch step at the entrance, but you can see just about everything inside through the front and side windows. Even if you can't manage the step, it's worth a gander.

Save some time to wander along Main Street, which is fairly level. Most of the business along this street have level access, although it's not always at the front door. Many of the historic building have alternate entrances in back, so make sure and watch for signs. A number of small shops and boutiques line the street, and there's no shortage of places to sample some fresh apple pie or other tasty treats.

If you'd like to get the insider's scoop on historic Julian, then sign up for a personalized walking tour with David Lewis (www.julianhistory.com). He's happy to tailor his tours to individual needs. Says David, "Some of the terrain in Julian is pretty steep, but we will figure out how to get you to wherever you need to go."

Orchard Hill Country Inn
2502 Washington Street
Julian, CA 92036
(800) 716-7242
www.orchardhill.com

GPS Coordinates
N 33.08016
W 116.60198

Shower in room 2 at the Orchard Hill Country Inn

Apples Bed & Breakfast Inn

Big Bear Lake, CA

Built in 1993, Apples Bed & Breakfast Inn is the brainchild of Jim and Barbara McClean. This 19-room Victorian style country home features large, comfortable rooms, as well as some very pleasant public spaces. The focal point of the 15,000 square-foot house is the gathering room, which features a wood burning fireplace, a baby grand piano, a game table and a library of books, games and movies. Guests are offered appetizers and apple cider here in the afternoon, and home made desserts and coffee in the evening. The décor throughout the house reflects the apple theme, but it's not overdone. It's just a very comfortable place to hole up for a few days.

Access Details

There's ramp access up to the back door, with level access into the gathering room. The accessible Crabapple Room is located on the main floor, and is furnished with a 28-inch high king-sized bed and two recliners. It also features a bay window which offers a good view of the grounds, and a gas fireplace to snuggle up in front of on those chilly nights.

The oversized bathroom is equipped with a tub/shower combination with grab bars, a hand-held showerhead and a fold-down shower seat. Toilet grab bars are located on the back and left walls (as seated), and the bathroom also features a lowered vanity and a roll-under sink.

It's just a short roll to the dining room, where breakfast is served; and all of the main floor public spaces offer good access. All in all, it's a very comfortable place to rest your head.

Candy's Take

The McClean's get a big thumbs-up for knowing how to make guests really feel welcome. They are friendly, but not over solicitous, and they always know just when to offer something or strike up a conversation. They also know when to give folks a little privacy, which is equally important. And then there was breakfast, which was just divine. It began with fresh cranberry applesauce, and included a cereal course of muesli, some apple dumplings, and a delicious vegetable quiche. They even had turkey sausage for me, since I don't eat red meat. It's the little touches like that, that really made my stay extra pleasant. Seriously, the McCleans could teach a course on hospitality.

Best Fit

Because of the height of the bed and the tub/shower combination, this

The gathering room at Apples Bed & Breakfast Inn

The Crabapple Room at Apples Bed & Breakfast Inn

property is best suited for slow walkers. That said, if you have some good upper body strength, and are traveling with someone else, you can probably manage the bed. If you absolutely, positively have to have a roll-in shower, then this property isn't for you. Since Big Bear Lake is home to the premier adaptive skiing program in the US, it's a good choice for anyone who wants to learn to ski. In fact, the United States Adaptive Recreation Center (www.usarc.org) at Bear Mountain Resort offers a full menu of snow sports, including downhill skiing, snow shoeing and snowboarding. They have a large collection of adaptive skiing equipment and they are a member school of the Professional Ski Instructors of America.

Nearby

Big Bear Lake is also home to the Alpine Pedal Path. This 3½-mile trail starts at the Stanfield Cutoff, runs along the north shore of the lake, and ends near the Solar Observatory. It's paved, mostly level and a great choice for wheelers and slow walkers.

There are a number of different access points along the trail, but one of the most accessible choices is Juniper Point. Located just east of the Big Bear Discovery Center, it features plenty of accessible parking and an accessible restroom. You will need to purchase an Adventure Pass at the Big Bear Discovery Center in order to park at any of the access points; however, if you have an America the Beautiful Access Pass you can just display that on your vehicle.

Although you can go either direction on the Alpine Pedal Path from Juniper Point, the section to the right is fairly level and it includes a short boardwalk section and a nice view of the lake. The portion of the trail to the left of the parking area is equally scenic, however the initial downhill section may be too steep for some wheelers.

If you'd like to enjoy some fun on the lake, the United States Adaptive Recreation Center also offers adaptive water skiing, jet skiing, stand-up paddle boarding, sailing and fishing during the summer months. If you love the outdoors, then Big Bear Lake is for you.

Apples Bed & Breakfast Inn
42430 Moonridge Road
Big Bear Lake, CA 92315
(909) 866-0903
www.applesbigbear.com

GPS Coordinates
N 34.24160
W 116.87664

Bathroom in the Crabapple Room at
Apples Bed & Breakfast Inn

Glorietta Bay Inn

Coronado, CA

Originally the stately home of John Dietrich Spreckels, the Glorietta Bay Inn is located just across the bay from San Diego on upscale Coronado Island. The 11-room Italian Renaissance mansion was constructed in 1906, and over the years it's had a variety of owners. In 1975 a group of San Diego businesspeople acquired it, renovated it and converted it to a hotel. Today this historic landmark boasts a large accessible suite in a new wing, so now everyone can enjoy this elegant old property.

Access Details

Accessible parking is available near the lobby, with a barrier-free pathway to the main building. Although steps grace the front entrance of this former estate, a wheelchair-accessible entrance has been added in the back. Just follow the signs.

Room 443 is a good choice for wheelchair-users and slow walkers. It's located behind the main building, with accessible parking close to the front door. The one-bedroom suite features good pathway access, wide doorways and plenty of space. The living area is furnished with a 14-inch high king-sized sofa bed, a desk with a chair, and a dining table with three chairs. The adjacent kitchen is equipped with everything you need to prepare a tasty dinner, and it includes a stove with an oven, a microwave, a refrigerator and a coffee maker. There is also a bar with two stools in the corner.

The spacious bedroom features a king-sized bed with access on both sides, and a lowered closet rod in the closet. The bathroom is equipped with a roll-in shower with a hand-held showerhead, grab bars and a fold down shower seat. The toilet grab bars are located on the left and back walls (as seated), and there is a sink and a large vanity in the alcove just outside the bathroom.

There is good pathway access to the public areas of this garden-like property, and the swimming pool is equipped with a pool lift. Best of all, it's located right across the street from the ocean.

Candy's Take

I love the old world feel to the public areas of this historic property, and the fact they were able to make it accessible without destroying that. It's also just across the street from the beach, which means you can park your car for the length of your stay. Driving can be a pain on the island, as there's a lot of traffic, and the timed restrictions on certain left turns

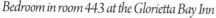

Bedroom in room 443 at the Glorietta Bay Inn

Bathroom in room 443 at the Glorietta Bay Inn

follow no rhyme or reason. The location of this inn just couldn't be better for beachgoers.

Best Fit

This property is a good fit for all abilities, as a lot of thought was put into the access upgrades. The accessible suite is very roomy, and with the sofa bed in the living room, there's plenty of room for an attendant. It's also a good choice for families, as the full kitchen allows folks to dine in and cut down on restaurant expenses. It's a very comfortable and homey suite.

Nearby

The big attraction on Coronado Island is the beach, and although sand and wheelchairs usually don't mix, that's not the case on Coronado Beach.

If you'd like to explore the beach, just follow the sidewalk from the Glorietta Bay Inn out to the Central Lifeguard Station, where power beach wheelchairs and surf chairs are available for loan.

The power beach wheelchairs are a cross between a manual beach wheelchair and a power wheelchair. They have big balloon tires, but they operate with a joystick, just like a power wheelchair. Even if you don't use a power wheelchair on a daily basis, after a brief orientation you'll be tooling along the beach in no time.

If you'd like to go into the water, then you might want to check out the hippocampe surf wheelchair. It looks like a sports wheelchair with off-road tires, and it has one small wheel in the front and a push bar in the back. If you can self-propel yourself in a manual wheelchair, you can self-propel in the hippocampe. If not, then the push bar in back allows easy access for an attendant. Either way, you can go out into the water in the hippocampe, and when the chair starts to float you can get out and swim. Then when you're ready to go back to shore, just climb back in the hippocampe, and repeat the process in reverse.

To borrow these beach toys, just use the intercom at the lifeguard station, and let them know what you'd like. It's that easy. The equipment is usually available on a walk-up basis during the week, but it's best to call the lifeguard station at (619) 522-7346 and reserve it if you plan to visit on the weekend.

Glorietta Bay Inn
1630 Glorietta Boulevard
Coronado, CA 92118
(619) 435-3101
www.gloriettabayinn.com

GPS Coordinates
N 32.68176
W 117.17638

Shower in room 443 at the Glorietta Bay Inn

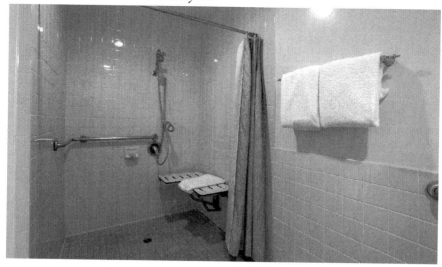

Miramonte Resort

Indian Wells, CA

Located in Indian Wells, just 30 miles from Palm Springs, Miramonte Resort offers luxurious accommodations in a Mediterranean village setting. This Southern California resort features 215 rooms housed in individual villas, on 11 park-like acres filled with olives trees, rose gardens and citrus groves. No only is there good access throughout the lush gardens that surround the villas, but access in the rooms is also nicely done.

Access Details

There's plenty of accessible parking near the lobby, with level access to the front entrance. From there, it's just a short drive to the villa that houses accessible Room 1251.

There is accessible parking in front of the villa with level access to the room. Inside, you'll find wide doorways and good pathway access to a very spacious room, furnished with a 28-inch high king-sized bed, with wheelchair access on both sides. Other furnishings include a desk, table and chair, an easy chair and a refrigerator.

55

The bathroom has a roll-in shower with grab bars, a hand-held showerhead and a portable shower chair. The shower is 41 inches wide and 47 inches deep, with plenty of room for most transfers. The bathroom also includes a toilet with grab bars on the left and back walls (as seated). A roll-under sink is located in an adjacent alcove, and there's even a lowered make-up mirror on the counter.

A sliding glass door with a level threshold leads out to a semi-private patio shielded by a hedgerow. It's furnished with a table and two chairs, however they can easily be moved to the grass for better pathway access.

Behind the building there's the adults-only Piedmont pool, which features good access around the pool, and lifts for the pool and the hot tub. The main pool, which is located near the lobby, is equally accessible. There is ramp access up to the hot tub area, and barrier-free access around the main pool and cabanas. Although this is the family pool, the kids are a well behaved lot, so it's still a pleasant place to relax. And if you want to ramp up the relaxation a bit, there's also level access to the spa from the main pool area.

Candy's Take

I love the healthy vibe of this spa property, which even extends to the Grove Restaurant. The menu includes a selection of fresh healthy foods, and the servers are happy to substitute healthier side dishes on request. It's

Room 1251 at the Miramonte Resort

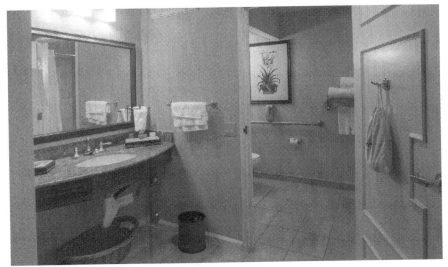
Bathroom in room 1251 at the Miramonte Resort

the perfect way to embrace the "Live Well Be Well" philosophy that makes the Miramonte Resort such and relaxing and refreshing retreat. And of course, like the rest of the property, the restaurant is wheelchair-accessible.

Best Fit

The spacious ground floor accessible room is big enough for larger wheelchairs and scooters, and the paved level pathways throughout the campus are ideal for slow walkers. Bottom line, this property is a good choice for all wheelchair-users and slow walkers. Because of the spa and the healthy menu in the Grove Restaurant, it's a good choice for a wellness weekend or a spa getaway. And because of the secluded adults-only pool, it's also a good pick for a romantic retreat.

Nearby

The Palm Springs Aerial Tramway (www.pstramway.com) is a must-see while you're in the area. There's plenty of accessible parking at the Valley Station, which is the lower terminus of the tramway. Although the front entrance to the station has three flights of stairs, there's also a stair lift for folks who can't manage them. Inside the station there is barrier-free access to the ticket counter and roll-on access to the tram.

The tram travels 2.5 miles up Chino Canyon to the Mountain Station in Mt. St. Jacinto State Park. The view along the way is spectacular, and the tram cars have a rotating floor, so you can see the whole canyon. And if you'd prefer to sit, there are also a few benches on board.

Up at the top you can grab a bite to eat and enjoy the view. There is also a small museum and a movie about the tram. Access at the Mountain Station is pretty good, with level access to most of the viewing areas, shops and facilities. Stay as long as you want, then take the return tram back at your leisure.

Miramonte Resort
45000 Indian Wells Lane
Indian Wells, CA 92210
(760) 341-2200
www.miramonteresort.com

GPS Coordinates
N 33.72060
W 116.33094

Toilet and shower in room 1251 at the Miramonte Resort

Hotel deLuxe

Portland, OR

Located on the fringe of Portland's downtown district, the Hotel deLuxe simply oozes charm. Formerly the Hotel Mallory, this 1912 property underwent an $8 million renovation in 2006. Today the posh lobby features a13-foot LCD screen that flashes glamorous images from Hollywood's Golden Age, while the adjacent hallways are adorned with black-and-white matinee idol photos. It's a touch of nostalgia tastefully done. And the good news is, they didn't skimp on access when they remodeled this stately old gem.

Access Details

Although stairs grace the front entrance of the property, a street level elevator runs up to the basement, and connects with another elevator that serves the lobby and guest rooms. Upstairs, there's barrier-free access to the front desk, Gracie's restaurant and The Driftwood Room lounge.

The property offers a number accessible guestrooms with roll-in showers or tub/shower combinations. They feature wide doorways, lever handles, lowered peepholes and good pathway access. There's also plenty of room for a wheelchair on either side of the beds. The bathrooms are equally spacious and feature a full five-foot turning radius; and are equipped with toilet and shower grab bars, hand-held showerheads and roll-under sinks. And they didn't forget the little things — like angled mirrors and lowered robe hooks — which make the bathrooms usable as well as accessible.

The accessible tub/shower combination units also have a unique two-way fold-down shower seat. Actually it's two shower seats, mounted on two different walls. One seat folds down perpendicular to the tub edge, while the other folds down parallel to it. The addition of the extra seat allows for a wider variety of transfer options, and makes the tub/shower combination accessible to more people. It's a good solution to an all too common problem.

Candy's Take

This is just a cool retro property. Everywhere you go there are pictures and film clips from Hollywood classics. I also have to say that the staff is first-rate. When I discovered that my jewelry pouch was missing after I departed, the hotel sent someone back up to my room lickity split to search for it. Of course I felt like an idiot when I found it in the outside pocket of my suitcase, but the helpfulness of the employees really impressed me. And don't miss happy hour in The Driftwood Room

Vendors at Pioneer Courthouse Square

Bathroom in an accessible room at the Hotel deLuxe

lounge, where you can enjoy a bottle of wine, one of their signature drinks or a light bite from the menu. It's the perfect start to a night on the town, and a must-do on any Portland visit.

Best Fit

This property is an excellent choice for anybody with a mobility disability, due to the variety of accessible rooms. Whether you prefer a roll-in shower or a tub/shower combination, you'll find exactly what you need at the Hotel deLuxe. It's also an great choice for old movie buffs. And if you'd like to explore Portland sans car, there's a bus stop right around the corner. Public transportation is very plentiful and accessible in Portland. The property is also within walking distance of Pioneer Courthouse Square, which is home to a few pods of the over 500 food trucks in the city. If you want to eat like a Portlander, you just have to try a food truck or two.

Nearby

If you want to hang with the locals, then head on over to the Portland Art Museum (www.portlandartmuseum.org), located just a few blocks from Pioneer Courthouse Square. Although there are steps at the front entrance, there's also an accessible ramp on the left side of the museum. Once inside, you'll find elevator access to all floors and plenty of room to roll around in the galleries. As the oldest museum on the West Coast, it's known for its impressive collections of English silver, graphic arts and Native American art. It's just a fun place to linger.

The Oregon Zoo (www.oregonzoo.org) is also worth a visit, and it's just a short bus ride away. Access is good throughout the zoo, with barrier-free pathways to all areas. That said, it's built in a canyon and covers a lot of ground, so pick up a zoo map and plan your route carefully. Save some time for a ride on the Zoo Train, which makes a 10-minute loop around the perimeter, and is equipped with a wheelchair-accessible car.

Of course no visit to the City of Roses is complete without a visit to the International Rose Test Garden. Located on the other side of Washington Park, the test garden features more than 9,000 plantings of 560 rose varieties; and on a clear day, you'll also get a great view of nearby Mt. Hood. There's ramp access down to the garden near the Rose Garden Store, with good access to most areas of the garden. Although there are a few steep ramps and steps here and there, you can still get a good look at things no matter what your ability.

Hotel deLuxe
729 SW 15th Avenue
Portland, OR 97205
(503) 219-2094
www.hoteldeluxeportland.com

GPS Coordinates
N 45.52099
W 122.68770

The International Rose Test Garden in Portland, Oregon

Pana Sea Ah Bed and Breakfast — *Depoe Bay, OR*

Built in 1999, the Pana Sea Ah Bed and Breakfast is located smack dab in the middle of the Oregon Coast, in the charming town of Depoe Bay. If you like coastal views, scenic drives and a casual, unpretentious atmosphere, then this is the place for you. In fact, innkeepers Bob and Mary Hauser relocated from Southern California several years ago, precisely because of those attributes. Since then they've built another house nearby, so guests now have full run of this 3,200-square foot property. So although the Hauser's are very attentive, you can rest assured you'll have all the privacy you need to enjoy a very romantic getaway on the beautiful Oregon Coast.

Access Details

The ground-floor Tuscany Suite features level access from the nearby garage. That said, the driveway is steep; so steep that a car door will not stay open by itself. To make access easier, Mary is able to leave the garage open upon request, and from there it's a short level roll to the front door.

Access features in the two-room suite include a 32-inch wide entry door and good pathway access throughout the unit. The queen-sized bed is 30 inches high, however Mary will gladly make up the 18-inch high futon in the sitting room. She can also bring in an upright chair to the sitting room, if the futon is too low for a comfortable transfer.

The tiled bathroom features a roll-in shower with a fold-down shower seat and a hand-held showerhead. There are grab bars in the shower and on the left side of the toilet (as seated). There is also a roll-under sink in the spacious bathroom, and a stackable washer and dryer just outside.

Additionally, the suite is equipped with all the creature comforts, including a cozy fireplace, a refrigerator and a microwave. It's also pet-friendly, and there's access to fresh drinking water right outside the front door.

Breakfast is served upstairs, on the second floor; however there is a level entrance from the back parking lot. Although breakfast can be deliverd, it's well worth the short drive around to the back, as the ocean view is magnificent.

Candy's Take

It's very easy to settle down with a good book and linger on the deck for hours. Since there are only four rooms in this property, it's not busy, and it's a great place to get some undisturbed me-time. Mary also knows the area very well, and she's spot-on with her dining and attraction suggestions, which is always a welcome attribute in an innkeeper.

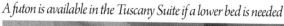

A futon is available in the Tuscany Suite if a lower bed is needed

Riverview Trail at Tillamook Forest Center

Best Fit

This property will work for most wheelchair-users and slow walkers. The suite is certainly spacious enough for most wheelchairs, however since the front door only has 28-inches of clearance space, it might not work for folks with larger wheelchairs. This is a nice place for a quiet romantic getaway, but only if you like the ocean. Because it's so quiet, it's also a good choice for a personal retreat.

Nearby

One of the main attractions in the area is the scenic coastal drive up Highway 101. Tillamook, which is located just a one-and-a-half-hour-drive north, is a good choice for a day trip. Not only is it a very scenic drive, but there are several accessible attractions to visit once you arrive.

The Tillamook Air Museum (www.tillamookair.com) tops the list, as it has over 30 restored warbirds on display, in a former durgible hangar. There is level access to the hangar, which also features exhibits about soldiers stationed at NAS Tillamook during World War II.

Just up the road you'll find the Tillamook Cheese Factory (www.tillamook.com), which features accessible parking near the entrance with level access to the front door. Inside, there's good access to the restaurant and elevator access to the second floor, which overlooks the production area. After a short self-guided tour be sure to sample some cheese downstairs, and pick up your favorites in the gift shop.

Last but not least, don't miss the Tillamook Forest Center (www. tillamookForestCenter.org), which is located about 20 minutes outside of town. This interpretive center tells the story of the devastating forest fires of 1933, 1939 and 1945 — otherwise known as the Tillamook Burn. There's level access to the visitor center, and wheelchairs are available for loan at the front desk. Outside, you can pick up the accessible Riverview Trail near the parking lot. This short trail winds through a section of lush forest along the river. As an added bonus, there are also some accessible picnic tables along the way, so pack along a lunch and enjoy some quality time with Mother Nature.

Pana Sea Ah
Bed and Breakfast
4028 Lincoln Avenue
Depoe Bay, OR 97341
(514) 764-3368
www.panaseah.com

GPS Coordinates
N 43.73300
W 59.78906

Bathroom in the Tuscany Suite at Pana Sea Ah Bed and Breakfast

Crater Lake Lodge
Crater Lake National Park, OR

The historic Crater Lake Lodge dates back to 1915, when this lakeside beauty welcomed travelers who journeyed for days over unpaved trails and roads to visit the caldera lake. Back then accommodations at the lodge were minimal, but tourists gladly accepted the substandard accommodations, as they were just happy to have a bed after their arduous trip. Over the years more creature comforts were added, but sadly the structure itself was in danger of failing. Finally in 1991 an ambitious $15, 000,000 renovation project began. Over the next four years the building was gutted and a new structural support system and modern hotel amenities were added. Today the property is once again the grand old lady of the lake, only now she sports some upgraded access features.

Access Details

At first glance the front entrance of the lodge doesn't look very accessible, with steps leading up to the front door; however there's also a ramp tucked away on the left side. There is a drop-off area in front, and the accessible parking spot is located on the side, close to the accessible room. Best bet is to

67

use the drop-off area, go in and register, then drive around to the accessible parking spot. Accessible Room 107 is just a short walk from the side door.

The room features a wide doorway and a lowered peephole, and is furnished with a 26-inch high bed with wheelchair access on both sides. Other furnishings include a desk with a chair, and a side chair. There's plenty of room to navigate even the largest wheelchair in the spacious room.

There's a wide doorway to the bathroom which is equipped with a tub/shower combination with a fold-down seat, grab bars and a hand-held showerhead. The toilet grab bars are on the back and right walls (as seated), and there is also a roll-under sink in the bathroom. As with the guest bedroom, there is plenty of space in the bathroom.

There is also good access to the public areas of the lodge, including the great hall, the terrace and the dining room. Guests can enjoy a selection of beverages, appetizers, soups, salads and desserts in the great hall or on the terrace; or indulge in a full menu of Northwest specialties in the dining room. The terrace offers the best views of the lake, but you'll also get an eyeful if you snag a window table in the dining room.

Candy's Take

The property exudes the charm of a 1920s lodge, and although it's a bit rustic it has all the comforts of a modern day property. The public spaces are very comfortable and I absolutely love the terrace. It's the perfect place

Room 107 at Crater Lake Lodge

Crater Lake in Crater Lake National Park

to enjoy a glass of wine or a light snack and watch the sunset over the lake. There's also a nice paved trail in front of the terrace that offers a number of different views of the lake.

Best Fit

The accessible room is large enough to accommodate a wheelchair or a scooter, however if you need a roll-in shower this property won't work for you. It's ideally located to explore Crater Lake, and unlike some of the chain hotels near the park, it has a rustic outdoorsy feel to it. Book early though, as it's a very popular choice.

Nearby

There are plenty of accessible things to see in Crater Lake National Park (www.nps.gov/crla) and the best place to begin your visit is at the Rim Visitor Center, just down the road from Crater Lake Lodge. There's level access to the building, which has interpretive exhibits, an information desk and a great view of the lake.

The most accessible way to enjoy Crater Lake is to take the Rim Drive, a 31-mile loop that circles the caldera. For the best windshield views take the drive in a counterclockwise direction starting with West Rim Drive. The most accessible viewpoint is Discovery Point, which has accessible parking with curb-cut access to the lower viewpoint. The entire drive takes about an hour if you drive it straight through, but allow extra time to stop along the way.

If you'd like to leave the driving to someone else, there is an accessible trolley tour which travels clockwise around the lake and stops at four viewpoints. This two-hour ranger guided tour departs from the Community House at Rim Village. It is conducted in a lift-equipped trolley, with space for two wheelchairs. Ticket sales begin at 9 a.m. for the first tour, which departs at 10 a.m.

And if you'd like to take hike, the Godfrey Glen Trail is the most accessible trail in the park. This 1.1-mile loop is rated as "accessible with assistance", and it travels through an old growth mountain hemlock and shasta fir forest. The hard-packed trail has some ruts and tree roots along the way, but most are passable. The biggest obstacle is the steep grade along some sections. Best bet it to travel in a clockwise direction, and double back when it gets too steep. Even if you can't complete the whole trail, you'll still get some nice canyon views along the way.

Crater Lake Lodge   **GPS Coordinates**
565 Rim Drive   N 42.91278
Crater Lake National Park, OR 97604 W 122.07224
(541) 594-2255
www.craterlakelodges.com

Bathroom in room 107 at Crater Lake Lodge

South Beach State Park Yurts

Newport, OR

Although yurts are quite common in Oregon state parks, South Beach State Park has the largest selection, including five wheelchair-accessible units. These domed structures with wooden floors, which are common in Mongolia, offer a great alternative to tent camping. Not only does South Beach State Park offer this rustic lodging option, but it also boasts a bevy of accessible recreational opportunities along the scenic Oregon coast.

Access Details

The yurts are located in the Cooper Ridge Loop, and since there are only eight units there, it's the quietest section of the campground. All of the accessible yurts have the same features, but Yurt 8 offers the most privacy, as there are no neighbors on one side.

There's level parking on a hard-packed dirt pad in front of the yurt, with an accessible path over to the ramped porch. The yurt has a wide doorway and is furnished with a table and two chairs, a bunk bed with a double on the bottom and a single above (bedding not included), and a futon that folds out. The futon and bottom bunk are 21 inches high, with wheelchair access on one side when the futon is folded up. The yurt also has electricity and a heater.

Although there are no cooking facilities in the yurt, there's plenty of room to set up a camp stove on the spacious front deck. There is also a picnic table with two benches and two chairs on the deck, and an accessible fire ring and another picnic table in a level area next to the yurt.

An accessible porta-potty is located between yurts 4 and 6; but flush toilets and showers can be found in Loop A, which is adjacent to the Cooper Ridge Loop. There's a level path with good signage leading to the bathhouse, and although it's a bit bumpy in places, it's doable for most folks.

An accessible family shower room is located in back of the bathhouse. It features a wide doorway with plenty of room to maneuver a large power wheelchair or scooter, and it's equipped with a roll-in shower with grab bars, a hand-held showerhead and a fold-down shower bench. The toilet grab bars are located on the back and right walls (as seated), and there is also a roll-under sink with a lowered mirror in the spacious room. The whole room is well designed, and it's also very private, with plenty of room for an attendant.

Candy's Take

A lot of places have accessible yurts, but I was thrilled to find some great

Inside Yurt 8 at South Beach State Park

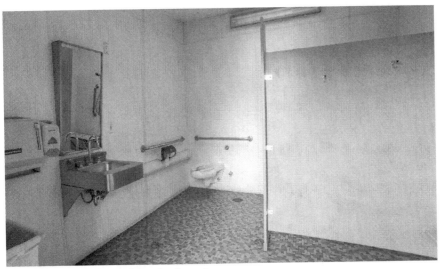
Family bath/shower room located in Loop A

accessible trails near this one. In fact, you can park your car for your entire stay and still manage to enjoy the beach. I also like the fact that recreational vehicles are prohibited in the Cooper Ridge Loop, so there's no generator noise. And the yurts are very affordable. It's a great place to commune with nature; in fact, we were lulled to sleep by the sound of barking sea lions.

Best Fit
The yurt will work for wheelchair-users and slow walkers, but it would be tight for a wheelchair with the futon folded out into a bed. The accessible shower room is very spacious, and will accommodate large wheelchairs and scooters. It's a good choice for a family getaway, even though the playground is located in another loop. It's perfect for a multigenerational getaway, or you could rent out the whole yurt loop for a family reunion.

Nearby
There are a number of accessible trails in South Beach State Park but the best way to get out to the beach is to take the quarter-mile paved trail which begins next to space A10. This wide level trail leads through a woodland area, then opens up to an accessible boardwalk over the dunes. Once you reach the beach overlook, there's an accessible viewing platform with a bench to sit and enjoy the view.

If you'd rather drive to the trailhead, the accessible beach boardwalk is about 400 yards from the day use area, just off the accessible South Jetty Trail. There's plenty of accessible parking in the day use area, with barrier-free access to some picnic tables on a level grassy area. There is an accessible stall in the nearby restroom, and although it has grab bars, it doesn't have enough turning space for a wheelchair or scooter.

The South Jetty Trail continues past the accessible boardwalk turnoff, and ends at the South Jetty. This mile-long multi-use trail is paved and level, and it's a great choice for wheelers and slow walkers. Down at the South Jetty there is an accessible porta-potty, and plenty of room to roll around and enjoy the jetty views. And if you'd like to do the trail in reverse, you can also access the South Jetty area from a nearby parking lot.

South Beach State Park Yurts
Newport, OR 97366
(541) 867-4715
www.oregonstateparks.org/index.cfm?do=parkPage.dsp_
parkPage&parkId=149

GPS Coordinates
N 44.60518
W 124.06067

Shower in the family bath/shower room

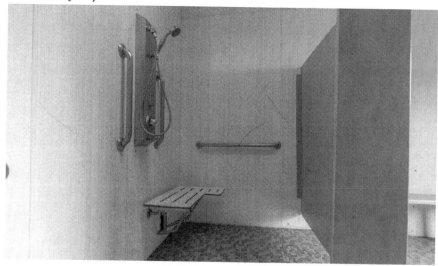

Skamania Lodge

Stevenson, WA

Located 45 minutes from Portland, Skamania Lodge is situated on 175 acres of prime real estate high above the Columbia River. The property is named for the Chinook word for "swift water", which seems appropriate, as there are over 70 waterfalls nearby. Suffice it to say that the views are spectacular from just about every corner of the property. But the scenery is only half the story at Skamania Lodge — the architecture is the other half. Built in 1993, the building was modeled after the great lodges of the early 1900s, with a high-pitched roof, exposed beams, wood paneling and lots of native stone. The lobby is typical of the architectural style, with a massive 85-foot tall andesite rock fireplace, black wrought iron artistic highlights and comfortable furnishings. This creative use of materials and nostalgic design evokes memories of yesteryear, and makes Skamania Lodge a very comfortable, yet rustic retreat.

Access Details

There is an accessible pathway to the lobby from the nearby parking area, and a convenient drop-off area near the front entrance. The property features good pathway access to all the public areas, including the gift shop, restaurants, library and adjacent conference center. This 254-room mountain resort boasts 11 accessible rooms; including eight with a tub/shower combination and three with a roll-in shower.

The accessible guest rooms all have good pathway access, a lowered peephole, lever handles and lowered closet rods. The spacious bathrooms are equipped with either a tub/shower combination or a roll-in shower; and they include a hand-held showerhead, grab bars in the shower and around the toilet, a roll-under sink and a portable shower bench.

There's good access to the public areas of the lodge too, including the restaurants and meeting rooms. And don't miss the garden and back lawn area, which features ramp access from the back patio. It's the perfect place to enjoy the sunset, or to just sit back and settle in with a good book.

Candy's Take

I like the rustic feel of the lodge, and the fact that they used a lot of reclaimed materials, to really give you the feel of days-gone-by. The Gorge Room floor is made from salvaged wood from a 200-year old building, while the timber columns came from the former Bumble Bee Cannery in Astoria. And the stone for the lobby fireplace was salvaged from a nearby abandoned quarry. I also love the outdoor areas of the lodge; it's as if the lodge extends out onto the patio and back lawn. And last but not

Accessible room at Skamania Lodge

Shower and sink in an accessible room at Skamania Lodge

least, Skamania Lodge gets a big thumbs-up for including those often-overlooked access details, like lowered soap dishes in the roll-in showers.

Best Fit

Because of the selection of accessible rooms, this property will work equally well for slow walkers and wheelchair-users. Just be aware that some accessible rooms have a tub/shower combinations, while others have a roll-in showers, so make sure and specify your needs when you make a reservation. This is also a great place for people who like to enjoy the outdoors, but prefer to retreat to more comfortable quarters for the evening. And since there's no shortage of scenic drives in the Columbia River Gorge, Skamania Lodge also works well for road-trippers.

Nearby

The big attraction in the area is Multnomah Falls, located a little over eight miles east of Crown Point on the Oregon side of the Columbia River. The falls are spectacular; however a word of warning about access. You may see signs directing you to take exit 31 off Interstate 84 for this attraction; however that exit takes you to a remote parking lot. For best access, take Highway 30 and park near the falls. You'll get a great view, with level access and less walking. Additionally, try and hit this top attraction as early in the day as possible, to avoid the crowds.

If you'd like to sample some local wines, then hop back over to the Washington side of the river and stop in at the Maryhill Winery (www.maryhillwinery.com). There is accessible parking near the entrance, and although the lot is gravel, the accessible spaces are on cement slabs. The tasting room features level access, as does the patio and back deck. Sit down and enjoy a glass of one of their premium red wines out on the patio, or gather around the fireplace inside. Although the winery looks unremarkable from the front; the view of the mountains, river and vineyards from the back deck will really wow you.

For a unique end to a very scenic drive, head up the road to Maryhill Stonehenge; the most unusual attraction along the Columbia River Gorge. Located just past the Highway 97 junction on the south side of Highway 14, this full-size replica of Stonehenge was erected as a memorial to local soldiers who died in World War I.

There's no striped parking, but you can drive right up and park near the monument. Most of the areas are pretty level and quite wheelable; plus, like everything else along the gorge, it boasts a spectacular view.

Skamania Lodge
1131 SW Skamania Lodge Way
Stevenson, WA 98648
(509) 427-7700
www.skamania.com

GPS Coordinates
N 45.68562
W 121.90524

Toilet in an accessible room at Skamania Lodge

Hotel Murano

Tacoma, Washington

Named for the famous Venetian glass, the Hotel Murano is located smack dab in the middle of Tacoma's vibrant museum district, just a short walk from the cornerstone Museum of Glass. This boutique property is decorated with the works of prominent artists, and like the other Provenance properties, it showcases the city's local culture. Each floor is dedicated to a specific artist, with their works prominently displayed in the rooms, as well as the public areas of that floor. From the moment you walk in the door, it feels like you've entered a gallery.

Access Details

There is level access to the ground floor lobby, with elevator access to the upper floors. Room 1900 is a very spacious accessible suite, with wide doorways and good pathway access throughout it. The living area is furnished with a dining table and chairs, two easy chairs and a sofa that opens out into a king-sized bed.

The bedroom has a 27-inch high king-sized bed with wheelchair access on one side. There is level access to the large bathroom, that is equipped with a roll-in shower with grab bars, a fold-down shower bench and a hand-held showerhead. Other access features include a roll-under sink, a toilet with grab bars on the left and back walls (as seated), and a lowered mirror.

A second bathroom, located just off the living area, features a standard tub/shower combination, a toilet, and a pedestal sink. It's all very nicely done, and you can even close off the front part of the suite for more privacy if you are traveling with an attendant.

There is also level access to the Bite Restaurant down on the fourth floor, which serves Pacific Northwest dishes prepared with fresh local ingredients.

And even though it's located up a slight hill from Pacific Avenue, there is a barrier-free route down the accessible Link train from the hotel. Just take a right on Broadway in front of the hotel, head down to 15th Street, cross the street and enter the Convention Center. From there take the elevator down to Commerce Street and catch the Link train.

Candy's Take

I just love the artsy flair of this property — it's very refreshing, and definitely not a cookie-cutter property. The food at the Bite is tasty, but the view of Mt. Rainier from the restaurant just can't be beat. And speaking of views, you can even see the Chihuly Bridge of Glass from Room 1900.

Bedroom in room 1900 at Hotel Murano

Bathroom in room 1900 at Hotel Murano

Best Fit

Wheelchair-users and slow walkers will be equally comfortable here, as the access is top-drawer. It's a great choice if you'd like to park the car for a few days and explore the museum district on foot, as there are many attractions, shops and restaurants within walking distance. The free Link train, which features roll-on access, is just a short walk away. It's also a good choice for anyone traveling with an attendant, as you can close off the living area to make it a true two-room suite.

Nearby

There are several top-notch attractions within walking distance of the Hotel Murano. Tacoma Art Museum (www.tacomaartmuseum.org) boasts an impressive Chihuly collection, and includes over 400 pieces of glass artwork from the Paul Marioni collection. Access is good throughout the museum, with level access at the Pacific Avenue entrance. Accessible parking is available in the back parking lot, with elevator access up to the back entrance.

Union Station, which is right next door to the art museum, also features some unique Chihuly pieces. The rotunda boasts a trademark Chihuly chandelier, while the windows are adorned with orange floats and reeds. Access features include a level threshold, good pathway access inside, and elevator access to the upper floors. There's no admission charge, but since the building now houses a courthouse, a valid ID is required.

Out back there is ramp access to the Chihuly Bridge of Glass, which connects Union Station with the Museum of Glass. The bridge begins with on overhead collection of shapes and forms, then transitions to two large columns of blue-green glass, and concludes with a showcase of individual Chihuly pieces.

And don't miss the Museum of Glass (www.MuseumofGlass.org), which features ramp access down to the front entrance from the glass bridge, and level access to the front lobby. Take a few minutes to enjoy the glass installation in the front fountain, which features a collection of floats and other objects. Inside, there's barrier-free access to all areas of the museum, which showcases the works of 20th and 21st century glass artists.

Hotel Murano
1320 Broadway Plaza
Tacoma, WA 98402
(253) 238-8000
www.hotelmuranotacoma.com

GPS Coordinates
N 47.16140
E 122.44146

Mount Rainier view from room 1900 at Hotel Murano

Kalaloch Lodge

Forks, WA

Named for the Quinault word for "a good place to land", Kalaloch Lodge sits on a coastal strip of Olympic National Park. Although the property has traditional lodge rooms, the rustic wood-sided cabins that dot the oceanside bluff are the premium accommodations. Cozy and quaint, the cabins have all the comforts of home, yet they are refreshingly absent modern day electronic distractions. You won't find phones, televisions or wifi in any of the cabins, and that's a definite plus. What you will find is a quiet sanctuary to relax and enjoy the magnificent Pacific coast.

Access Details

Accessible parking is available in front of the lodge, with ramp access up to the Creekside Dining Room. There are two steps down into the gift shop (which doubles as the office), so it's best to go around to the accessible sliding door on the left.

The accessible cabin (Cabin 40), is located close to the office, with a wide parking area in front. It's not striped, but it's reserved for cabin guests, and there's plenty of room for an accessible van. There's ramp access to the front door of this duplex cabin, with good pathway access inside.

The full kitchen features a roll-under counter and sink, and is equipped with a refrigerator, stove, microwave and coffee maker. It has all the pots, pans, dishes and utensil you could possibly need. A tall table with four bar stools sits just off the kitchen, and bar seating is also available.

The adjacent living room has an 18-inch high double futon, two easy chairs and a wood burning stove. Although the dining room table is not accessible, a fireside meal is a nice alternative. A separate bedroom has two 30-inch queen-sized beds with an access aisle between them, a night stand and a dresser.

There is a wide doorway into the spacious bathroom that is equipped with an oversized roll-in shower with grab bars, a hand-held showerhead and a lowered soap dispenser. The shower is four feet deep and over six feet long, and there is a full five-foot turning radius outside the shower. There is a toilet grab bar on the right side (as seated), and the bathroom also includes a roll-under sink and a portable shower chair. Even the small touches, like a lowered mirror and lowered robe hooks were included.

Outside there is an accessible picnic table on the grass. And if you'd like to explore a bit, you'll also find a flashlight, walking sticks and binoculars in the cabin.

There is good access to the public areas, including the mercantile and the Creekside Dining Room. An accessible family restroom is also located next to the mercantile.

Living room in Cabin 40 at Kalaloch Lodge

Bedroom in Cabin 40 at Kalaloch Lodge

Candy's Take

I like the quiet isolation of this place, and its close proximity to the Olympic National Park (www.nps.gov/olym) beaches. I also like the healthy choices available in the Creekside Dining Room. The calories are printed on the menu, and they have gluten-free, dairy-free, heart healthy and organic selections. From gluten-free buckwheat pancakes for breakfast, to a full selection of soups, salads and sandwiches for lunch, there's something for everybody. And the dinner menu offers tasty selections like weathervane scallops, penn cove mussels and chicken stuffed with walnuts and feta. They also have a light eater menu, which features smaller portions.

Best Fit

The cabin has excellent access, with one of the largest roll-in showers I've ever seen, so it's a good pick for all wheelchair-users and slow walkers. And if you travel with an attendant, the futon in the living room will give you both an added bit of privacy. Because it's a duplex cabin it might not be the best choice for a romantic getaway, but it would be perfect for a family vacation. You can also reserve the other half of the duplex for a larger family gathering, as there is a door to the adjoining cabin from Cabin 40.

Nearby

The dramatic coastline is the big draw of the area, and you can get a good view from the gazebo on the property. There is a slight bump up to it, but most folks can manage with a little assistance. There is also a picnic table on the grass near the gazebo that offers an equally spectacular view.

Just down the road you'll find Beach 4, which has accessible parking and restrooms, as well as a level hard-packed dirt trail out to a beach overlook. There are a few ruts and rocks near the first part of the trail, but most are easy to dodge. There is also a picnic table on a grassy area near the parking lot, and although it's a little high you can always set your food on the bench.

Ruby Beach is also a must-see. It has accessible restrooms, and level access from the dirt parking lot to the overlook. From there you'll get an impressive view of the log-strewn beach below. Although there are a few bumps along the way, it's doable for most people. There is also a picnic table at the top of the drive, before the asphalt road gives way to a dirt path. It's located on a level grassy area, and it's a good place for a lunch break.

Kalaloch Lodge
157151 Highway 101
Forks, WA 98331
(360) 962-2271
www.thekalalochlodge.com

GPS Coordinates
N 47.60290
W 124.36965

Toilet and Shower in Cabin 40 at Kalaloch Lodge

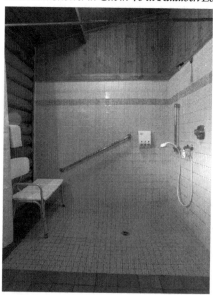

Lake Crescent Lodge

Port Angeles, WA

Built in 1915, Lake Crescent Lodge started out life as a tavern with seven sleeping rooms upstairs. Today the original tavern serves as a restaurant and lobby, while the upstairs rooms have been remodeled, and a variety of outbuildings have been added. Although it's still the oldest lodge in Olympic National Park, the most recent renovation included the addition of some modern accessible rooms. It's a far sight more accessible than it was when President Roosevelt visited in 1937, and that's due in part to the actions of former Manager Todd Gubler. Says Gubler, "I really try to connect with my guests, and our access improvements are a direct result of guest feedback." And that responsive customer service approach led to a very comfortable and accessible property.

Access Details

There's ramp access up to the historic main building, with level access into the lobby. The most accessible rooms are located in the Marymere lakeside building, which is just a short walk away. Accessible parking is located near the building, with a barrier-free path to the front door of Room 101.

Inside, there's good pathway access on both sides of the two 24-inch high queen-sized beds. The other furnishings, including the chest of drawers, are placed well outside the path of travel.

There's a wide doorway into the bathroom, which is equipped with a tub/shower combination, with grab bars, a hand-held showerhead and a wooden tub bench. The bench is removable, and a plastic shower chair is available upon request. The toilet grab bars are located on the back and right walls (as seated), and the bathroom also has a roll-under sink. And they even remembered the lowered robe hooks. Best of all, thanks to the choice of burnished copper grab bars, the room lacks the institutional feel common in many accessible rooms.

There is level access out to the shared back porch, which offers a nice view of the lake. Room 102, which is located next door, has the exact same access features.

There is also a barrier-free path over to the main lodge, good access to the restaurant, and level access out to the adjacent dock.

Candy's Take

I really like that they were able to make the historic main building accessible, yet keep the character of it. The glassed-in porch, which is just off the lobby, is a nice place to have a glass of wine and some appetizers,

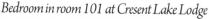

Bedroom in room 101 at Cresent Lake Lodge

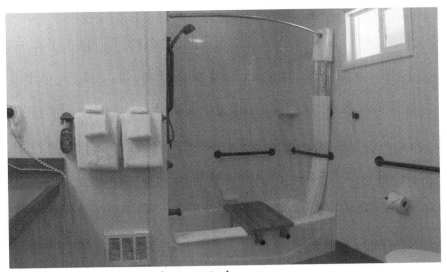

Tub / Shower in room 101 at Lake Cresent Lodge

and enjoy what is often described as "the best view of Olympic National Park". The servers in the restaurant are also very attentive. When I was obviously suffering from a cough and laryngitis, our server thoughtfully offered me some hot water and honey. As an added bonus, there are no televisions or telephones in any of the guest rooms, so you can really enjoy the natural surroundings and get away from it all. Plan accordingly though, as the lodge is only open from May to January.

Best Fit

The accessible room and bathroom can certainly accommodate a large power wheelchair or scooter, however it won't work for folks who absolutely need a roll-in shower. This property just screams "romantic retreat" with the beautiful lake views and a nice porch to enjoy the sunset. Add in a quiet dinner in the dining room and you have the perfect anniversary celebration.

Nearby

The accessible room is just a short walk away from the barrier-free Moments in Time Trail. Just follow the paved pathway along the lake till you reach the trailhead. This 2/3-mile hard-packed dirt trail travels along the lakeshore and through the forest. Although there are a few tree roots at the beginning, you can definitely go around them, and after that there are no obstructions on the trail. Interpretive plaques and benches along the way encourage visitors to stop and reflect in that moment in time.

If you'd like to explore an often overlooked area of Olympic National Park (www.nps.gov/olym), then hop in your car and head over to Madison Falls. Take Highway 101 towards Port Angeles, turn right on Elhwa Creek Road and follow the signs to Madison Falls.

There's accessible parking in the lot, and accessible vault toilets near the beginning of the trail. There are also accessible picnic tables on a shaded level grassy area near the parking lot, The .1-mile paved trail winds through a deep forest and emerges at the Madison Falls overlook. There's a bench at the overlook, and railings are lowered so wheelchair-users can get unobstructed views of the cascading falls. It's a favorite spot for photographers, so take some time to sit back and enjoy the beauty of it all. And don't miss the view of the Elhwa River, from the hard-packed dirt area across the street from the parking lot.

Lake Crescent Lodge
416 Lake Crescent Road
Port Angeles, WA 98363
(360) 928-3211
www.olympicnationalparks.com/
accommodations/
lake-crescent-resort.aspx

GPS Coordinates
N 48.05897
W 123.79783

Toilet in room 101 at Lake Cresent Lodge

Barrier-Free Travel
Olympic and Mount Rainier
National Parks

for Wheelers and Slow Walkers

Penned by accessible travel expert Candy B. Harrington, this handy guide includes detailed access information about trails, sites and attractions in two popular Washington state national parks. Information on accessible lodging in and near the parks, along with lots of accessible room photos are also included. This guide will help you find an accessible room that works for you, and plan a accessible itinerary based on your abilities. Find out which of the "accessible with assistance" park trails are doable for wheelchair-users and slow walkers, and which ones present substantial obstacles. Don't leave home without this essential resource.
www.barrierfreeolympic.doc

Kestner Homestead on the Kestner Homestead Trail in Olympic National Park

Lake Quinault Lodge

Quinault, WA

Although it's just outside of Olympic National Park, Lake Quinault Lodge makes an excellent home base for exploring the park and the Olympic National Forest. This rustic lodge was built in 1926 on the south shore of Lake Quinault. Over the years there have been a number of upgrades and additions to the property, including the recent renovation of the accessible lakeside rooms. Today the lodge offers good access for wheelchair-users and slow walkers in a relaxed and comfortable setting. It's almost like being at home, only you don't have to cook and clean.

Access Details

There's accessible parking and level access to the main lodge, which houses the lobby, gift shop, Roosevelt Dining Room and office. From there, it's a short drive around back to the accessible parking area near the lakeside rooms.

Room 402 features a wide doorway, a level entry and good pathway access throughout the spacious unit. It's furnished with a 27-inch high queen-sized bed and a 12-inch high double sofa bed. There is level access out to the secluded terrace, and a wide doorway into the bathroom.

The bathroom has a roll-in shower with grab bars, a hand-held showerhead and a shower chair. The toilet grab bars are located on the right and back walls (as seated), and the bathroom also has a roll-under sink. Best of all, the bathroom is just as roomy as the guest room, with a full five-foot turning radius.

There is good pathway access around the well manicured property, and barrier-free access throughout the main lodge building. The indoor heated pool also features level access, and it is equipped with a lift.

Candy's Take

I was simply wowed by General Manage Hiedi Olson's knowledge on accessible trails in the area. She took the time to check them out and she shared her evaluation of them with me, and presumably other guests. I also love the lobby area, with the big comfortable chairs and massive fireplace. It's the perfect place to curl up with a good book, and enjoy the stately charm of this historic property.

Best Fit

The accessible lakeside room offers excellent access with plenty of room to navigate a wheelchair or scooter, and a large bathroom with a roll-in shower. In short, it will work for just about anybody. It's a great place for a romantic dinner, and a moonlight stroll near the lake, but it's also a good

Room 402 at Lake Quinault Lodge

The Maple Glade Rain Forest Trail in Olympic National Park

choice for anybody who loves nature and the great outdoors.

Nearby

There are several accessible trails to enjoy near the lodge. The closest one is the Rain Forest Nature Loop, which is just up the road. There's accessible parking, an accessible restroom and an accessible picnic table near the trailhead; and although the trail is rated as accessible, Hiedi Olson expressed her reservations about that.

And Olson was spot on in her assessment; as although the first part of this half-mile loop is doable for wheelchair-users and slow walkers, after the Willaby Creek overlook it's an access nightmare. Not only does the grade increase to a sustained 1:5, but there are exposed tree roots and even steps along the second part of the trail. That said, it's still worth a stop, as the first stretch features a beautiful walk through the rain forest on a level hard-packed dirt trail.

For a truly accessible hike, head over to the north shore of Lake Quinault, inside Olympic National Park, where you'll find two accessible trails near the ranger station. There is also an accessible restroom and a picnic table on a level grassy area near the ranger station..

The shorter of the two trails is the Maple Glade Rain Forest Trail. Technically this trail is rated as "accessible with assistance", but in reality it's more accessible than the Rain Forest Nature Loop. The half-mile loop is covered in hard-packed dirt and travels under a forest canopy filled with fern draped trees and moss covered logs. The trail is level with a few bumps here and there, but mostly doable in dry weather. As an added bonus, there are bridges and boardwalks over the wetter areas.

The longer Kester Homestead Trail travels a 1.3-mile loop from the ranger station past the 1891 Anton Kestner homestead. This level hard-packed dirt trail is covered with crushed granite in places, and is doable for just about everyone. The homestead, which is a collection of old farm buildings, is located about halfway along the loop. There is also a picnic shelter there, but none of the tables are accessible. From there the trail travels through the rain forest, before it joins the first part of the Maple Glade Rain Forest Trail. You can do one or both trails, and take a break for lunch along the way. And if you're lucky, you'll almost have the forest to yourself, as many people entirely overlook this pristine area of the park.

Lake Quinault Lodge
345 South Shore Road
Quinault, WA 98575
(360) 288-2900

GPS Coordinates
N 47.46695
W 121.92184

www.olympicnationalparks.com/accommodations/lake-quinault-lodge.aspx

Toilet and Shower in room 402 at Lake Quinault Lodge

Paradise Inn

Ashford, WA

Located in Mount Rainier National Park, the Paradise Inn first opened its doors on July 1, 1917. Back them it was a modest property with just 33 guest rooms, none of which had private baths. Still it was considered one of the "Great Lodges of the West", with a cavernous two story lobby framed with exposed cedar logs, massive French doors and a very imposing fireplace. After decades of snow damage this grand old lady started to show some wear, so in 1979 a $1.75 million renovation project was launched. During that time the inn got a total makeover, from foundation to finish work. Today the property has 121 rooms and boasts modern access features, yet still retains the flavor of yesteryear.

Access Details

Accessible parking is located near the entrance, with level access to the lobby. Room 331, which is located on the ground floor, features wide doorways and good pathway access. It's furnished with two 27-inch high double beds with an access aisle between them, a desk and chair, a chest of drawers and a night stand. A roll-under sink is located just outside the bathroom.

There is level access to the bathroom through a wide doorway. It is equipped with a roll-in shower with a fold-down shower bench, a hand-held showerhead and grab bars. The toilet grab bars are located on the left and back walls (as seated), and although the five-foot turning radius extends into the shower space, there's plenty of room to navigate in a wheelchair.

The public spaces are equally accessible, with barrier-free access through the lobby, and in the gift shop and the Taboosh Cafe. The main dining room has steps down into it, but there is a wheelchair lift on the side. Additionally, there is an accessible family restroom on the first floor, as well as accessible stalls in both the men's and women's restrooms.

Candy's Take

The lobby is my favorite place on the property. Not only does it have a rustic north woods feel to it, but some of Han Fraehnke's vintage woodwork pieces are on display there. Fraehnke was the German carpenter who crafted the 14-foot grandfather clock, the rustic piano and the imposing cedar chairs and tables that fill the lobby. I also love the view of the wildflowers in the adjacent meadow. It's the perfect location for a lodge.

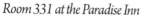
Room 331 at the Paradise Inn

Mount Rainier view from Sunrise

Best Fit

This property is the most accessible choice in Mount Rainier National Park, and because of the roll-in shower it's good for wheelchair-users or slow walkers. It's also a family friendly lodge, and although the accessible room would be cozy with a few kids, the large lobby is a great place to gather and do puzzles or play board games. It's also in a good location for exploring the park; but plan ahead, as the inn is only open from May to October.

Nearby

Mount Rainier National Park (www.nps.gov/mora) offers a number of accessible sightseeing choices. For a good overview of the park stop by the Paradise Visitor Center and pick up a park map or chat with a ranger. It's located right across the parking lot from the Paradise inn, and it features accessible parking, level access, accessible restrooms and an elevator.

A good way to enjoy the diversity of the park is to take the drive from Paradise up to Sunrise. It takes about three hours round-trip, but allow extra time to stop and enjoy the windshield views along the way. The route travels through the forest, and features canyon and waterfall vistas, before it culminates at Sunrise Day Lodge at 6,400 feet.

Accessible parking is available near the Sunrise Visitor Center, but it's best to drive behind the restrooms and park near the accessible side door, as there are steps along the route from the parking lot. There's barrier-free access inside the building, and a lowered viewing scope aimed at nearby Mt. Rainier. There's also some picnic tables on the terrace to the left of the building, and ramp access to the snack bar at the other end of the parking lot. The best plan of action is to drive directly to Sunrise, then stop for the views — especially Sunrise Point and Reflection Lakes — on the way down.

The most accessible trail in the park is located about five miles from the Nisqually entrance, at Kautz Creek. Accessible parking, vault toilets and picnic tables are located across the street from the Kautz Creek Trail. The short boardwalk trail travels about 100 feet through the recovering forest and opens up to a crushed granite-covered viewing area over Kautz Creek. Along the way interpretive plaques detail the devastation caused by the 1947 glacial debris flow. There are benches to sit and relax and enjoy the forest, and the viewpoint offers yet another perspective of Mount Rainier.

Paradise Inn
98368 Paradise-Longmire Road
Ashford, WA 98304
(360) 569-2275
www.mtrainierguestservices.com

GPS Coordinates
N 46.78544
W 121.73828

Shower and toilet in room 331 at the Paradise Inn

100

Zephyr Cove Resort

Zephyr Cove, NV

Billed as a refreshing alternative to the large hotels that line the overcrowded South Lake Tahoe strip, Zephyr Cove Resort offers a quieter, more relaxed lodging option. Granted, the cabins that dot this lakeshore retreat are outfitted with modern amenities; however the historic nature of the 1900s property has been retained through numerous upgrades, renovations and repairs. And although Zephyr Cove is also a popular day use area, nothing beats overnighting at this pristine lakeside property.

Access Details

Accessible parking is available near the main building, with ramp access up to the general store and restaurant. The general store, which doubles as the lodge office, features level access from the front porch. There are also accessible restrooms across from the general store and in the restaurant.

Cabin 29, a nice two-story model with a lake view, is the most accessible cabin in the complex. It features accessible parking on an asphalt pad, with ramp access up to the front porch. There are also low-rise stairs for slow walkers in front.

Access features include wide doorways and plenty of room to navigate a wheelchair on the first floor. Two downstairs bedrooms each have a 30-inch high queen-sized bed with wheelchair access on both sides, as well as a dresser, night tables and a side chair.

The spacious bathroom, which is located between the bedrooms, is equipped with a roll-in shower with a fold-down shower bench, grab bars and a hand-held showerhead. It measures 33 inches wide by 32 inches deep. There is also a separate tub/shower combination with grab bars, a hand-held showerhead and a fold-down tub seat. The toilet grab bars are located on the back and right walls (as seated), and the bathroom also includes a roll-under sink with plenty of knee space and a lowered mirror.

The cabin features a full kitchen with a lowered eating bar. It comes with a refrigerator, stove, oven, sink, microwave and coffee maker; and is stocked with plenty of pots, pans, dishes and utensils.

The adjacent great room is furnished with a large dining table and a 13-inch high sofa bed. And if you'd like to dine al fresco, the front porch has a built-in charcoal grill and a picnic table. The large second floor bedroom is only accessible by stairs, and it is furnished with a twin, a double and a queen bed. Two roll away beds are also stored in the downstairs closet.

Great Room in Cabin 29 at Zephyr Cove Resort

One of two downstairs bedrooms in Cabin 29 at Zephyr Cove Resort

Access is good around the property too, with asphalt pathways leading to all of the cabins and public areas. There is also a paved pathway near the accessible cabin that leads over to the Beach Bar and Grill. The restaurant serves casual fare, and features level access to the deck and dining room, and an accessible restaurant in the rear.

Candy's Take

I love the kitchen in this cabin, because it's a full kitchen, not a kitchenette. You can certainly cook up some gourmet meals there, if that's your pleasure. There's also a great view of the lake from the front porch, and with no street lights to pollute the night sky, you can really see the stars.

Best Fit

This cabin is a good choice for just about any disability as the large bathroom has a roll-in shower and a tub/shower combination. You also have your choice of bed heights between the queen beds, roll away bed and sofa bed. And since the cabin can sleep up to 10, it's perfect for a family getaway. If you want to gather the whole clan you can always rent nearby cabins and make this the party cabin.

Nearby

Of course you can certainly pass the time at Zephyr Cove just sitting on the deck and enjoying the view, however if you want to get up-close-and personal with Lake Tahoe, hop aboard the MS Dixie II (www.zephyrcove.com/msdixie.aspx). Docked next to the Beach Bar and Grill, this Mississippi-style paddle wheeler offers daily cruises around the largest alpine lake in North America.

There's level access out to the dock, with a ramp up to the outside deck. Once aboard you'll find ramp access over the coaming (lip) to the main deck cabin, which has table-and-chair seating, a very roomy accessible bathroom and lots of windows. There's only stair access to the upper decks, but the view is great from below.

The one-and-a-half-hour cruise takes passengers over to Emerald Bay and back. And with narration by "Mr. Tahoe" and a few fun games, there's never a dull moment aboard. There's also a full bar and a restaurant in the main cabin, if you'd like to enjoy an adult beverage or have a little snack. The only problem with the cruise is that it goes by much too quickly.

When you get back to shore make sure and explore the accessible trail that runs alongside the lake. It starts near the dock, and although there are steps down to the beach, the views from the trail are well worth the walk.

Bathroom in Cabin 29 at Zephyr Cove Resort

Zephyr Cove Resort
760 Highway 50
Zephyr Cove, NV 89448
(775) 589-4907
www.zephyrcove.com

GPS Coordinates
N 39.00940
W 119.94726

Toilet, tub / shower, and shower in Cabin 29 at Zephyr Cove Resort

Whitney Peak Hotel

Reno, NV

Located just a stone's throw from the famous arch, the Whitney Peak Hotel is Reno's first non-smoking, non-gaming property. In its former life the building was first Fitzgerald's Hotel and Casino, and then CommRow, an outdoor adventure complex. The most recent renovation sought to bring out the best of both incarnations, as the climbing wall on the front facade was retained, while the old guestrooms were given a fresh new face. And in keeping with their motto, "Turning Reno Outside In", the whole property has a very outdoorsy feel to it.

Access Details

Access is good throughout the property, with level access from the Commercial Street (side) entrance, and a barrier-free pathway to the front desk. Valet parking is available curbside, and self-parking is available in the garage down the street. Either way, guests can leave their car at the valet stand while they check in.

There's plenty of room to roll around on the cement floor in the lobby, with elevator access to the upper floors. Room 1126 features a wide doorway, and it's furnished with a 21-inch high king-sized bed with plenty of room for a wheelchair on both sides. Other furnishings include a chair and ottoman, a desk and a dresser. And even with all of that furniture there's still plenty of room for a large power wheelchair or even a scooter.

There is level access to the bathroom, which is outfitted with a tub/shower combination with a hand-held showerhead and grab bars. The toilet grab bars are in a frame, with grab bars on both sides and the back, There is 24 inches between the two side grab bars, and the back grab bar is 15 inches from the wall. Other access features include a roll-under sink, and a portable shower chair (upon request).

Candy's Take

Reno is undergoing a rebirth of sorts, with a total redevelopment of the downtown area. This property — with it's non-smoking non-gaming theme — embodies the hip new attitude of this evolving city. The Heritage Restaurant, located just off the lobby, is a favorite of mine, as it serves up dishes that celebrate the heritage of Northern Nevada. The menu is filled with lots of healthy choices, locally sourced products and even some gluten-free selections. And although the Whitney Peak Hotel represents the new Reno, you can still get a good view of old Reno's florescent jungle (otherwise known as Virginia Street) from Room 1126.

Room 1126 at the Whitney Peak Hotel

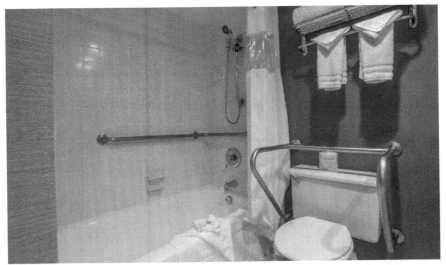

Tub/shower in room 1126 at the Whitney Peak Hotel

Best Fit

Although the bathroom has a five-foot turn around, some of it extends under the sink area, which may make the turn a little tight for larger power wheelchairs and scooters. Still, there's room enough to maneuver if you take it slowly. Additionally, the side grab bars may be to close together for some larger people. And if you absolutely have to have a roll-in shower, this property isn't for you. That said, it will work for a large number of people, and because it's off Interstate 80, it makes a great road trip stop. Baby Boomers will just love the nostalgic feel of Reno.

Nearby

Although Reno is often touted as a gambling venue, there's still plenty to do even if you never enter a casino. At the top of the list is the excellent National Automotive Museum (www.automuseum.org). Located along the Riverwalk, the museum features accessible parking with a level pathway to the entrance. Inside, the spacious galleries feature cars and trucks from all decades. You know you're in for a treat when you spot the gold plated De Lorean in the lobby.

Another Reno cultural must-do is the Nevada Museum of Art (www.nevadaart.org). Access is good at the museum with accessible parking near the entrance and level access to the front door. There's elevator access to the upper floors, where the exhibits are located, and barrier-free access to the first-floor restaurant and gift shop.

Constructed in 2002, the museum has a large collection of contemporary art by American artists, Michael Heizer, Dennis Oppenheim and Takako Yamaguchi, as well as new media works by Korean artist Jongsuk Lee and British artist Chris Drury. The permanent collection also contains more than 1,000 contemporary landscape photographs.

Save some time for a stroll along the Riverwalk, located just a few blocks from the hotel. There's ramp access down to the river level, with plenty of spots to stop and rest along the way, and a tantalizing selection of eateries up on the street level. It's just a pleasant — and very accessible — place to stroll.

Whitney Peak Hotel
255 N. Virginia Street
Reno, NV 89501
(775) 398-5400
www.whitneypeakhotel.com

GPS Coordinates
N 39.52786
W 119.81384

Toilet in room 1126 at the Whitney Peak Hotel

Mountain States

Hualapai Lodge

Peach Springs, AZ

Hualapai Lodge is a bit off-the-beaten-path, but that's part of its charm. Located on an original stretch of Route 66, halfway between Flagstaff and Kingman, this Peach Springs property is situated entirely on Hualapai land. The architecture reflects the native culture, with a cozy river rock fireplace in the lobby, and walls adorned with Hualapai artwork. Although it's not a luxury resort, it certainly has all the comforts of home. Plus it's the perfect place to base yourself if you'd like to explore a little-know driving route to the bottom of the Grand Canyon.

Access Details

There's accessible parking in front of the property, with level access to the building. Accessible Room 117 is located just off the lobby. This extra large room features wide doorways and good pathway access, and is furnished with two 25-inch high double beds, with wheelchair access on both sides. Other furnishings include an easy chair, a desk and a chest of drawers.

The bathroom features a wide doorway and is equipped with a roll-in shower with a hand-held showerhead and a fold-down shower bench. Toilet grab bars are located on the back and left walls (as seated), and a roll-under sink is located in an alcove just outside the bathroom.

There's good access to the public areas, including the pool and spa, which have lifts. There is also level access to the Diamond Creek Restaurant, just down the hall from lobby. The menu features Native American specialties as well as American favorites. A continental breakfast in the restaurant is included with the room rate, or you can upgrade to a full breakfast for $5.

Candy's Take

I love the feeling of yesteryear at this place. It's as if you dialed back the clock to the 1930s when the Mother Road was the main east-west U.S. artery. The historic Peach Springs Trading Post and Gas Station, which was built in the 1920s, is a prime example of this nostalgic feel. Located next to Hualapai Lodge, it once did a thriving business during the heyday of Route 66. Now it's on the National Register of Historic Places, and although the old buildings aren't open, it's a hoot to walk around and peer into them.

Best Fit

The spacious ground floor accessible room, roll-in shower and barrier-free access throughout the property makes Hualapai Lodge a good choice for

Room 117 at the Hualapai Lodge

Hualapai Cultural Center in Peach Springs

wheelchair-users and slow walkers alike. And because of the Route 66 heritage, it's the perfect place to rest your head while exploring the Mother Road. It's also a very family-friendly pick.

Nearby

Peach Springs is the gateway to the 19.5-mile driving route to the bottom of the Grand Canyon. It's an excellent choice for wheelchair-users and slow walkers, as you can get some great windshield views from the comfort of your own vehicle. A permit, which is required to drive to the bottom of the canyon, can be purchased at Hualapai Lodge. A package deal that includes overnight lodging, a picnic lunch and a driving permit is also available.

The drive begins just across the street from Hualapai Lodge, as it winds through a residential area on a paved road. About a mile down the road, the pavement gives way to a graded dirt road. Although you don't need a four-wheel-drive to make the trek, it's not recommended for low clearance vehicles, as it gets rougher as you get closer to the river.

Along the way you'll pass Diamond Peak, and as you descend you'll notice a marked change of landscape, from juniper in the upper reaches to cactus down near the river. Shaded picnic tables are located about a mile from the river. Depending on weather conditions, the last stretch of the road may not be passable in a vehicle. There are also a couple of picnic tables on the beach, but even if you don't make it that far, it's still a beautiful drive. If you visit from April to September, you'll probably share the beach with some rafters, but during the rest of the year you'll most likely have it to yourself.

Hualapai Lodge
900 Highway 66
Peach Springs, AZ 86434
(928) 769-2230
www.grandcanyonwest.com

GPS Coordinates
N 35.52890
W 113.42445

Shower and toilet in room 117 at the Hualapai Lodge

Hualapai Ranch

Peach Springs, AZ (Grand Canyon West)

Although Hualapai Ranch technically has a Peach Springs address, it's actually located at Grand Canyon West, a three-hour drive from Peach Springs proper. Billed as the newest development in the Grand Canyon, Grand Canyon West is located outside the national park boundary on tribal land. It's also the location of the infamous Grand Canyon Skywalk, a u-shaped glass bridge which offers unparalleled views of the canyon. As the closest accommodation to the skywalk, Hualapai Ranch makes the perfect home base for exploring yet another side of the Grand Canyon. Getting there is fun too, as the route passes through a massive Joshua tree forest.

Access Details

Hualapai Ranch is located in a re-created western village which features old time store fronts, horse stables, covered wagons and employees outfitted in western gear. Lodging is provided in rustic western cabins at the far end of the village. Guests check-in at the telegraph office, which can be accessed through the gift shop next door. There is no parking in front of the cabins, but guests can park there to drop off their luggage. Guest parking is available in the remote dirt parking lot, which is not striped.

It's just a short walk to Cabin 19, which features ramp access up to the front porch, a wide doorway and wood floors. It's furnished with a 27-inch double bed with wheelchair-access on one side, and a 27-inch high twin bed in an alcove.

The bathroom has a wide pocket door and a full five-foot turning radius. It's equipped with a 35-inch square roll-in shower with a hand-held showerhead, grab bars and a portable shower chair. The toilet grab bars are located on the right and back walls (as seated), and a lowered mirror is located above the pedestal sink.

There is a large bench on the front porch, with plenty of room to maneuver a wheelchair around it. A fire circle is located nearby, where the cowboys make s'mores and entertain guests in the evenings.

Breakfast, which is served in the accessible dining room, is included with your stay. It includes scrambled eggs, sausage, fruit, toast and hot or cold beverages.

Candy's Take

I think the tribe should be commended for adding access features to the property, as technically they weren't required to do so. Since the property is on tribal land, it's exempt from the Americans with Disabilities Act,

Cabin 19 at Hualapai Ranch

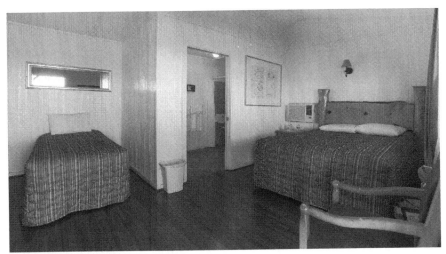
Inside Cabin 19 at Hualapai Ranch

so everything they've done access-wise has been voluntary. And they've done a really good job of it. Plus, after all the day trippers have departed, Hualapai Ranch is a very quiet and peaceful place to spend the night.

Best Fit

This is a good choice for all abilities, as the accessible cabin has a roll-in shower with ample room to navigate a wheelchair. It's the perfect family choice, as the twin bed is over in an alcove for a little more privacy. Plus, kids absolutely love the wranglers who teach visitors the finer points of roping, or show them how to toss a tomahawk.

Nearby

The Grand Canyon Skywalk is just a short drive from the western village, with accessible shuttle bus service to and from it. Private vehicles are prohibited in the park, and the shuttle busses carry visitors from Hualapai Ranch to the Main Terminal, Eagle Point and Guano Point. The shuttle busses can accommodate up to four wheelchair-users and they are equipped with ramps and tie-downs. Shuttle bus transportation is included with all Grand Canyon Skywalk admission tickets.

The Grand Canyon Skywalk is located at Eagle Point. Named for the eagle rock formation on the canyon wall, Eagle Point is a very sacred place to the Hualapai people. They believe that the spirit of the eagle delivers prayers from people to the heavens. Out of respect, they have kept the canyon rim in pristine condition, so you won't find the requisite sidewalks and guard rails that are prolific on the South Rim.

Although the parking area is covered in gravel, it's a level roll from the shuttle bus stop over to the canyon rim. It's a little bumpy, so some people may need assistance, but the view is great from just about every spot along the rim. Additionally, you'll find Hualapai ambassadors dressed in traditional clothing at all the shuttle stops.

There is ramp access up to the Grand Canyon Skywalk line, and level access to the adjacent locker area. Nothing is permitted out on the skywalk, so all purses, cameras, backpacks and bags must be left in the lockers. Ambulatory visitors are asked to wear disposable booties on the skywalk, but there are no restrictions for wheelchair-users.

From the locker area, you can just roll right out to the skywalk, which extends out over the canyon, for a bird's eye view of it all. It's truly a once-in-a-lifetime experience, and you can spend as much time on the skywalk as you want. And since cameras are prohibited on the skywalk, staff photographers are on hand to capture the memory for visitors.

Hualapai Ranch
Peach Springs, AZ 86434
(928) 769-2636
www.grandcanyonwest.com

GPS Coordinates
N 35.92531
W 113.80870

Toilet and shower in Cabin 19 at Hualapai Ranch

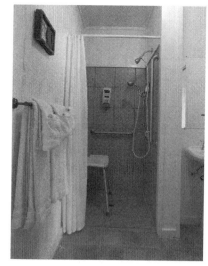

Thunderbird Lodge

Grand Canyon Village, AZ

Built in the 1960s, Thunderbird Lodge is perched on the South Rim of the majestic Grand Canyon. The interior brick walls reflect the style of the era, and the guest rooms are equipped with all the creature comforts travelers expect in a modern hotel. As an added bonus, the property is within walking distance of all the restaurants, gift shops, trails and attractions that make Grand Canyon Village one of the most touristed spots in this popular national park. Even better — Thunderbird Lodge is the only South Rim property that has an accessible room with a canyon view.

Access Details

There's no front desk at the Thunderbird Lodge, but guests can check-in at nearby Bright Angel Lodge. There's accessible parking in the Bright Angel parking lot, and although the main entrance to the lodge has steps, the canyon-side entrance is barrier-free.

It's just a short drive from Bright Angel Lodge to Thunderbird Lodge, and accessible parking is available in the rear of the property. Thunderbird

121

Lodge has several accessible room choices.

Room 6213 has wide doorways and good pathway access. It's furnished with a 26-inch high queen-sized bed, with good pathway access on both sides. There is a sliding door to the bathroom, which is equipped with a roll-in shower with a hand-held showerhead, grab bars and a portable shower chair. The toilet grab bars are located on the back and right walls (as seated), and the bathroom also has a roll-under sink.

Room 6211 and Room 6209 have the same access features as Room 6213; except that Room 6211 has a second door which opens on the canyon side, and Room 6209 has a tub/shower combination instead of a roll-in shower.

Although there are no in-house restaurants at Thunderbird Lodge, there are several accessible choices nearby. There is ramp access to the El Tovar Dining Room, which is located inside the historic El Tovar Lodge. The upscale Arizona Room, which sits on the canyon between Thunderbird Lodge and Bright Angel Lodge, has an accessible entrance on the canyon side. And if you'd like something a bit more casual, the Bright Angel Restaurant features ramp access from the main hotel lobby.

Candy's Take

You just can't beat the location of this property — right on the canyon rim. I also like the extra thought that went into the access features. Seldom

Mather Point on the Rim Trail in Grand Canyon National Park

Hopi House on the Rim Trail in Grand Canyon National Park

found amenities, such as electronic draperies, were included in the accessible rooms. The draperies can be easily opened from a switch near the thermostat, so getting a beautiful canyon view can literally be done with the touch of a finger.

Best Fit

The Thunderbird lodge is a good choice for everybody, as it has accessible rooms with roll-in showers or tub/shower combinations. The rooms are very spacious, so there's even room for a large wheelchair or a scooter. Plus it's in the perfect location to explore several accessible trails along the rim. And if you'd like to check out other areas of the park, you can just hop on the wheelchair-accessible shuttle bus. You can park your car for your entire stay and still see all of the South Rim attractions.

Nearby

There are a number of accessible things to do in Grand Canyon National Park (www.nps.gov/grca) within rolling distance of Thunderbird Lodge. A half-mile stretch of the paved Rim Trail starts at Hopi House and passes by El Tovar Hotel, Kachina Lodge, Thunderbird Lodge, the Arizona Room and Bright Angel Lodge. Not only is it an easy and accessible way to get to the other lodges and restaurants, but there are some great canyon views along the way.

If you'd fancy a longer stroll, the 1.3-mile Trail of Time runs along a section of the Rim Trail from the Yavapai Geology Museum to Verkamp's Visitor Center. The paved level trail winds along the rim of the canyon and helps visitors understand the magnitude of geologic time. The geologic timeline is marked by brass medallions embedded in the pavement; and interpretive exhibits and displays along the way encourage visitors to connect the visible rocks in the canyon to the geologic timeline. Wheelchair-height viewing scopes are available, and accessible pictograms point out the wheelchair-accessible route.

And don't miss the, the Yavapai Geology Museum, which features level access with plenty of room to maneuver a wheelchair inside. The building was constructed in the 1920s, when a group of geologists chose this site as the best representation of Grand Canyon geology. Today the structure houses exhibits about the geology of the area, and offers a great canyon view. Accessible restrooms are located near the parking lot (just follow the directions on the sign), and there are also benches to sit down and rest inside the museum.

Thunderbird Lodge
10 Albright Avenue
Grand Canyon Village, AZ 86023
(888) 297-2757
www.grandcanyonlodges.com

GPS Coordinates
N 36.05674
W 112.13935

Toilet and shower in room 6213 at the Thunderbird Lodge

Barrier-Free Travel
THE GRAND CANYON FOR
WHEELERS AND SLOW WALKERS

Penned by accessible travel expert Candy B. Harrington, this handy access guide includes detailed access information about trails, sites and attractions in one of America's most visited national parks. Along with information on accessible sites on the North and South Rim, the book also includes hard-to-find access information about Grand Canyon West, which is located outside of the national park on Hualapai land. Accessible lodging choices in and near the park are also included; and if you'd like to ride the rails to the South Rim, there's information on how to do that too.
barrierfreegrandcanyon.com/

Sedona Rouge

Sedona, AZ

Located along Sedona's main drag, Sedona Rouge is far from your garden variety hotel. Very far. As soon as you enter the lobby you notice a definite sense of style and sophistication that sets it apart from the crowd. The luxury property is an eclectic mix of ancient Roman, French, Mediterranean and North African cultures; with Tunisian wrought iron window work and an interesting mix of Moroccan and Moorish decor. Couple that with a collection of top-drawer amenities and a very accommodating staff, and you have all the ingredients for a perfectly relaxing retreat.

Access Details

There's plenty of accessible parking in front, and level access to the courtyard and front lobby. There's also a drop-off zone in front, if you can't manage the walk from the parking area. From the lobby, there's elevator access up to accessible Room 213, which overlooks the first-floor courtyard.

This corner room features wide doorways and good pathway access, and is furnished with two 29-inch high queen-sized pillow top beds, a chair, an ottoman and a desk.

The oversized bathroom has a large roll-in shower with grab bars, a shower chair and a hand-held showerhead. There is also an overhead rain shower, with the controls within easy reach. The shower measures a whopping 78 inches by 54 inches, and includes a four-foot-wide opening. And it's not like they took the room out of the rest of the bathroom either, as it still boasts a very healthy five-foot turning radius. Other access features include toilet grab bars on the left and back walls (as seated), a roll-under sink, and a lowered make-up mirror.

There is also level access to a small balcony that overlooks the courtyard. Additionally, all areas of the property, including the first-floor courtyard and Reds restaurant, feature barrier-free access.

Candy's Take

You really get the feeling that you are staying in a private villa at Sedona Rouge. It was very relaxing to leave the balcony door open and listen to the fountain while I nodded off to sleep. This is the perfect place to unwind and revel in the spiritual energy that engulfs Sedona.

Best Fit

Because of the huge roll-in shower this property is a good choice for just about everyone. The one drawback is that the balcony on this corner

Room 213 at Sedona Rouge

Toilet and Shower in room 213 at Sedona Rouge

room is a bit tight for a wheelchair; however there are many other pleasant public spaces with plenty of room. This property is a good choice for a spa weekend, and the perfect pick for a romantic getaway.

Nearby

Gallery hopping is a popular activity in Sedona, and as luck would have it Sedona Rouge is just down the road from the Tlaquepaque Arts and Crafts Village (www.tlaq.com), which houses a eclectic collection of unique galleries. Patterned after the Mexican village of the same name, the complex features level access to most of the shops, plenty of accessible parking, and lots of room to wheel around the peaceful courtyards. It's a fun place to spend the day, do a little shopping, visit with the artists and get a bite eat.

Save some time to enjoy Sedona's famous red rock formations. There's no better place to get a gander at them then at Bell Rock, which is located just up the road from the Visitors Center in the Village of Oak Creek. It's one of the more accessible red rock areas, as the upper part of Bell Rock Trail is wide, level and made of hard packed dirt. It's doable for most wheelchair-users, however you can also get a great view of the formation from the parking lot overlook.

If you love animals, then make sure and visit Out of Africa Wildlife Park (www.outofafricapark.com), located 30 miles south of Sedona in Camp Verde. This remote refuge is home to hundreds of exotic mammals, birds and reptiles from around the world. The 40-minute tour is conducted in an accessible open-air bus, which allows visitors to get an intimate look at the zebras, Watusi cattle, antelope, giraffes and addax in the Masai Mara enclosure. And don't miss the signature Tiger Splash show, which features Bengal and Siberian Tigers that interact with their caretakers in the water.

Finally, no visit to red rock country is complete without an excursion on the Verde Canyon Railroad (www.verdecanyonrr.com), located just west of Sedona in Clarkdale. The four-hour train trip winds through a 680-foot tunnel, passes over towering trestles and chugs past Indian ruins.

There is lift access to the train, and wheelchair-users can opt to stay in their own wheelchair or transfer to a seat for the ride. The lift can only accommodate wheelchairs that are less than 25-inches wide, but loaner wheelchairs are available. The lift can also not accommodate loads over 300 pounds, so sometimes power wheelchair batteries must be removed; however the staff is very accommodating and they are willing to work with guests so everyone can enjoy this scenic ride. It's a great day trip and probably the most accessible way to enjoy the beautiful red rock formations that surround Sedona.

Sedona Rouge
2250 W. State Route 89A
Sedona, AZ 86336
(928) 201-4111
www.sedonarouge.com

GPS Coordinates
N 34.86411
W 111.79920

Casa de San Pedro

Hereford, AZ

L ocated 90 miles southeast of Tucson, in the small hamlet of
Hereford, Casa de San Pedro Bed & Breakfast attracts birders from
around the world. The reason is simple. Not only is this remote
property adjacent to the San Pedro Riparian National Conservation
Area, but it's also located along a major migratory path between Mexico
and Canada. But this little piece of paradise isn't just for bird lovers; in
fact, innkeepers Karl Schmitt and Patrick Dome have made it into a cozy,
romantic retreat that just about anyone can enjoy. Top that off with some
added access features, and you can easily see why this rural resort is the
perfect choice for wheelchair-users and slow walkers.

Access Details

Accessible parking is located near the office of this 11-room property,
with barrier-free access to the office and gift shop. From there, you'll find
level access around the courtyard to Room 6, which will work well for
most wheelers and slow walkers.

Access features include wide doorways, lever handles, a level threshold and wheelchair access between the two 21-inch high double beds. As an added bonus, the beds both have electric blankets, a very welcome feature on those chilly nights.

The bathroom has a wide doorway and is equipped with a roll-in shower with grab bars and a hand-held showerhead. There is a slight one-inch lip on the shower, but because of the placement of the toilet, it's easy to transfer to the portable shower bench. The toilet has grab bars on the right and back walls (as seated), with a shorter than usual grab bar on the right side. And although the sink is not a roll-under sink, it does have some knee space underneath.

There is a table with two chairs just outside the room, facing the courtyard fountain. Additionally, the room is located next door to the great room, which features level access and offers a computer and printer, a fireplace, lots of reading materials and a TV. A scrumptious and filling breakfast is served next door in the dining area, which also features level access.

Candy's Take

I like the remoteness of this property, and the fact that we were able to barbeque our own dinner there. There is a guest refrigerator and a microwave in a small room near the office, and level access out to an outdoor grill. There's also a large selection of dishes, utensils, pots and pans for guests to use. We had a nice intimate dinner in the courtyard, and

Room 6 at Casa de San Pedro

Breakfast room at Casa de San Pedro

then topped it off with a sampling of the yummy desserts that Karl and Patrick set out.

Best Fit

Karl and Patrick are very up front about the limitations of their accessible room, and they are quick to note that it is not "ADA accessible". There are two main drawbacks in the bathroom; the slight lip on the roll-in shower and the lack of a truly roll-under sink. That said, there is some knee space under the sink and the shower lip is doable with assistance. Although it's a huge birding property, I felt it was a very nice romantic retreat. Karl and Patrick live off site, which gives guests a high degree of privacy. And privacy and seclusion can be pretty romantic.

Nearby

Of course birding opportunities abound near the property. There's a hard-packed gravel trail to the adjacent San Pedro Riparian National Conservation Area, which attracts over 335 species of birds. The trail runs through the grassland and over to the river, and although it gets a bit bumpy in places, it's doable for most power wheelchairs and scooters.

There is also level access to a pleasant pond near the BBQ area, which attracts a fair share of birds. Peak birding season is during the spring and fall migrations, but you'll certainly find year-round residents there in the off season. In fact, we spotted a covey a Gamble's quail as we were eating breakfast one morning. You never know what you'll see, and to be honest that's part of the beauty of this nicely accessible property.

Casa de San Pedro is also just a 45-minute drive from Karchner Caverns State Park (www.azstateparks.com/parks/kaca/), which features good wheelchair access. All of the cave tours are wheelchair-accessible, however wheelchairs must have seats less than 18-inches wide, while scooters must be less than 30 inches long. If your mobility device exceeds these dimensions, loaner wheelchairs are available.

The tour starts with a tram ride up the hill to the cavern entrance. The open-air tram features one car with ramp access, with plenty of room for your entire party. From the tram stop there's level access to the cave entrance, with paved pathways and plenty of benches along the tour route. Although there are a few steep sections inside the cave, alternative viewing points are available if you can't manage them. And quite frankly it's one of the most pristine caves I've ever seen. Plan ahead though, as tickets sell out fast at this popular attraction.

Casa de San Pedro
8933 S. Yell Lane
Hereford, AZ 85615
(520) 366-1300
www.bedandbirds.com

GPS Coordinates
N 31.40872
W 110.10677

Bathroom in room 6 at Casa de San Pedro

Cat Mountain Lodge

Tucson, AZ

L ocated on the outskirts of Tucson, Cat Mountain Lodge is the perfect place to soak up a little sun, enjoy the evening stars and generally get away from it all. This southwestern style B&B features a peaceful courtyard surrounded by five guest rooms, including one which will work for many wheelchair-users and slow walkers.

Access Details

There is a signed accessible parking place near the entrance, however since the parking lot is gravel, it's not striped. Some wheelchair-users may need a little help over the gravel, but once you get to the flagstone sidewalk, there's barrier-free access to the courtyard. There is a sliding glass door to the public Arizona Room, which features a computer and printer, books, magazines and coffee to enjoy around the kiva fireplace

The accessible Fiesta Room is located just a few steps away. It features a wide doorway; however there is a one-inch lip at the entrance. Inside, the tile floors are accented with throw rugs, and the room is decorated with a definite southwestern flair. Furnishings include a love seat, a table and chairs, a chest of drawers, and two nightstands. There is wheelchair access on both sides of the 21-inch high king-sized bed, and the room also has a small refrigerator.

There is a wide doorway into the bathroom, which is outfitted with a shower with grab bars and a hand-held showerhead. The shower has a one-inch lip, and although it's 56 inches wide and 28 inches deep, because of the layout of the bathroom, there's only 27-inches of clearance space to the shower. The toilet grab bars are located on the right and back walls (as seated); and the room also includes a 36-inch high pedestal sink with a lowered mirror.

Guests are also treated to breakfast at the Coyote Pause Cafe, which is just a short walk from the lodge. Although the route is level, it's best to drive if you use a wheelchair, as the gravel surface makes for tough rolling. There's accessible parking in front of the cafe, with level access to the building. Menu selections range from southwestern specialties like huevos rancheros and mesquite pancakes with prickly pear syrup, to traditional favorites like bacon and eggs or omelets.

Candy's Take

My favorite spot on the 13-acre property is the patio area that's furnished with a swing and some chairs. It features level access and it's a nice place to enjoy the sunset. Spencer's Observatory, where guests can book an

The Fiesta Room at Cat Mountain Lodge

Patio at Cat Mountain Lodge

optional star gazing session, is also located there. Although there is a three-inch step up to the observatory, there's also a table and chairs outside, so you can certainly enjoy the night sky on your own.

Best Fit

Although the bathroom will work for many people, it's not the best setup for power wheelchair-users, mostly because of the narrow clearance to the shower. Even though the accessible room is spacious, some folks may need to move a piece or two of furniture for better access. In the end, this property is a good choice for slow walkers and part-time wheelchair-users. The property is very quiet, with mostly couples as guests. It's a good road trip property, and it's incredibly popular with Baby Boomers.

Nearby

The property is pretty remote, so there's not many things within walking distance. That said, Cat Mountain Station, which houses a number of shops, is located next to the Coyote Pause Cafe. There is level access to Cat Mountain Emporium, The Trading Post, and the galleries that compose the 4,500-square foot shopping center. It's a good place to find locally crafted jewelry, art work and textiles.

The Arizona Sonora Desert Museum (www.desertmuseum.org) is just a short drive away. This combination zoo, botanical garden and aquarium features more than 230 animal species and 1,200 types of plants.

There is barrier-free access throughout most areas of the garden, with plenty of accessible parking near the entrance, and barrier-free access to the entrance patio.

Save some time to visit a section of Saguaro National Park (www.nps.gov/sagu), which is just up the road. The Tucson Mountain District of this national park features the accessible Desert Discovery Trail, which focuses on desert ecology; and the Bajada Loop Drive, which offers a very scenic view of an impressive Saguaro cactus forest.

Cat Mountain Lodge
2720 S. Kinney Road
Tucson, AZ 85735
(520) 578-6085
www.catmountainlodge.com

GPS Coordinates
N 32.18920
W 111.10100

Toilet and shower in the Fiesta Room at Cat Mountain Lodge

Adobe and Stars B&B

Taos, NM

This pueblo style property is located halfway between Taos and Taos Ski Valley, in the wide open spaces of Northern New Mexico. Decorated with southwestern furniture and regional art, the guest rooms feature high beamed ceilings and traditional kiva fireplaces, while the public areas are spacious and inviting. Best of all, the inn was designed so guests can enjoy the spectacular mountain and mesa views, with large windows, decks and patios to take it all in.

Access Details

There's barrier-free access to the inn from a level sidewalk in front of the property, and a wide door into the accessible lobby. Parking is located in the back of the inn on a gravel area, but it's best to unload the car from the drop-off area in the front, as that's the most accessible route.

The Pegasus Room, which is located near the lobby, features wide front and back doors, good pathway access, and a tile floor for easy wheeling. It is furnished with a king-sized bed with wheelchair access on both sides. There is also level access to the small back porch, but there is a one-inch lip down to the gravel parking area.

The tiled bathroom is equipped with a roll-in shower with a built-in shower bench, grab bars and a hand-held showerhead. The toilet has grab bars on the back and right walls (as seated), and the bathroom also has a roll-under sink with an accessible angled mirror. It's a very spacious bathroom, with a full five-foot turning radius.

Guests are treated to a get acquainted happy hour in the lobby, and a full breakfast in the adjacent dining area. Both areas are wheelchair-accessible, and although breakfast was good, somehow the get acquainted happy hour never materialized during our stay.

Candy's Take

The small back patio is a nice place to enjoy the beautiful scenery and the sunset. And because of the remote location of the property, there's not a lot of light pollution, so it's also a good spot to take in the night sky. It's not a private patio, but it gives guests some semi-private outdoor space.

Best Fit

The only real access drawback is the lip down to the back parking area, but if you travel with someone who can bring the car around to the front, it's not really a problem. The bathroom is also spacious enough to accommodate just about any size wheelchair or scooter. Although

The Pegasus Room at the Adobe and Stars B&B

the accommodations are upscale, the innkeepers are a chatty bunch at breakfast, so I wouldn't really recommend the property for a romantic getaway. It's a good spot to base yourself to explore historic Taos, as the southwestern architecture and furnishings really help set the mood.

Nearby

Taos Pueblo (www.taospueblo.com) is the most popular attraction in the area. This living Native American community, which is located at the base of the Sangre de Cristo Mountains, dates back over 1,000 years. The adobe homes are passed down from generation to generation and they are still used for cultural and religious activities. Today approximately 150 people live in the pueblo full time, while others use their family homes to sell hand-crafted wares or native food.

There is accessible parking in a dirt lot near the registration building, with level access over to the building where the entrance fee is collected. Accessible restrooms are located behind the registration building, and although the modern stalls are accessible, the cement ramp up to the building is a bit on the steep side. Still, with a little assistance it's doable. There are also porta-potties located throughout the pueblo, but none of them are accessible.

The dirt pathways through the pueblo are level, and although there are a few bumps along the way, it's pretty easy to navigate around the obstacles. You can wander through the pueblo on your own, or join one of the walking tours conducted by tribal members. If you go it on your own, remember that this is a living community, so be careful not to wander into any restricted areas.

Be sure and stop at the St. Jerome chapel, which features level access at the front door. Built in 1850, the sanctuary houses a Virgin Mary statue that was brought over by Spanish missionaries. Other sites worth a visit are the San Geronimo church ruins and graveyard, the north and south houses and the plaza.

There's no shortage of vendors inside the pueblo, and although some of the adobe houses are a tight fit, many are accessible to wheelchair-users and slow walkers. Don't miss the drying racks with corn husks, fruit and meat in the plaza, and the large bee hive adobe ovens used to bake bread, pies and meats.

There are a few benches to sit and rest along the perimeter, and you can do the self-guided walking tour at your own pace. And although not all of the inside areas are accessible, the best views of the pueblo can be had from the outside. It's an interesting look at a unique culture, and as an added bonus many of the residents are eager to share their tribal history with visitors.

Adobe and Stars B&B
584 State Highway 150
Taos, NM 87571
(800) 211-7076
www.taosadobe.com

GPS Coordinates
N 36.51121
W 105.57997

Shower in the Pagasus Room at the Adobe and Stars B&B

Toilet and sink in he Pegasus Room at the Adobe and Stars B&B

Snow Mountain Ranch Yurt

Granby, CO

O perated by the YMCA of the Rockies, Snow Mountain Ranch
is located 80 miles west of Denver, between Winter Park Ski
Resort and Grand Lake. The 5,000-acre ranch has a variety of
lodging choices, from campsites to lodge rooms, but their wheelchair-
accessible yurt is the most unique choice. This round domed structure
includes a number of creature comforts, but because of its location there's
a real wilderness fee to it all.

Access Details

There's level access to the main lodge, where yurt guests check-in. From
there it's just a short drive to the yurt village, which features accessible
parking in front of the Red Fox Yurt. There's ramp access up to the wide
front door, and plenty of room to navigate a wheelchair on the wooden
floor inside.

The yurt is furnished with a 23-inch high open-framed queen-
sized bed, two sets of bunk beds, a table and chairs, a microwave and a
refrigerator. Bedding and towels are also included, which isn't necessarily

143

the case at all yurts, And if you'd prefer to cook out under the stars, there's an accessible grill and a picnic table on a cement pad just outside the door.

There is an accessible shower room in the nearby bathhouse. It features a toilet with grab bars on the back and right walls (as seated), and a low-step shower with a hand-held showerhead and a fold-down shower bench. There's plenty of room to roll around in the private shower room, which also has a locking door.

Outside there's a large sink to rinse off your dishes, and a emergency phone which is connected directly to the office. So even though the location is a bit remote, you can still easily access the office if there's an emergency.

Candy's Take

The yurts are in their own little village, and I really like the fact that there's plenty of room around them. I never felt crowded, and I didn't even see any other guests during my stay. I also love the fact that there is a nice indoor pool near the main lodge. And since this is a YMCA property, the pool was accessible long before it was ever required. It has a nice cement ramp and a water wheelchair for loan. There's no lift to mess with — you can just transfer to the water wheelchair and roll on it.

Inside the Red Fox Yurt at Snow Mountain Ranch

Pool, access ramp and water wheelchair at Snow Mountain Ranch

Best Fit

Although the yurt is certainly very accessible, the low-step shower in the shower room may not work for some people. That said, there is plenty of space in the shower room for an attendant, if you need assistance. Alternatively, the pool locker rooms pool have roll-in showers. You have to drive over there, but it's always an option. The yurt is a good choice for people who like soft adventure and the outdoors, but still want to sleep in a bed.

Nearby

Snow Mountain Ranch makes a good home base for exploring nearby Rocky Mountain National Park (www.nps.gov/romo). The most accessible way to experience the park is to drive across Trail Ridge Road, which bisects the park, and passes the 12,183-foot summit. You'll get some spectacular windshield views in either direction, and you won't even have to get out of your car to enjoy them.

If you'd like to stretch your legs a bit, the mile-long Coyote Valley Trail is a good choice. Located four miles from the west park entrance, this hard-packed dirt trail follows the the Colorado River and affords great views of the Never Summer Mountains.

On the other side of the park, the .9-mile Lilly Lake Loop offers equally stunning views of waterfowl, wildflowers and of course the lake. The level trail is covered with crushed granite, and features strategically placed benches. The area is especially scenic in late spring and early summer, when you'll find it filled with wildflowers.

Another trail that will work for some slow walkers is the half-mile trail around Bear Lake. There are some level overlooks near the trailhead, and a short part of the trail to the left is level and covered in crushed granite. After that it gets fairly steep, so enjoy the overlooks and turn back when the trail loses its access.

Last but not least, don't miss the half-mile trail around Sprague Lake. This fairly level trail is covered with crushed granite, and there are benches and accessible fishing platforms along the way. You can get a great view of the Continental Divide from this trail. Accessible restrooms, parking and a picnic table are also available there, so it makes a great spot for a midday meal.

Snow Mountain Ranch
1101 County Road 53
Granby, CO 80446
(970) 887-2152
www.snowmountainranch.org

GPS Coordinates
N 39.99256
W 105.92638

Lilly Lake Loop trail

Golden Gate Canyon Yurt

Golden, CO

Located just 30 miles from Denver, Golden Gate Canyon State Park is a bit off-the-beaten-path, but that's a very good thing. Although Rocky Mountain National Park entices out-of-state visitors, the locals tend to prefer this low-key 12,000-acre paradise. With electrical hook-ups and tent sites in two different campgrounds, stocked fishing ponds and plenty of picnic areas, it has all the requisite features of a mountain retreat. Add in a nice accessible yurt, some breathtaking views of the Continental Divide and trails appropriate for wheelers and slow walkers, and you have the near perfect alpine venue for people of all abilities.

Access Details

The accessible yurt is located in Reverend's Ridge Campground, which is located in the northeastern part of the park. There's level access to the campground office, and from there it's just a short walk to Yurt 1 (also known as the Bobcat Yurt). There's a large parking space in front of the yurt, with ramp access to the roomy front porch.

There's good access inside too, with plenty of room to maneuver a wheelchair. It's furnished with a 23-inch high double bed, a twin bed, a pair of bunk beds, and a table and chairs. There are lights, electrical outlets and a propane heater in the yurt, but all cooking must be done at the fire ring outside. There's also an accessible picnic table near the fire ring.

Although this yurt lacks a refrigerator and a microwave, it's still pretty comfortable; and the front porch is a very pleasant addition. Remember to bring your own bedding and towels though, as they are not provided for yurt guests.

An accessible restroom is just a short level walk away, but the showers are located on the other side of the campground. It's best to drive to the showers, as there isn't a good accessible path to them.

There is a roll-in shower with a fold-down shower bench in the men's and women's bathhouses. The showers are coin-operated, and the coin slot can be easily accessed from a seated position. It's costs about $2 for a good shower, and there's usually plenty of hot water, which is not always the case with coin-operated showers. There are also accessible toilet stalls in both bathhouses.

Candy's Take

My favorite feature of this yurt is the large front porch. There's plenty of room for camp chairs and wheelchairs on it, and although the yurt is close to the office, it's off the main path. It nice to have some semi-private outdoor space, yet still be close to the restrooms.

Inside the Bobcat Yurt at Golden Gate Canyon State Park

The view at Panorama Point

Best Fit

The yurt is very roomy, and although the showers are pretty basic, they will work for just about everyone. I heard about this place from a (now deceased) friend who used a power wheelchair and a ventilator, and she was quite pleased with the access. She loved to vacation there with her partner, her daughter and her attendant, and at just $70 a night, she could afford to stay a whole week. This is a great choice for people who love the outdoors, and absolutely perfect for families.

Nearby

Make sure and take the short drive from the campground up Gap Road to Panorama Point, as it's aptly named. There is accessible parking, with level access to picnic tables, and a nice boardwalk out to the overlook. It's the ideal place to enjoy the sunset.

If you'd like a short nature walk, then go south on Mountain Base Road, turn left on Highway 46, and head to the Visitors Center. There's accessible parking outside, with barrier-free access to the building, and good access around the interpretive exhibits inside.

Outside, the quarter-mile Show Pond Trail features paved access around the trout-filled pond. Pack a picnic lunch and enjoy it on an accessible picnic table on the back patio. There's a great view of the pond, and it's a blissfully peaceful place to relax.

Golden Gate Canyon
92 Crawford Gulch Road
Golden, CO 80403
(303) 582-3707
www.cpw.state.co.us/placestogo/Parks/goldengatecanyon

GPS Coordinates
N 39.83086
W 105.41053

Show Pond Trail

Estes Park Center

Estes Park, CO

Part of the YMCA of the Rockies, this family resort is located between Rocky Mountain National Park and Estes Park, Colorado. Although both group and family guests are welcome year round, this retreat center is a favorite for family reunions. Not only does it offer something for just about every family member, but it also has some nicely accessible lodge rooms.

Access Details

Accessible parking is available near the administration building, where guests check-in. From there it's just a short drive up to Longs Peak Lodge, which features the most accessible rooms on the property. There's plenty of accessible parking in front, with level access up to the lodge entrance. Guests actually enter on the second floor, and accessible room 8101 is located just one floor down, near the elevator.

The room features wide doorways and good pathway access. It's furnished with two 26-inch high queen-sized beds, with an access aisle between them. It also has a table and two chairs, but in keeping with the rustic atmosphere, it's pleasantly devoid of a TV. A single futon mattress is also available, which bumps up the maximum occupancy to five.

There is level access through a wide door to the oversize bathroom, which is equipped with a roll-in shower with a hand-held showerhead, grab bars and a fold-down shower bench. Toilet grab bars are located on the back and right walls (as seated), and there's even an extra perpendicular grab bar on the side wall. Round it out with a roll-under sink and you have a very accessible bathroom.

Longs Peak Lodge also features a nice common area around the fireplace in the lobby. It's good for an informal get together, or for chatting with friends and family till the wee hours of the morning.

The Aspen Dining Room is located near the administration building, and although there is path down from the Longs Peak Lodge, it's a bit steep and rocky. Best bet is to drive down if you have mobility issues. There is level access to the dining room, which offers a breakfast, lunch and dinner buffet.

Candy's Take

This is a very affordable family oriented property, and I really like the whole dining arrangement. There are lots of large tables with plenty or room for families or groups to sit down and enjoy their meals together. Plus there's enough variety in the food to satisfy everyone, from toddlers

Room 8101 in the Longs Peak Lodge at Estes Park Center

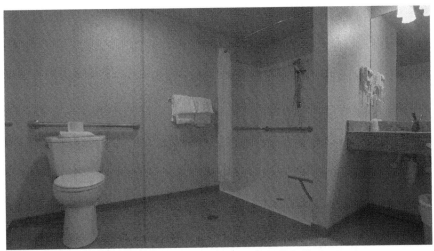

Bathroom in room 8101 in the Longs Peak Lodge at Estes Park Center

to grandparents; and if you want go the healthy route, they also have a nice salad bar. And even though everyone seems to converge on the dining room at the same time, the employees are able to manage the crowds quite efficiently.

Best Fit

Variety is the key word here, because if a roll-in shower won't work for you, they also have accessible guest rooms with tub/shower combinations. So disability-wise this lodge will work for just about everyone. It's the perfect family reunion venue, as there are plenty of activities to keep the kids occupied, and lots of space for parents and grandparents to just sit back and visit. And if you are a novice at reunion planning, Estes Park Center offers a Family Reunion University in the off season, which teaches you everything you need to know.

Nearby

Let's face it, Estes Park Center is the destination, as although you can certainly strike out and explore the surrounding alpine forests, there's plenty of activities to keep the kids busy at the lodge. In fact the YMCA of the Rockies prides itself on providing day camps that enable kids to learn, play and grow together. And although some of the day camp activities are not accessible, with advance notice many of them can accommodate children with access needs.

The day camp groups are divided by age. The Bennett Beavers offers full-day or half-day programs for preschoolers who are able to spend a few hours away from their parents. Activities include short hikes, nature activities, crafts, story time and playing with blocks and games. Older children can participate in a variety of full-day programs which include activities from swimming and archery, to crafts, scavenger hunts and even team building activities.

In the end, the day camps provide a good opportunity for kids to bond, learn a little about nature, and get some exercise; and for adults to enjoy a much coveted slice of alone time. Truly it's a winning combination for everyone.

Estes Park Center
2515 Tunnel road
Estes Park, CO 80511
(888) 613-9622
www.ymcarockies.org/lodging

GPS Coordinates
N 40.34005
W 105.57339

Nordic Inn

Crested Butte, CO

Known as the last great Colorado ski town, Crested Butte beckons skiers of all ages and abilities. And the Nordic Inn, is the perfect place to rest your head while you hit the nearby slopes. This 28-room property is located close to the "mountain", and owners Kim and Ken Stone went the extra mile to make sure accessibility was considered in all renovations. In fact, they consulted with the experts at the Adaptive Sports Center after they purchased the lodge in 2012, to make sure they didn't miss anything. The end result is a very accessible and comfortable ski chalet.

Access Details

The two accessible rooms (114 and 115) are located near the ramped north entrance, just around the corner from the lobby and dining area. Access features include wide doorways, wood floors, wheelchair access to the beds, and extra wide pocket doors to the bathrooms.

Both bathrooms are outfitted with a roll-in shower with grab bars and a hand-held showerhead; and a toilet with grab bars on the back and right walls (as seated). Other access features include a roll-under sink and a portable shower chair.

Room 114 is furnished with a king-sized bed (that can be converted to two twins), and Room 115 has 2 queen-sized beds. All the beds are 29-inches high, and because of the furnishings and configuration, Room 115 has more floor space. Even the small things — like accessible make-up and shaving mirrors — weren't overlooked. Once again, that's evidence that the Stones got advice from the real experts.

A hearty continental breakfast is served each morning in the dining room, and the lobby is a pleasant place to linger after a long day on the slopes. It's just the perfect little ski lodge.

Candy's Take

I think the location of the lodge is excellent, no mater what you want to do in Crested Butte. If you want to ski, the free Crested Butte Mountain Resort electric shuttle stops right outside the accessible rooms. Although you have to transfer to a seat, the driver is happy to stow your wheelchair. And if you'd like to go down and explore the "village", The Mountain Express departs from Mountaineer Square, just a short walk from the lodge. The bus is free, and it makes several stops in Crested Butte. Best of all, every Mountain Express bus is wheelchair-accessible.

Room 114 at the Nordic Inn in Crested Butte

Crested Butte, Colorado

Best Fit

The lodge is a good choice for all wheelchair-users and slow walkers, as a lot of thought was put into the accessible features of the property. The guest rooms are very large, and the roll-in showers are nicely done. And of course the property is an excellent choice for a ski holiday.

Nearby

You don't have to go far to hit the slopes, as Crested Butte Mountain Resort is well known for its challenging terrain, bowl skiing and of-the-beaten-path Nordic routes. The resort is also home to the Adaptive Sports Center (www.adaptivesports.org), a top-rated adaptive ski program. Founded in 1987, this well respected non-profit organization offers adaptive skiing, snowboarding and Nordic programs, to just about anyone who wants to give them a try.

Rest assured though, it's all very safe; in fact, Marking Director, Mike Neustedter, emphasizes the professionalism of his team. "Unlike other adaptive programs, that are volunteer-based, we are instructor-based; meaning that only instructors, not volunteers, give lessons. Additionally, 100 percent of our instructors are certified by the Professional Ski Instructors of America."

Equipment is just as individualized, and the Adaptive Sports Center offers a wide range of monoskis and biskis. Says Neustedter, "Snowboarding is really increasing in popularity, and we even have special boot fittings for that." The folks at the Adaptive Sports Center also realize that one size doesn't necessarily fit all, and each piece of equipment is customized as needed for their clients. Adds Neustedter, "We go through a lot of duct tape in the winter, as it's a great tool to quickly customize equipment."

Best of all, no experience is needed to give adaptive skiing a try. Says Neustedter, "It's all mental. If you think you can do it, you can do it. If you can get over the mental hurdle, we can help you get over the physical ones."

Nordic Inn
14 Treasury Road
Crested Butte, CO 81224
(970) 349-5542
www.nordicinncb.com

GPS Coordinates
N 40.03455
W 105.46509

Toilet and shower in room 114 at the Nordic Inn

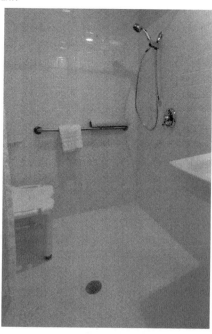

Glenwood Hot Springs Lodge

Glenwood Springs, CO

L ocated just 150 miles west of Denver along Interstate 70, Glenwood Springs is home to the largest mineral hot springs pool in the world. Established in 1888, the main pool spans the length of a football field and contains over a million gallons of natural mineral water. Doc Holiday reportedly visited the hot springs to ease his tuberculosis, Theodore Roosevelt summered there one year, and during WWII the hot springs pool was used by physiotherapists to rehabilitate injured soldiers. Although there's still a definite historic feel to the Glenwood Hot Springs Lodge, modern access upgrades have been added over the years, which makes it a good choice for wheelchair-users and slow walkers.

Access Details

Located across the street from the historic bathhouse, the Glenwood Hot Springs Lodge features level access to the front lobby, which is located on the second floor. After check-in, guests can park in an accessible space in the underground parking garage and take the elevator to the third floor, where accessible Room 325 is located.

Access features of the room include wide doorways and excellent pathway access. It's furnished with a 26-inch high king-sized bed with wheelchair access on both sides, an easy chair, a desk, an armoire, a small refrigerator and a microwave. There is also level access out to the patio through a large sliding glass door. Although it's not technically a private patio, it's pretty secluded and surrounded by shrubs, and it's a nice spot to enjoy a glass of wine after a relaxing soak.

The bathroom is very spacious with a full five-foot turning radius. It's equipped with a roll-in shower with grab bars, a hand-held showerhead and a fold-down shower bench. The toilet grab bars are located on the left and back walls (as seated) and the bathroom also has a roll-under sink.

Hot springs access and a full cooked-to-order breakfast are also included with all rooms, which makes it an almost all-inclusive vacation package.

Candy's Take

The folks at Glenwood Hot Springs get a big thumbs up for retaining the historic feel of the bathhouse, while adding modern access features. It's a great place to relax, work out the kinks and just take in the beautiful surroundings. I also really like the patio space in the lodge room. Although it's not totally private, it's a nice place to relax, as the room is tucked away in the back of the property.

Room 325 at Glenwood Hot Springs Lodge

Bathroom in room 325 at Glenwood Hot Springs Lodge

Best Fit

The room is beyond comfortable, and the extra large bathroom can accommodate even large scooters and power wheelchairs. The property is good for all abilities, as there is even access to the historic pools. It's the perfect pick for a spa getaway or even a romantic retreat.

Nearby

Enjoying the hot springs is truly the thing to do at this resort. Although it's just a short walk from the lodge to the pools, there are several flights of stairs along the route, so it's best for wheelchair-users and slow walkers to just drive over. There are several accessible parking places in front of the bathhouse, with good pathway access up to the front door. Inside, there's plenty of room to roll around, with level access to the gift shop and changing areas.

Both the men's and women's changing rooms have an accessible toilet stall and a roll-in shower; however there is also a family changing room on the ground floor which has a roll-in shower with a fold-down shower bench.

Outside, there are two pools: a large main pool and a small therapy pool. Lift access is available to both, so your choice depends on your water temperature preference. The main pool is usually around 93 degrees, while the therapy pool heats up to 104 degrees. Most of the kids tend to keep to the big pool, so the therapy pool is usually a lot calmer. Still, because of access modifications, the choice is entirely yours.

And if you'd like a bite to eat, be sure and stop by the Grill, located behind the main pool. There's level access from outside, with plenty of room to navigate in the restaurant. They serve up cooked-to-order omelets and eggs during the breakfast hour, and have a variety of sandwiches soups, pizzas and treats to choose from the rest of the day. You can even dine outside if that's your preference.

Glenwood Hot Springs Lodge
401 N. River Street
Glenwood Springs, CO 81601
(800) 537-7946
www.hotspringspool.com

GPS Coordinates
N 39.54962
W 107.32360

Pool lift at the hot springs

The Broadmoor

Colorado Springs, CO

L ocated in Colorado Springs, this Grand Dame of the Rockies spans over 3,000 acres and includes more than 700 rooms. The property made its debut in 1891 as a casino, but the current incarnation was built in 1918 by Spencer Brown. Over the years, it has seen many additions, improvements and upgrades, and the end result is top-drawer access.

Access Details

The most accessible rooms are located in Broadmoor West, one of the newer buildings on the property. There's barrier-free access to the lobby, with valet parking available. Room 4359 features wide doorways and good pathway access, and is furnished with two 32-inch high double beds. There is also a king-sized sofa bed in the large sitting area, along with two easy chairs and a desk. And the extra large walk-in closet has room for a car-full of luggage, with plenty of room to spare.

The bathroom has a roll-in shower with a hand-held showerhead, grab bars and a portable shower seat. It also features a roll-under sink and a toilet with grab bars on the back and right walls (as seated). It's all very spacious, with plenty of room to navigate a wheelchair or scooter.

Rooms 4158 and 4259, which are located in the same building, also have the same bathroom configuration, but they are furnished with 22-inch high king-sized beds. As with everything else, you have choices in accessibility at The Broadmoor.

There's also good access around the property, and to the restaurants, bars, shops and outdoor areas. There is level access to the spa, and all of the pools have lifts. The outdoor zero-entry pool also has a water wheelchair. Truly, there's no limit to what you can do at the Broadmoor.

Candy's Take

I really love the refined elegance and luxurious feel of the property, but beyond that, the employees go the extra mile with special requests. For example, they can arrange to raise or lower your bed, or provide extra equipment like bed rails or raised toilet seats. Says Allison Scott, Director of Communications, "There's very little we can't do as far as access accommodations are concerned." And that's reason enough to choose The Broadmoor.

Best Fit

Between the extras that the staff can offer, and the good access in the room

Room 4359 at the Broadmoor

Bathroom in room 4359 at the Broadmoor

and around the property, The Broadmoor will work for just about any wheelchair-user or slow walker. It's my top pick for a romantic getaway, and it would be absolutely perfect for a special anniversary.

Nearby

The Pikes Peak Cog Railway (www.cograilway.com) is a must-do while you are in the area. This historic railway departs from nearby Manitou Springs and travels up almost nine miles of track, to the summit of Pikes Peak. The trip lasts just over three hours, and includes a little time on top to take in the view from one of Colorado's 54 "fourteeners".

Accessible parking is available near the depot, with an attendant on duty to direct folks. If you have any questions, don't hesitate to ask, as the employees are very helpful. Access is good on the train too, with ramp access and transfer plates. You can stay in your own wheelchair or transfer to a train seat. If you want to stay in your wheelchair, you'll be seated in the last row, with your companion in front of you. There are no tie-downs on the train, but the train only goes eight miles-per-hour, so it's really not a problem. Plan ahead though and use the accessible restrooms at the station, as there are no toilet facilities on the train.

During the ride, you'll be treated to a narrative about the history and geography of the area. The train schedule is somewhat weather dependent, and in inclement weather it only goes up to the 10,000 foot stop. Still you can get out and roll-around and enjoy the view; however there aren't any toilet facilities there. Gladly the latter issue isn't a problem at the summit station, where you'll also get sweeping views of the Rockies.

The Broadmoor
1 Lake Avenue
Colorado Springs, CO 80906
(855) 634-7711
www.broadmoor.com

GPS Coordinates
N 38.79078
W 104.85055

Level boarding on the Pikes Peak Cog Railway

Ridgway State Park Yurt

Ridgway, CO

Located 15 miles from Ouray in Southwestern Colorado, Ridgway State Park is known for its beautiful reservoir, extensive trail system and diverse wildlife. Lauded for the barrier-free design of its facilities, the park has a good collection of accessible trails, and a nice accessible yurt. And with striking views of the San Juan Mountains, it's the perfect place to spend a few days and bask in Mother Nature's glory.

Access Details

The accessible Beaver Lodge Yurt (Yurt 10) is centrally located in the Dutch Charlie area of the park, in the Dakota Terraces Campground. Check-in is relatively easy, as there's no campground office, and no forms to complete. Visitors are e-mailed the yurt key code with their confirmation, so after you pick up a map at the self-pay fee station, you can drive directly to the yurt in Loop A.

There's accessible parking in front of the yurt with a sidewalk leading up to the porch. The yurt has a wide doorway and a threshold ramp, and there's plenty of room to wheel around inside. Furnishings include two queen-sized futons, a bunk bed (bedding not included), and a table and chairs. The kitchen area has a counter with a small refrigerator and a microwave. It's also equipped with lights and a gas stove for heat.

Out front there is an accessible picnic table and a grill on a cement pad. There is also a 15-inch high tent platform on the side. The restroom is just a short walk away along a level path. Both the men's and women's restrooms have a large stall with grab bars on the back and left walls (as seated).

The bathhouse is located near the entrance to Loop A, which is a bit farther down the road. There's accessible parking in front, if you'd prefer to drive there. Each bathhouse has a roll-in shower with a fold-down shower bench, a hand-held showerhead and grab bars. The coin slot for the shower is within easy reach while seated, and there is also a roll-under sink and an accessible toilet stall in each bathhouse. The toilet grab bars are located on the back and right walls (as seated) on the women's side, and on the back and left walls (as seated) on the men's side. There's also plenty of room for an attendant to assist in the shower and toilet areas.

Candy's Take

This is one of the nicer campgrounds that I've stayed in, and the hosts do a good job of keeping the showers and restrooms clean, and the trash

Inside the Beaver Lodge Yurt at Ridgway State Park

Western Bluebird on the Forest Discovery Trail

picked around the campsites. It's also very quiet. I also really like the raised tent platform at the accessible yurt, as it's not a feature you often see. And there's a lot of room between the yurts, so you get plenty of privacy.

Best Fit

Although the yurt is certainly large enough for just about any wheelchair or scooter, the speed bumps along the campground road make it difficult to wheel to the bathhouse. That said, if you are able to drive down there, it's not a problem. The yurts have electricity, so you can recharge your wheelchair or scooter batteries there, and heat from the gas stove is a real plus on cold mornings. This is a good choice for a family vacation. Fisherman will also love Ridgway State Park, as the area below Ridgway Dam is stocked with rainbow trout.

Nearby

There are plenty of accessible trails to explore in the park. For a good orientation, stop by the Visitor Center in the Dutch Charlie area. There's level access to the building, with interpretive exhibits and a ranger information desk inside. Outside, there is a short paved trail to an overlook which offers a good view of the reservoir and surrounding forest.

The Forest Discovery Loop is also located near the Visitor Center, and a portion of this half-mile loop is doable for most wheelchair-users and slow walkers. The hard-packed trail is covered in crushed granite, and the first half of it is pretty level. After that the grade increases and there are ruts and rough spots along the way. Additionally, it can get pretty muddy after a storm.

Down by the marina, the Mears Trail is a good accessible choice. This one-mile paved trail is fairly level, and runs alongside the lake. It's not really too scenic in dry years when the lake is low, but if it's a normal rainfall year it's very pleasant.

Over in the Pa-Co-Chu-Puk area at the north end of the park, you'll find a short paved pathway along the Uncompahgre River. It's four feet wide, with benches along the way. Additionally a portion of the Oak Leaf Trail, which leads to the walk-in campground, is also paved and level.

Last but not least, the accessible Marmot Run Trail is located in the Dallas Creek area in the south end of the park. This 1.8-mile paved level trail runs alongside the reservoir, and when the lake is full it's a good riparian habitat. There is also an accessible restroom and picnic site along the trail at Cookie Tree, so pack along a lunch and enjoy the day at the lake.

Ridgway State Park Yurt
28555 Highway 550
Ridgway, CO 81432
(970) 626-5822
cpw.state.co.us/placestogo/Parks/ridgway

GPS Coordinates
N 38.19685
W 107.74172

Toilet and shower in the men's bathhouse at Ridgway State Park

Grouse Mountain Lodge

Whitefish, MT

From the aroma of the fire to the exposed beams and vaulted ceilings, you know you're in a real wilderness retreat the moment you enter the lobby of Grouse Mountain Lodge. Located along the Whitefish Lake Golf Course, this 143-room luxury property first opened its doors on June 30, 1984. Ever since then, it's welcomed guests year after year to enjoy the majestic scenery of nearby Glacier National Park. And thanks to some very vocal local advocates, the access at this upscale mountain retreat is first-rate too.

Access Details

There is accessible parking near the front door, with ramp access up to the lobby. Room 103, which is located on the first floor, features wide doorways, a lowered peephole, and good pathway access. There's even a lowered clothing rod in the closet. It's furnished with two 30-inch high beds with an access aisle between them, a refrigerator, a desk and a side chair.

The spacious bathroom has a full five-foot turning radius, and is outfitted with a roomy roll-in shower with grab bars and a hand-held showerhead. A portable shower chair is also available. Other access features include a roll-under sink, and a lowered towel rack. The toilet grab bars are located on the right and back walls (as seated). Round it out with a lowered mirror, and you have a nicely accessible bathroom.

Access is good throughout the public areas of the lodge too, including Logan's Grill, which is located just off the lobby.

Candy's Take

This property has a nice rustic feel, but with high-end amenities. I totally enjoyed just relaxing by the fireplace in the lobby. I'm also very partial to the food at Logan's Grill. It's easy to eat healthy there — I had a delicious cedar planked salmon, while Charles enjoyed a braised rainbow trout. Try and snag a seat by the cozy fireplace if you can; but truthfully there's not a bad seat in the house.

Best Fit

This place was recommended by a local who uses a wheelchair, and I have to say her evaluation of the access was spot-on. The oversized bathroom with a roll-in shower makes it a good choice for anybody. Plus, it has much better access than any of the properties inside Glacier National Park, but it's close enough for day trips. If you love the outdoors, you'll love this property. It's also a good choice for a romantic retreat.

Bathroom in room 103 at the Grouse Mountain Lodge

View at Logan Pass on Going-to-the-Sun Road in Glacier National Park

Nearby

There are many accessible things to see in nearby Glacier National Park (http://www.nps.gov/glac). At the top of the list is the drive across the summit on Going-to-the-Sun Road. Although it's only 50 miles long, allow a full day for this drive, as there are many viewpoints and overlooks along the way. Even if you never get out of your car, you can catch some great vistas of this beautiful national park.

If you'd like to get a little more active, the Apgar Bicycle Path is a good introductory trail. It begins behind the Apgar Visitor Center, near the west entrance to the park. This wide, level asphalt path winds through the forest, and out to McDonald Creek, before it loops back out to Main Street. From there, it's a level roll back to the Visitor Center.

If you'd prefer a longer hike, the .7-mile Trail of the Cedars is a good choice. It's located up the road from McDonald Falls on Going-to-the-Sun Road. The bulk of this loop trail is a wide level boardwalk, but there is a short section of asphalt in the middle. There are interpretive plaques and viewing platforms along the trail, and the boardwalk features low bumpers instead of high railings, for unobstructed views of the surrounding forest.

Running Eagle Falls Nature Trail, which is located on the east side of the park, is the newest accessible trail. To get to the trailhead, take Highway 49 to Two Medicine Junction, then follow the spur for about five miles towards Two Medicine. This hard-packed dirt trail travels for a-third-of-a-mile to a rocky beach where you can get a good view of Running Eagle Falls. There's also a bench there, so you can sit down and take it all in.

Last but not least, don't miss the trail out to Goat Lick Overlook, which is located along the west border of the park, on Highway 2, about two-and-a-half miles east of the Walton Ranger Station. A short paved path leads out to an overlook along the Middle Fork of the Flathead River. Across the way, you'll spot mountain goats, elk and deer that come to lick the mineral laden cliffs. Don't forget your binoculars, and try to come early in the day when the animals are more active.

Grouse Mountain Lodge
2 Fairway Drive
Whitefish, MT 59937
(406) 892-2525
www.grousemountainlodge.com

GPS Coordinates
N 48.40960
W 114.35999

Trail of the Cedars in Glacier National Park

The View Hotel

Monument Valley, UT

Located in an isolated stretch of Monument Valley, The View Hotel is aptly named, as every room has a magnificent view of the beautiful red rock formations that dot this tribal land. The property, which is between Mexican Hat, Utah and Kayenta, Arizona off of Highway 163, is technically in Arizona, although it sports a Utah address. Still it's not hard to find as there aren't very many structures in this neck of the woods. And that's part of the beauty of it all — the isolation. If you've ever seen a western movie, chances are you've seen Monument Valley. In fact, while driving through this remote patch of Navajo land, you can almost picture a band of warriors lined up on the ridge. And again, that's part of the beauty of it all.

Access Details

There's plenty of accessible parking in front of the property, with level access to the lobby. Room 103, which features wide doorways, a lowered peephole and lever handles, is located just around the corner. It's furnished with a 28-inch high queen-sized bed, with wheelchair access on both sides. An easy chair, desk, refrigerator, microwave and a chest of drawers round out the furnishings.

The bathroom is equipped with a roll-in shower with a built-in bench, grab bars and a hand-held showerhead. There is a slight one-inch lip on the shower threshold, but most people won't have any problems with that. And with the full five-foot turning radius in the bathroom, there's plenty of room to navigate even the largest wheelchair. Other bathroom access features include a roll-under sink and toilet grab bars on the right and back walls (as seated).

There is good access throughout the public areas of the property, with elevator access to The View restaurant and The Trading Post gift shop on the second floor. A loaner wheelchair is also available at the front desk.

Candy's Take

The best thing about this property is of course the view. I love the balcony, as it's a great place to sit back and enjoy the sunset. From the hotel, you can also take the 17-mile drive through Monument Valley; however the road is unpaved and bumpy and not really recommended for low clearance vehicles. No matter where you look, the scenery is nothing short of spectacular.

Room 103 at the View Hotel

View from the balcony in room 103 at the View Hotel

Best Fit

The bathroom is certainly large enough to accommodate power wheelchairs and scooters, but it should be noted that the placement of fixtures partially blocks the transfer space for the built-in shower bench. That said, if you can roll over the one-inch lip on the opposite side of the shower, it won't be a problem. Other than that, it's smooth sailing access-wise. This property is the perfect choice for a road trip, as Highway 163 makes for a very scenic drive with lots of Native American vendors along the roadside.

Nearby

Of course the hotel is ideally located for exploring Monument Valley Tribal Park (navajonationparks.org/htm/monumentvalley.htm). Known as "the place where the earth meets the sky", this chunk of Navajo land boasts an impressive collection of sandstone formations towering as high as 1,000 feet above the desert.

A Welcome Center and a Navajo Market are located near the park entrance. Accessible parking is available in front of the Welcome Center, with level access up to the front door. Inside, there are interpretive exhibits about the history of the area, and about the many films and commercials that were made there. There's barrier-free access throughout the building, and to the terrace out back, which offers a panoramic view of the Mitten Buttes and Merrick Butte.

Next door there's also accessible parking near the Navajo Market, which features a variety of local vendors, and boasts everything from artwork and jewelry to baskets and even wood carvings. There is level access to many of the shops, and although some are a bit small, most vendors will happily bring items out to you. It's a good place to shop for native wares, as the quality is good and the prices are reasonable.

And then of course, there's always the view.

The View
Indian Route 42 East
Monument Valley, UT 84536
(435) 727-5555
www.monumentvalleyview.com

GPS Coordinates
N 36.98188
W 110.11210

Toilet and shower in room 103 at the View Hotel

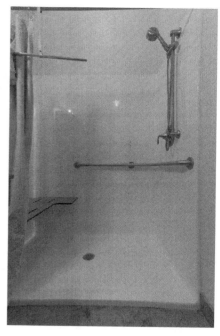

Zion Lodge

Springdale, UT

L ocated in Zion National Park, Zion Lodge has quite the history. The original lodge was built in the 1920s, however it was destroyed by fire in 1966. It was quickly rebuilt, but the new design lacked the rustic appeal of the original structure. In 1990 the exterior of the lodge was restored to its classic appearance, and today the property offers modern access features yet retains its historic character. Truly, it's the best of both worlds.

Access Details

There's level access to the main lodge building, and a barrier-free path to the registration desk. The four accessible guestrooms are located in Building A, which is just a short walk or roll from the main lobby. There's plenty of accessible parking in the nearby lot, but there's also an accessible drop-off area in front of Building A.

The accessible guestrooms are quite spacious, and feature wide doorways, lowered peepholes and plenty of room to navigate around the two queen-sized beds. The rooms also boast a private back porch, which offers a great view of the surrounding canyon.

Two of the accessible rooms have a roll-in shower with a fold-down shower bench, and two are equipped with a tub/shower combination with a portable shower chair. Other bathroom access features include grab bars in the shower and around the toilet, a hand-held showerhead and a roll-under sink.

There is also good access to the public areas in the main lodge, including the gift shop, the coffee bar and the Castle Dome Cafe. Additionally, there's elevator access to the Red Rock Grill, located on the second floor. All in all it's a very comfortable, convenient and accessible property.

Candy's Take

This property is literally surrounded by Zion Canyon, and the red rock views are nothing short of magnificent. I also like the fact that, unlike the lodging options in nearby Hurricane, Zion Lodge is pretty quiet. Plus you can actually see the stars. It's also a very popular pick, especially in the summer, so make your reservations early to avoid disappointment.

Best Fit

Since guests have their choice of accessible bathroom configurations, Zion Lodge is a good choice for everybody. The accessible guestrooms are very

Bathoom in an accessible room in Building A at Zion Lodge

View along the Riverside Walk in Zion National Park

spacious, and there's plenty of room for even the largest assistive device in them. It's the perfect home base if you want to explore Zion Canyon, and it's also a great choice for a family vacation.

Nearby

Although vehicle traffic is prohibited the Zion Canyon portion of Zion National Park (www.nps.gov/zion), visitors with confirmed reservations at Zion Lodge can drive to the lodge. After that, guests must park their cars and take the free accessible shuttle bus to explore Zion Canyon. It's a very scenic route through the canyon, with several accessible trails along the way.

The closest trail to Zion Lodge is the Lower Emerald Pool Trail, which is located across the street. A level bridge leads to the wide .6-mile paved trail that winds along the river. Although it's not rated as accessible, many folks will be able to do at least the first part of it. After that it gets pretty steep, but even if you can't do the whole trail, take some time to enjoy the river from the bridge at the trailhead.

Another good trail for most wheelchair-users and slow walkers is the Riverside Walk, located near the Temple of Sinawava shuttle bus stop. This two-mile round-trip hike runs alongside the Virgin River at the bottom of a narrow canyon. Although it's rated as wheelchair-accessible, after about the first half-mile you'll encounter some short, steep sections. It's probably doable for most folks in power wheelchairs and scooters, but manual wheelchair-users may need some assistance through the steeper parts. Still, it's a great trail to try, as it's paved and there are benches along the way; and you can always turn back if it proves too much of a challenge.

The most accessible trail in the park is the Pa'rus Trail. This 1.8-mile trail, which runs along the Virgin River, is wide and flat and a good choice for all ability levels. It runs from the Canyon Junction shuttle bus stop to the Zion Canyon Visitors Center. There is also a branch over to the Human History Museum, however you have to be able to do about 15-20 steps to take that fork. Still the Pa'rus Trail is a very pleasant way to enjoy the park; but you have to be committed to going the distance, as there's no place to exit along the way.

Zion Lodge
1 Zion Canyon Scenic Drive
Springdale, UT 84767
(435) 772-7700
www.zionlodge.com

GPS Coordinates
N 37.25019
W 112.95650

The Pa'rus Trail in Zion National Park

Coming Soon

Barrier Free Travel
Utah's National Parks
for Wheelers and Slow Walkers

Penned by accessible travel expert Candy B. Harrington, this handy access guide includes information about accessible trails, sites and attractions in and near Utah's five national parks. Detailed information about accessible lodging near Canyonlands, Arches and Capitol Reef national parks, as well as lodging in and near Zion and Bryce Canyon national parks is also included. Plus, get some inside tips on where to go for the best windshield views, accessible picnic spots and sunset photos. Don't leave home without this essential resource.

www.barrierfreeutahparks.com

Delicate Arch at Arches National Park

Iron Gate Inn

Cedar City, UT

Located in the heart of Cedar City, Utah, The Iron Gate Inn is housed in an 1897 building that's been completely restored. Says owner Susan Wooten, "I made sure we included an accessible room in the renovation plans, because my father was in a wheelchair and I remember how hard it was for him to find truly accessible accommodations." Susan did a great job with the access features, and today this nine-room inn is a good choice for wheelchair-users and slow walkers alike.

Access Details

Although there are steps up to the front door of this historic property, ramp access is available from the parking area. And Susan will happily reserve the space closest to the ramp for slow walkers. Just let her know that you need that accommodation when you make your reservation.

Inside, there's barrier-free access throughout the tastefully decorated home, with plenty of room to maneuver a wheelchair. It's not cluttered like many historic B&Bs, and the clean lines give it a very modern feel.

The accessible Grace Mary Room, which is located on the first floor, features wide doors, wood floors and good pathway access. It's furnished with a 25-inch open-frame queen-sized bed, with good wheelchair access on both sides.

The bathroom features a full five-foot turning radius and is equipped with a roll-in shower with grab bars and a hand-held showerhead. The toilet grab bars are located on the back and right walls (as seated), and the bathroom also has a roll-under sink. And if you need a portable shower chair, just let Susan know when you make your reservation, and it will be in your room when you arrive.

There's also good access to the breakfast area, and level access out to the adjacent patio. A full breakfast is included with the room, and in nice weather guests can enjoy it outside.

Candy's Take

My favorite place on this property is the patio area. It's a nice spot to sit and relax, or enjoy a glass of wine. They even have a wine hour there in the afternoon. I also like that Susan is very tuned in to access needs of all kinds, and she goes above-and-beyond for her guests.

Best Fit

Because of the good design, large bathroom and the roll-in shower, this

The Grace Mary Room at Iron Gate Inn

Bathroom in the Grace Mary Room at Iron Gate Inn

property will work for people of all abilities. It's more of an adult property, and it's nice and quiet, with no kids underfoot. It's a good home base for exploring the surrounding countryside, and it's absolutely the perfect place to stay for the Utah Shakespeare Festival. They even host some of the actors for breakfast every now and then, so guests can get the inside scoop on the productions.

Nearby

If you'd like to do a little wine tasting while you're in town, Utah's newest winery is located just across the parking lot. Winemaker Doug McCombs opened the doors to the Iron Gate Winery (www.igwinery.com) in 2012. There's level access to the winery, plenty of room to roll around inside, and a large accessible bathroom.

Doug features a wide range of wines to choose from including Riesling, Chardonnay, Viogner, Roussane, Cabernet Sauvignon, Tempest (red blend), Syrah, Mourvedre, Tempranillo and Zinfandel. And although you can certainly taste wines at this location, it's too close to a church to be a retail outlet. Doug solved that problem nicely, as he opened up a small store for retail transactions just down the block. It's only a short walk, and although there's a small step up at the entrance, the employees are happy to bring your purchase out to you.

Additionally, the property is just a few blocks from Southern Utah University, where the Utah Shakespeare Festival is held (www.bard.org).

All of the venues there are wheelchair-accessible, and if you plan things right, you can see six plays in three days. The festival runs from late June through October, and in addition to the plays, patrons can also attend a variety of seminars, ranging from props and costumes to a general review of the previous nights performance. All of the seminars are free, and they are held in accessible venues.

Iron Gate Inn
100 N. 200 W.
Cedar City, UT 84720
(435) 867-0603
www.theirongateinn.com

GPS Coordinates
N 37.67913
W 113.06480

Jugglers perform at the Green Show at the Utah Shakespeare Festival

Wasatch Mountain State Park Cabin — Midway, UT

L ocated in Heber Valley in Northern Utah, Wasatch Mountain
State Park is the most developed state park in the beehive state.
This 23,000-acre preserve is a favorite for the locals, but somewhat
overlooked by out-of-staters. And at 5,900 feet, the accessible ridge top
camping cabin is the perfect place to take a break on a road trip. It's a nice
change of pace from the interstate motels, and since it's just four miles
from US 40, it's a perfectly doable option.

Access Details

The Falcon's Ledge cabin is appropriately named, as it's perched on a
mountaintop in the Pine Creek Campground. There's no dedicated
accessible parking, but the parking spot reserved for the cabin is two
spaces wide, and roomy enough for even the largest van. From the parking
area, there's a paved level path to the front porch, and barrier-free access to
the cabin.

The cabin is furnished with a table and two chairs, a queen-sized
futon and a bunk bed (bedding not included), a refrigerator and a

microwave. It also has electricity, an air conditioner and a heater. Outside, there is a water pump near the picnic table and the grill.

The restrooms are located across the parking lot, just a short walk from the cabin. There is ramp access to the restrooms and there is an accessible stall with grab bars and a roll-under sink in both the men's and women's restroom.

The showers are located in the nearby Cottonwood Loop, between spaces 40 and 42. Although it's just a short walk, it's best to drive over because of the grade. There's accessible parking in front of the bathhouse with level access to the unisex accessible shower room, which features a roll-in shower with a fold-down shower seat, and a lowered showerhead and controls. Accessible sinks, mirrors and outlets are located just outside of the shower room.

Accessible restrooms with large stalls and grab bars are also located there. The men's restroom has toilet grab bars on the right side (as seated), and the women's has them on the left (as seated).

Candy's Take

I really enjoyed the view from the cabin, and it was nice to sit on the front porch sip my coffee and watch the sunrise, before hitting the road again. The down side to this otherwise comfy cabin is that it's located across the parking lot from the group campground, and these group campers tend to be a bit

Inside the Falcon's Ledge cabin at Wasatch Mountain State Park

Inside the Visitor Center at Wasatch Mountain State Park

on the noisy side. On the hand, if there are no group campers there, it's far removed from the other sites; but then again, that a roll of the dice.

Best Fit

The cabin itself will certainly work for just about everyone, but because of a few other access glitches this is really only a good choice for slow walkers or part time wheelchair-users. The cabin picnic table can't be accessed in a wheelchair, and the path to the bathhouse would be tough going for most wheelers. Add in the lack of access to the trails and sites in the park, and that's three strikes. This is a good family choice, and if you have little ones in tow, you'll feel right at home there. And even though the scenery is very conducive to romance, the campers here are a very chatty bunch, so it's really not a good couples getaway. Truthfully it's best suited for a one-night break on a road trip.

Nearby

Wasatch Mountain State Park offers a few historic sites, but to be honest it's more of a "rest and relax" park than a "get up and explore park". Still a stop at the Visitor Center is a must. There's level access to the building, which has interpretive exhibits and an information desk inside.

Outside there's a very peaceful pond, surrounded by a nice grassy area. There are several picnic tables around the pond, and it's a level roll out to them, so pack along a picnic lunch and enjoy the scenery. And although it is a Visitor Center, it also seems to be one of the quieter places in the park.

Slow walkers will also want to head over to Huber Grove, where the historic Huber farmhouse and creamery still stand. Built in the late 1800s by the Huber family, these historic buildings have a step up into them, but they are still worth the short walk even if you don't go inside.

There's no accessible parking, but then again it's just a dirt parking lot. From the parking lot it's just a short walk to the apple tree grove, but there is a 12-inch step up to the bridge to cross the creek. Truly it's only doable for slow walkers, but there are some picnic tables in a level area near the grove, so it might be a good lunch option for some people. If you can manage it, it's worth the walk.

Wasatch Mountain State Park Cabin	**GPS Coordinates**
1281 Warm Springs Road	N 40.55654
Midway, UT 84049	W 111.49030
(435) 654-3961	
www.stateparks.utah.gov/park/wasatch-mountain-state-park	

Shower and toilet in the men's bathhouse at Wasatch Mountain State Park

Red Cliffs Lodge

Moab, UT

Nestled on the banks of the Colorado River in Eastern Utah, Red Cliffs Lodge is smack dab in the middle of red rock country. And although the main lodge is a work of art itself with its 20-foot high ceilings, wood paneled walls and rustic log furniture, the drive there is even more dramatic. As Highway 128 winds along the Colorado River, red rock cliffs line the opposite side of the road and create a very scenic approach to the property. The property itself boasts a decidedly western ambiance, but it's outfitted with all the comforts of home, and it includes a very nice accessible suite.

Access Details

There is ramp access to the main lodge building, with good access to all of the public areas. The accessible riverside king suite (Room 101) is just a short walk from the lobby, with accessible parking directly in front of it. The spacious suite features a large sleeping area, a living area; and a kitchenette equipped with a microwave, a sink and a refrigerator.

There is barrier-free access throughout the unit, which has tile floors,

wide doorways, lowered closet rods and level access to a private patio that overlooks the river. The bathroom features a roll-in shower with grab bars, a hand-held showerhead and a portable shower bench. It also comes equipped with a roll-under sink and toilet grab bars on the right and back walls (as seated). Great attention was paid to access details, and they even remembered a lowered soap dish in the shower.

There is barrier-free access to the Cowboy Grill, which is located in the main building. This intimate restaurant serves up a hearty selection of regional favorites accompanied by locally produced Castle Creek wines. And the views of the red cliffs and the river from the restaurant are spectacular. For the best seating, be sure and make a reservation and request a table on the patio. It's a great place to enjoy the sunset.

Candy's Take

Although you just can't beat the views from the restaurant and the patio, my favorite thing about this property is the Moab Museum of Film and Western Heritage, located just off the main lobby. The accessible entrance is located around the back, but just ask at the front desk if you have any questions. The museum contains memorabilia from the over 120 movies shot in the area, including City Slickers II, Back to the Future III, Thelma and Louise and Indiana Jones and the Last Crusade. There's no admission charge and it's a fun stop for film buffs.

Room 101 at Red Cliffs Lodge

Bathroom in room 101 at Red Cliffs Lodge

Best Fit

The room is well done in the access department, and with the large roll-in shower it's a good choice for just about any wheelchair-user. It's a great choice for a family vacation as there's room for the whole brood in the suite, and you can even cook a few simple meals there. And the view from the deck makes it a good pick for anyone who enjoys the outdoors.

Nearby

Two of Utah's national parks — Arches and Canyonlands — are located near the property, so save a few days to explore both of them.

Arches National Park (www.nps.gov/arch) is at the top of the list scenery wise, as it features over 2,000 sandstone arches, along with a healthy smattering of what can only be described as unusual rock formations. There's level access to the Visitor Center, just off Highway 191, where you can pick up a map and browse through the interpretive exhibits.

From there, head north, past the petrified dunes and the rock pinnacles until you reach Balanced Rock, where an accessible .3-mile trail leads around the formation out to the overlook.

Truly most of the park can be seen from the main road as you'll pass by Ham Rock, the Parade of Elephants and other easily identifiable formations. And don't miss Delicate Arch, the most photographed formation in the park. The trail out to this arch is not accessible, but you can get a great view of it from the lower viewpoint.

Save another day for a visit to Canyonlands National Park (www.nps.gov/cany), located just north of Arches off of Highway 191. The most accessible section of the Park—Islands in the Sky—is a large mesa wedged in between the Green and Colorado Rivers. Be sure and pick up the self-guided CD audio tour at the Visitor Center, as it describes the major sites and provides a little history of the park.

Best bet is to head straight out to the end of the road to Grand View Point Overlook. There's plenty of accessible parking and a paved trail out to the overlook, which offers a panoramic view of the park. It's definitely is a grand view.

As you work your way back towards the park entrance, be sure and stop at Buck Canyon Overlook and Green River Overlook for more spectacular canyon views. Buck Canyon Overlook features accessible parking and a 200-foot paved pathway that leads out to the overlook, while the Green River Overlook also has accessible parking, with level access out to a spectacular canyon view. As with Arches National Park, this park also makes for a great scenic drive.

Red Cliffs Lodge
Mile Post 14, Highway 128
Moab, UT 84532
(435) 259-2002
www.redcliffslodge.com

GPS Coordinates
N 38.68262
W 109.45615

Park Avenue at Arches National Park

320 Guest Ranch

Gallatin Gateway, MT

Built in 1898, the 320 Guest Ranch is located 52 miles south of Bozeman, along a two-mile stretch of the Gallatin River. This historic property features 59 log cabins, outfitted with classic western style furnishings and decor. It's a good place to get away from the hustle and bustle of city life, and it's close enough to Yellowstone for a day trip. And although it's not totally accessible, one cabin will work for some slow walkers.

Access Details

There's barrier-free access to office, with plenty of room to navigate a wheelchair or walker inside. Riverview Cabin 12, which is the most accessible cabin on the property, is located just a short drive away. There's ramp access to the front porch from the parking area, and level access over the front threshold. Inside, there's plenty of room in this two-bedroom cabin, which has good pathway access and wide doorways.

The larger bedroom is furnished with a 21-inch high queen-sized bed, while the smaller bedroom features two double beds of the

197

same height. There's also a small sink and vanity area in the smaller bedroom. The living room has a fold-out sofa bed, which bumps the sleeping capacity up to eight. The adjacent kitchenette has a small stove, a refrigerator and a dining room table. And if you get chilly, there's a fireplace in the living room, and plenty of wood on the front porch.

And although the bathroom is not adapted, it will work for many people. It includes a tub and a separate low-step shower. The tub has vertical and horizontal grab bars, but you'll need to bring your own portable hand-held showerhead. The low-step shower doesn't have any grab bars, but it might work for some ambulatory folks. The toilet also has one grab bar on the left, (as seated).

A full buffet breakfast is included in the room rate (from June to September, and mid December to March only). It's served in the restaurant, which is a short walk from the cabin. Some folks may need assistance over a small grassy patch in front of the restaurant, and up the concrete ramp. There's one step at the front doorway, but there's level access to the back patio dining area. Since there's no access to the restaurant from the back patio, you'll have to have someone else fill your plate and bring it out to you. On the plus side, the employees are very accommodating, and are happy to assist guests.

Inside Riverview Cabin 12 at the 320 Guest Ranch

Bedroom in Riverview Cabin 12 at the 320 Guest Ranch

Candy's Take

I really like the location of the cabin, as you get a great view of the pasture from the front porch. It's very peaceful and has that real cowboy feel to it. As an added bonus, there's a picnic table and a BBQ in the large pasture just outside the cabin. It's the perfect place to soak up a little nature by day, or do some star gazing at night.

Best Fit

Because of the configuration of the bathroom, this property is a better choice for slow walkers and part time wheelchair-users. You need to be able to walk at least a step in order to use the low-step shower, and to access the restaurant. Still the cabin will sleep eight, so it's a good choice for a multigenerational getaway. It's also a nice choice for a family reunion, as you can book several cabins and have your meals at the picnic table in the pasture.

Nearby

The property is located near the north entrance of Yellowstone National Park (www.nps.gov/yell), which is just a short drive from one of the most dynamic thermal areas of the park — Norris Geyser Basin.

There's accessible parking near the Norris Geyser Basin Museum, with level access up to the museum. Inside, there are a number of interpretive exhibits which detail the thermal activity in the area. Although the boardwalks and trails around the geysers are not technically accessible, they are doable for many people — that is, if you follow the right route.

The trail to Back Basin is semi-accessible depending on the route and weather, while the trail to Porcelain Basin is not accessible at all, because of steep grades and steps. That said, you can get a great view of the area from the overlook in back of the museum. To access the overlook, go out the south entrance of the museum, turn right, then take the first right and follow it out to the overlook.

When you're done taking in the view, double back and follow the right branch of the trail. This is the most accessible part of the one-and-a-half-mile loop around Back Basin. The hard-packed dirt and boardwalk trail travels through a heavily wooded area and around an interesting collection of geysers, mud pots, steam vents and hot springs.

Some folks may need help over a few rough areas of the trail, but for the most part it's doable. Give it a try and go as far as you can. Eventually you'll hit some steps and you'll have to double back. Be sure and note the elevation change on the way down though, as you'll have to roll uphill on the way back.

32 Guest Ranch
205 Buffalo Horn Creek Road
Gallatin Gateway, MT 59730
(406) 995-4283
www.320ranch.com

GPS Coordinates
N 45.10324
W 111.21471

Bathroom in Riverview Cabin 12 at the 320 Guest Ranch

Explorer Cabins at Yellowstone
West Yellowstone, MT

Located just outside the west entrance to Yellowstone National Park, the Explorer Cabins at Yellowstone welcomed their first guests in July 2013. This 50-cabin property focuses on cabineering, a new lodging concept which offers the comforts of home and the perks of a hotel in a remote natural setting. The complex features two accessible cabins with top-drawer amenities and it exudes a definite mountain ambiance.

Access Details

There's no dedicated office for the cabins, so-check in is done at the Grey Wolf Inn & Suites in the winter and at the Yellowstone Park Hotel in the summer. Both properties have accessible parking in front and barrier-free access to the lobby. Luggage assistance is also available upon request.

Cabin 24 features ramp access to the front porch, and accessible parking in a nearby lot. This modern log cabin is furnished with a 14-

inch high sleeper sofa in the living room, and has a kitchenette with a refrigerator, microwave, cook top, sink and a full set of dishes and utensils. There's also a gas fireplace to snuggle up to if you get chilly. And in keeping with the rustic ambience, the cabin is pleasantly minus a television.

The bedroom is furnished with a 31-inch high king-sized bed, with 32 inches of clearance on one side and 26 inches on the other. There is level access to the bathroom, which features a wide doorway and a five-foot turning radius; and is equipped with a roll-in shower with grab bars, a hand-held showerhead, and a fold-down padded shower bench. Toilet grab bars are located on the left and back walls (as seated), and the bathroom also has a roll-under sink.

There is a table and a chair on the large front porch, but you can also enjoy the view through the floor-to-ceiling windows in the living room. Outside there is a paved level pathway around the complex to the fire circle, which is a favorite gathering spot for families.

Cabin 11 offers the same access features, but it's also pet friendly.

Candy's Take

What's not to love about this upscale cabin? Not only is it very spacious, but extra amenities like binoculars, walking sticks, flashlights and even a s'mores kit are included. Truly this is glamping at its finest.

Living room and kitchenette in cabin 24 at Explorer Cabins at Yellowstone

Bedroom in cabin 24 at Explorer Cabins at Yellowstone

Best Fit

Both of the cabins feature excellent access, and they will work for just about every slow walker and wheelchair-user. It's a very family-friendly property, and it's perfect for kids of all ages. It's also an excellent choice for a family national park adventure, as it's much more comfortable than tent camping.

Nearby

The Grizzly & Wolf Discovery Center (www.grizzlydiscoveryctr.com), which is just down the street from the cabins, is worth a stop while you are in West Yellowstone. There's accessible parking near the entrance and level access to the front door. Inside you'll find interpretive exhibits about wolves and bears, ranging from ecology, poaching and bear safety, to a brief run down on the bears of the world.

Outside there is level access to the enclosures, where you can get up-close-and-personal with the inhabitants. From bears, wolves and even bald eagles, there's certainly plenty to see. And if you can't do distances, a wheelchair is available for loan at the front desk. Best bet is to visit in the morning, as the animals are more active then.

The Yellowstone Museum (www.yellowstonehistoriccenter.org), which is located down the street, is also a must-do in West Yellowstone. Housed in the historic Union Pacific Railroad Station, it contains exhibits about Yellowstone, lots of old photos and even the original shoe shine stand from the depot. There's level access to the museum, and barrier-free access to the exhibits. Plan ahead though, as it's only open from May to September.

Over in Yellowstone National Park (www.nps.gov/yell), Old Faithful puts on a daily show that's not to be missed. There's level access to the Visitor Center, which has information about the next eruption; and plenty of room for wheelchairs in the geyser viewing area. There's also a .7-mile boardwalk and asphalt trail around the famous geyser.

After the show, take the barrier-free asphalt trail in front of the general store to Upper Geyser Basin. Even if you don't want to do the whole one-and-a-half-mile length, Castle Geyser and Crested Pool are just a short walk away.

Explorer Cabins at West Yellowstone
201 Grizzly Avenue
West Yellowstone, MT 59758
(866) 826-0138
www.visityellowstonepark.com

GPS Coordinates
N 44.65679
W 111.10298

Toilet and Shower in cabin 24 at Explorer Cabins at Yellowstone

Keyhole State Park Cabin

Moorcroft, WY

Known as a Mecca for migrating birds, Keyhole State Park also boasts a healthy population of mule deer, pronghorn antelope and wild turkeys. And if the wildlife isn't enough, the scenery will definitely win you over. Located on the western edge of the Black Hills, between Sundance and Moorcroft, it's within sight of Devils Tower National Monument. Add in a cute little camping cabin tucked away on the shore of Keyhole Reservoir, and you have all the ingredients for a very accessible outdoor adventure.

Access Details

Located in the Tatanka Campground, on the southeast shore of the reservoir, Cabin 4 features accessible parking on a cement pad with ramp access up to the deck. There level access to the cabin through the wide doorway, and although it's a bit tight, there's enough room to navigate a wheelchair inside.

The cabin is furnished with a 28-inch high double bed and a bunk bed (bedding not included), and a table and bench. There is wheelchair access on one side of the bed, and the cabin is equipped with air conditioning, lights and electrical outlets. There's also a glider and an accessible picnic table on the large deck, and a fire ring near the cabin.

It's just a short level walk to the accessible pit toilets, which have wide doorways and grab bars. There is also a water pump in front of the toilets. And since there aren't any showers in the campground, access isn't really an issue. It's a pretty basic cabin, but certainly comfortable enough. And even though it's near the day use area, it's very quiet in the evening.

Candy's Take

The cabin is in a great location with a nice view of the lake, and I really like the large deck. It's also close to Devils Tower, which is pretty remote, so you can easily get there early in the morning and beat the crowds. There's no gate to the park, so you can go as early as you want — you can even enjoy the sunrise there.

Best Fit

The inside of the cabin would be a tight fit for two wheelchair-users, and in the end it's probably best for manual wheelchair-users or part time wheelchair-users who can park their assistive devices out on the porch. Most of your time will probably be spent outside so it won't really be an issue except at night. And since there are no showers you should be

Inside Cabin 4 at Keyhole State Park

Cottonwood Bay near Cabin 4 at Keyhole State Park

prepared to rough it. Even though it's a bit rustic, it's still a good choice for a romantic getaway, because it's so secluded. And although it does have a bunk bed, it would be very cozy for a family. Keep in mind that the campground is only open from May 15 to September 15, so plan accordingly.

Nearby

Devils Tower National Monument (www.nps.gov/deto) is about a 45-minute drive from the park. This geologic feature, which seems to rise from the rolling prairie, is sacred to the Lakota people, and a favorite for rock climbers from around the world. You'll get a great view of the formation as you drive down Highway 24, just before you get to Highway 110.

There's accessible parking and restrooms near the Visitor Center, with level access to the building. Inside there's a collection of interpretive exhibits and a staffed information desk. There are also a few accessible picnic tables outside, if you'd like to pack along a lunch.

Although the trail around the monument is paved, it's too steep for wheelchair-users and slow walkers. That said there is a graded dirt road near the Visitor Center that leads to an alternative vantage point, for a very scenic view of the towering formation. There's no striped parking in the dirt lot, but it's usually not crowded as most folks only make it to the Visitor Center and completely miss this turnoff.

And don't miss the prairie dog town near the park entrance. There are level spots to pull out near the complex, but the paths out around the mounds are not accessible. Still, you can check out these cute critters from you car, or get some nice photos of them from the paved road. Be forewarned though, they will happily pose for you, but the moment you get close, they will dive back into their holes.

Keyhole State Park Cabin
353 McKean Road
Moorcroft, WY 82721
(307) 756-3596
wyoparks.state.wy.us/Site/SiteInfo.aspx?siteID=10

GPS Coordinates
N 44.34515
W 104.75341

Pit Toilet near Cabin 4 at Keyhole State Park

Buffalo Bill Village
Cody, WY

L ocated along the main drag in Cody, Buffalo Bill Village is part of a larger resort complex that includes the adjacent Holiday Inn and Comfort Inn. Although the hotels are a modern addition, Buffalo Bill Village dates back many years. The individual cabins still sport the original log siding, but the interiors have been completely refurbished. Access upgrades have also been added, so today wheelchair-users and slow walkers can enjoy this historic property in one of America's great wild west towns.

Access Details

There's accessible parking in front of the Holiday Inn, with level access to the Buffalo Bill Village office and gift shop. Accessible Cabin 365 is located just a short drive away, in the back of the complex. There's accessible parking near the cabin, with a paved level sidewalk to the front door.

There is ramp access to the cabin, which has a wide doorway and good pathway access. It's very spacious and is furnished with two 26-inch high queen-sized beds with an access aisle in the middle. Other furnishings include a sofa, a chest of drawers, a table and two chairs.

The bathroom has a wide doorway and includes a full five-foot turning radius. It's equipped with a roll-in shower with a hand-held showerhead, grab bars and a portable shower chair. The toilet is in a 36-inch wide alcove with grab bars on both sides. Other access features include a roll-under sink and a lowered mirror.

There is good access around the cabins, and level access to the Holiday Inn, which houses the accessible QT Restaurant.

Candy's Take

The cabin has a definite western feel to it, and I think if you visit Cody you should definitely go western. It's very large and comfortable, and it's located in a nice quiet corner away from the street noise. The bunny rabbits, which seem to love the lawn area in front of the cabin, are also pretty cute. It's the perfect place to set the mood for a Cody visit.

Best Fit

The cabin is roomy enough for even large power wheelchairs and scooters, and there's plenty of room to navigate around the spacious bathroom. That said, since the toilet is in a 36-inch alcove it may be problematic if you can only do a side transfer. There's probably room enough to scootch in (depending on your wheelchair) but it's unlikely you'll be able to get

Inside Cabin 365 at Buffalo Bill Village

Team roping at Cody Night Rodeo

perfectly parallel to the toilet. That said, since there are grab bars on both sides of the toilet, there are all kinds of possibilities. Buffalo Bill Village is a great choice for a family getaway, as the kids will love the western theme.

Nearby

The Buffalo Bill Center of the West (www.centerofthewest.org) is the perfect place to begin your Cody visit, as it has five galleries dedicated to the old west, including the impressive Buffalo Bill Museum. Other galleries include the Whitney Gallery of Western Art, the Plains Indian Museum, the Cody Firearms Museum and the Draper Museum of Natural History — all of which have level access, and present a comprehensive picture of the old west.

Of course no wild west visit is complete without a gunfight, so make sure and catch the show on the street in front of the historic Irma Hotel. Performances are held at 6 PM, Monday through Saturday during the summer. The show is free, and you can watch it from the sidewalk, but get there early to stake out a good vantage point.

If you'd like a little cowboy entertainment, then don't miss Dan Miller's Cowboy Music Revue (www.cowboymusicrevue.com). Located across the street from the Irma, this Branson style music show features lots of old cowboy tunes. There's level access to the theater with plenty of wheelchair seating up front. It really puts you in that "old west" mood.

And last but not least, make sure and take in the Cody Night Rodeo (www.codystampederodeo.com). There's plenty of accessible parking at the rodeo grounds, which also features accessible seating. It's a very patriotic family event, with lots of up-and-coming talent in the arena. The kids in the audience even get a shot at a little hands-on rodeo fun, so it's a great hit with everyone. It's also very affordable, which is a real bonus for families.

Buffalo Bill Village
1701 Sheridan Avenue
Cody, WY 82414
(307) 587-5544
www.blairhotels.com

GPS Coordinates
N 44.52707
W 109.05490

Toilet and Shower in Cabin 365 at Buffalo Bill Village

Lake Yellowstone Hotel

Yellowstone National Park, WY

After a two-year renovation project and a bill in excess of $28.5 million, a major restoration project on the Lake Yellowstone Hotel was completed in 2014. Built in 1889, this colonial revival property is listed on the National Register of Historic Places and is a member of Historic Hotels of America. And although the renovation wasn't an easy task, the contractors managed to preserve the historic nature of the property and still add modern access features.

Access Details

There's accessible parking near the front entrance, with level access into the lobby of the Lake Yellowstone Hotel. The new accessible rooms are located on the upper floors, and thanks to the recent addition of elevators, everybody can access them.

Room 126 is located on the second floor, and includes a wide doorway and good pathway access throughout the room. It's furnished with two 27-inch high queen-sized beds with wheelchair access on both sides, and includes a barrier-free pathway to the bathroom.

213

The bathroom has a roll-in shower, with grab bars, a hand-held showerhead and a portable shower bench. The toilet has grab bars on the right and back walls (as seated), and the spacious room also has a roll-under sink. The access features are nicely incorporated into the historic design of the room, and they even remembered to lower the soap dish in the shower.

Room 226, which is located one floor up, has the exact same access features, except that it has a tub/shower combination instead of a roll-in shower.

Down at the end of the hall, Room 202 features a 27-inch high king-sized bed with wheelchair-access on both sides. There's plenty of room to roll around this large corner room, which boasts a great view of the lake.

The bathroom is equipped with a tub/shower combination with grab bars and a hand-held showerhead. Other access features include a toilet with grab bars on the left and back walls (as seated), and a roll-under sink. Round it out with a portable shower chair and you have a nicely accessible room.

Access to the public areas is equally good, with plenty of room to wheel around the magnificent first-floor sun room and the lobby bar. There's a barrier-free pathway to the restaurant, and the tables are spaced far enough apart so there's good access to just about every seat in the house.

Guestroom 126 at the Yellowstone Lake Hotel

Candy's Take

My favorite thing about this property is that it's located right on the lake, and even if you don't have a lake view room you can still take it all in from the back porch or the sun room. The view is equally impressive from the Yellowstone Lake Hotel Dining Room, which features a healthy menu filled with fresh ingredients. And if you'd like to get a closer look at the lake, there's ramp access to a paved pathway down to the lakeshore, just outside the back door. It's just a gorgeous setting for this lovely old building.

Best Fit

Since they did such a good job with the access upgrades, this property will work well for just about every wheelchair-user and slow walker. There's a choice of bathroom configurations, and the rooms are very spacious. This stately old gem is perfect for an anniversary or a romantic retreat. The only bad thing about this property is that it's only open from May to October.

Nearby

Although the hotel is located in Yellowstone National Park (www.nps.gov/yell), it's also close enough to Grand Teton National Park (www.nps.gov/grte) for day trips.

There are several trails that will work for some wheelers and slow walkers in Grand Teton National Park, including the three-quarter-mile Lakeshore Loop Trail at South Jenny Lake. This paved trail is located behind the Visitor Center, and although it has a few undulations it's doable for most people.

The Laurance S. Rockefeller Preserve is also worth a stop as it boasts a short hard-packed trail through the forest. The trail ends at the nature center, which features barrier-free access and offers a variety of interpretive exhibits.

Last but not least, make sure you stop at Coulter Bay Village for the excellent David T. Vernon Indian Arts Museum, which features an impressive collection of Native American jewelry, baskets, beadwork, weaving and clothing. There's level access at the front museum entrance, but if you can't do stairs, you'll need to use the back door to access the lower level. There's also a nice barrier-free trail along the lakeshore, just behind the museum. Just park near the amphitheater and follow the path down to the lake.

And for a spectacular view of the Grand Canyon of the Yellowstone River, be sure and take the scenic South Rim Drive in Yellowstone National Park. Although there are some great windshield views along the way, Artist Point and Uncle Tom's Overlook are definitely worth a stop. There's a paved pathway out to the Artist Point overlook, which offers a good view of Lower Falls; and a boardwalk and hard-packed dirt trail out to the edge of Uncle Tom's Overlook, where you can get a spectacular view of Upper Falls.

Lake Yellowstone Hotel
1 Grand Loop Road
Yellowstone National Park, WY 82190
(307) 344-7311
www.yellowstonenationalparklodges.com

GPS Coordinates
N 44.555112
W 110.39574

Toilet and shower in guestroom 126 at the Yellowstone Lake Hotel

216

Central States

Chisos Mountains Lodge
Big Bend National Park, TX

If you have a hankering to get away from the maddening crowds, then Chisos Mountains Lodge is just the ticket for you. Located in Big Bend National Park in Southwestern Texas, it's the only property in this very remote national park. In fact to describe Big Bend as merely being remote is somewhat of an understatement, as it's more than 100 miles away from the nearest freeway, hospital or shopping mall. That said, the lodge boasts a bevy of creature comforts and offers several accessible rooms.

Access Details

There's accessible parking and level access to the main lobby, with plenty of room to navigate a wheelchair inside. The accessible rooms are located just a short drive away in the Casa Grande section of the property.

Accessible parking is located near these ground floor rooms, with barrier-free pathways to and from them. The accessible rooms feature wide doorways, lowered peepholes and tile floors. They are furnished with double beds, but there's certainly plenty of room to add a rollaway bed.

There's also level access to the back deck, which is a great place to relax and enjoy the sunset.

Bathroom access features include a tub/shower combination with a hand-held showerhead, grab bars in the shower and toilet areas, and a portable shower bench. A roll-under sink is located in the sleeping area, which frees up more floor space in the bathroom.

The Casa Grande rooms are also equipped with a refrigerator and a microwave, and the nearby camp store offers a good selection of easy-to-prepare meal items.

The Chisos Mountains Lodge Restaurant is located just a short walk away from the guest rooms; however since it's on an uphill grade it's best to drive. There's accessible parking in front of the main entrance, with barrier-free access through the lobby to the restaurant. The restaurant features a good variety of Tex-Mex dishes, and the deck is a great place to relax, enjoy a glass of wine and take in what can only be described as one of the best views in Texas.

Candy's Take

The spectacular view of the Chisos Mountains from the back decks of the accessible rooms is by far one of the best features of this property. Additionally it's not unusual to get a glimpse of the native wildlife just outside your back door. It's also pretty quiet, and thanks to very little light pollution it's a nice place to star gaze.

Best Fit

The accessible rooms are quite spacious, but if you have to have a roll-in shower they won't work for you. It's also important to note that you should book an accessible room if you use any kind of an assistive device, even if you don't need an adapted bathroom, because the accessible rooms are the only rooms with wide doorways. The lodge is a good family property, and it's the ideal home base for a Big Bend vacation, as day trips from even the nearest towns are just not practical.

Nearby

Save several days to explore Big Bend National Park (www.nps.gov/bibe) as there are a number of accessible things to see and do there. At the top of the list is the Window View Trail, which is located just across the parking

Enjoying the view on the Window Trail

lot from the Casa Grande rooms, near the camp store and Visitor Center. This trail gets its name from the "window" opening in the canyon that offers a great view of the valley below.

This .3-mile barrier-free trail features paved access, with a gradual descent to the window viewpoint. Benches are strategically placed along the trail, and it's just a very pleasant place to take in the spectacular canyon walls and the Chisos Mountains.

Be sure and stop in at the Visitor Center on your way back. It features a variety of interpretive exhibits and an information desk. There's level access to the building with good pathway access to all the exhibits. And if you're not staying at the lodge and have to drive, there's accessible parking nearby.

By far the highlight of any Big Bend visit is what's referred to as "the" drive in the park — the Ross Maxwell Scenic Loop. This 30-mile scenic drive leads to the Castolon Historic District and Santa Elena Canyon, and passes through some historic and geologic treasures along the way. The drive takes about 45 minutes one-way, but be sure to allow extra time for stops.

There are a number of scenic overlooks along the route, several of which are wheelchair-accessible. The Homer Wilson Ranch Overlook and Mule Ears Viewpoint both have accessible parking with barrier-free access out to the viewpoints. The former features views of the old ranch house and surrounding land, while the latter offers a good view of the iconic Mule Ears rock formation. No matter which way you look, you'll be treated to some very scenic vistas of the massive Chihuahuan Desert.

Chisos Mountains Lodge
1 Panther Lane
Big Bend National Park, TX 79834
(432) 477-2292
www.chisosmountainslodge.com

GPS Coordinates
N 29.12749
W 103.24254

Toilet and tub/shower in an accessible Casa Grande room

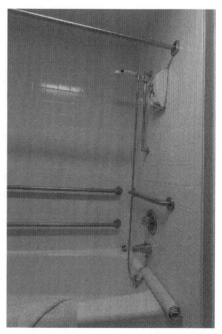

Hotel Sorella CityCentre

Houston, TX

L ocated in what's billed as Houston's hip Mecca for hot retail, upscale dining and luxurious living, the Hotel Sorella CityCentre features 13 accessible rooms, a very accommodating staff, and some fun public spaces. As an added bonus, this 244-room property is within easy rolling distance of a number of cool restaurants, cafes, bars and retail outlets. And that's no accident either; as it was planned that way from the get-go.

Access Details

There's barrier-free access to the ground floor of the property, with elevator access up to the second-floor lobby. Accessible parking is available in a nearby parking structure, but there is also a drop-off area in front of the hotel.

Room 305 is typical of the accessible accommodations you'll find at the property, with wide doorways, and good pathway access throughout the unit. The bathroom features a roll-in shower with grab bars and a hand-held showerhead, a roll-under sink, and toilet grab bars on the right and back walls (as seated). A portable shower chair is also available. All in all, it's a very spacious, comfortable and accessible room.

And if you'd prefer a tub/shower combination, accessible rooms with that bathroom configuration are also available.

There's good access to the public areas of the property as well, including the Monnalisa Bar which features musical entertainment; and the second-floor lobby lounge, where a complimentary Continental breakfast is served daily.

Candy's Take

I absolutely love that this hotel is located in the middle of a 37-acre retail complex. Even better, it doesn't feel like you are in a shopping center, as the hotel itself is very luxurious and quiet. But because of its location, a wide variety of restaurants are just a stone's throw away. Whether you're craving Mexican food, some hearty Italian fare or maybe just a few California Rolls, they've got you covered at CityCentre. They also did an excellent job with access around the complex, from pathways to entrances and even public spaces. It's nice to be able to park your car and just walk or roll to dinner.

Best Fit

Because of the variety of accessible rooms, this property will work for everyone — no matter if you need a roll-in shower or a tub/shower

Toilet in bathroom in room 305 at Hotel Sorella CityCenter

Sink and shower in bathroom in room 305 at Hotel Sorella CityCenter

combination. It's a good choice for a romantic getaway or just a kid-free weekend. It's also great choice for folks who want to do a little shopping or enjoy a few of Houston's museums.

Nearby

The best way to explore the trendy museum district from the hotel is to take the 131 bus to Main Street Square Station, then transfer to the red line train and get off at the Museum District Station. The trip takes about an hour, but it's much easier than searching for a parking space, especially on weekends. The Metro (www.ridemetro.org) buses all have ramps or lifts, and the rail cars feature level access with wheelchair spaces aboard.

The Contemporary Arts Museum Houston (www.camh.org), which is located just a few blocks from the Museum District Metro stop, makes a good first stop. This Houston icon features a large collection of international, national and regional art, dating back to the 1980s. Access is excellent in the museum too, with ramp access to the building and barrier-free access to all the galleries. Best of all, there's never an admission charge.

Just across the street, the Museum of Fine Arts, Houston (www.mfah. org), is equally accessible; with a wheelchair-accessible entrance, elevator access to all levels and plenty of room to roll around in the galleries. With over 56,000 works, this museum is massive; but make sure and save time for the excellent Asian, South Pacific and African collections.

And if all this museum hopping has worked up your appetite, be sure and stop for a bite to eat at Bodega's Taco Shop (www.bodegastacoshop. com). It's just a few blocks from the Museum of Fine Arts, at 1200 Binz, between San Jacinto and Caroline Streets.

This hidden gem of the museum district features ramp access on the side, with plenty of room to navigate inside. And you won't be disappointed with the fare either, as they serve up some very tasty made-to-order Mexican favorites and top-notch margaritas.

Hotel Sorella CityCentre
800 Sorella Court
Houston, TX 77024
(713) 973-1600
www.hotelsorella-citycentre.com

GPS Coordinates
N 29.77996
W 95.56136

The Contemporary Arts Museum in Houston, Texas

Creekhaven Inn

Wimberley, TX

L ocated 35 miles southwest of Austin in the heart of Texas Hill Country, Creekhaven Inn offers guests the best of both worlds. It's close enough to the Texas capital to enjoy its cultural highlights, but it's also pleasantly removed from urban congestion and noise. Nestled on the banks of Cypress Creek, this 14-room luxury B&B offers a much needed respite from the rigors of everyday life. And even though it's a relatively small inn, owners Pat and Bill Appleman still managed to squeeze in an accessible room.

Access Details

Although there are steps up to the front entrance of the main house, an accessible entrance is located at the top of the driveway in the rear of the building. The accessible Jasmine Room is located on the first floor of the Garden House, just around the corner.

Accessible parking is located near the ramp to the Garden House, with barrier-free access up to the Jasmine Room. Access features include wide doorways, good pathway access, and a tile floor for easy rolling.

The room is furnished with a 31-inch high bed, and it also includes a microwave and a refrigerator.

The bathroom has a roll-in shower with grab bars and a hand-held showerhead, toilet grab bars on the right and back walls (as seated) and a roll-under sink, The L-shaped shower has a three-foot square entrance, which leads around a beveled corner to a three-foot by five-foot shower area. Although many people will be able to navigate it just fine, the beveled corner may be problematic for power wheelchair-users. If you can walk a few steps, have assistance or have a small manual wheelchair you should be fine; as the turning area measures 41-inches diagonally at its widest point.

Outside, there's level access to a covered patio, just a short distance from the room. It's a great place to enjoy a glass of wine in the evening, but if you can't make it that far, the shared front porch just outside the room is equally pleasant.

A hot buffet breakfast, which is served in the dining room in the main house, is also included with the room.

Candy's Take

I really like the covered patio at this property. It's surrounded by lush vegetation, and you can hear the creek in the background. There's also a good smattering of wildlife around, from birds and squirrels to the occasional deer or two. It's just a very peaceful property, and a wonderful

Shower and sink in the Jasmine Room at Creekhaven Inn

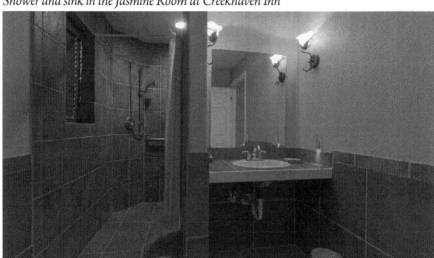

Toilet in the Jasmine Room at Creekhaven Inn

place to de-stress. The shared porch outside the cabin is also a nice spot to enjoy a morning cup of coffee,

Best Fit

Because of the shower configuration, this property is a better choice for slow walkers. Additionally, many slow walkers will like the higher bed that comes with a step stool. I'll also give the Creekhaven Inn high marks for romantic ambiance, and it's a great spot to enjoy a kid-free weekend.

Nearby

If you'd like a little dose of Texas history, then spend a few days in nearby Austin. For a good primer, begin your visit at the Bob Bullock Texas State History Museum (www.thestoryoftexas.com). There's plenty of accessible parking in the underground garage, and elevator access up to the museum. The museum features a variety of rotating exhibits and films which focus on Texas history — from the early days to modern times. There is barrier-free access to all the galleries, and accessible seating in the theaters. A loaner wheelchair is also available at the front desk.

The Lyndon Baines Johnson Presidential Museum and Library (www.lbjlibrary.org), located just a half-mile away, is also worth a visit. Access is excellent throughout the museum, with accessible parking near the entrance, level access across the plaza to the museum, elevator access to all floors and plenty of space to wheel around the galleries.

As with all presidential museums, a good chunk of the exhibits are devoted to the family history of the president and the first lady. Then there's the reproduction of the oval office, as it was during the president's term. But, Baby Boomers will especially enjoy the exhibits about the events of 1950s, 60s and 70s, as it's a great trip down memory lane. And if you visit on one of eight "free days" during the year (including August 27, which is LBJ's birthday), there's no admission charge.

And to give equal time to the other half of the Johnson team, make sure and plan a stop at the Ladybird Johnson Wildflower Center (www.wildflower.org). There's level access from the parking lot to the Visitors Gallery, where you'll find interactive exhibits and displays about the Lone Star State's diverse native flora.

Outside there are level pathways through the gardens. Additionally, there are two accessible trails on the grounds — the quarter-mile long John Barr Trail, and the mile-long Restoration Research Trail. Both trails are wide and level, and covered in crushed granite. You can do each trail as a loop or connect to the Restoration Research Trail midway along the John Barr Trail. No matter which route you take, you won't be disappointed with the colorful blooms. Spring is especially scenic, when the Bluebonnets are in bloom.

Creekhaven Inn
400 Mill Race Lane
Wimberley, TX 76876
(512) 847-9344
www.creekhaveninn.com

GPS Coordinates
N 30.00061
W 98.09279

Runnymede Country Inn

Fredericksburg, TX

Surrounded by wildflower-filled pastures, the Runnymede Country Inn is just three miles south of Fredericksburg, in rural Southern Texas. This English-style inn is located on a 10-acre country estate, and even though it's a bit out of the way, that's part of its charm. Innkeepers Anne Farrar and Jenny Farrar Jones live in a nearby cottage, and although guests certainly never want for anything, the sisters also give folks plenty of privacy.

Access Details

There's accessible parking next to the Chatsworth Garden Cottage, and barrier-free access up to the front door. Inside you'll find wide doorways, good pathway access and tile floors. The roomy cottage is furnished with a 23-inch high open-frame bed, a day bed, some easy chairs and an ottoman. Also included is a kitchenette with a wet bar, a microwave, a refrigerator and a coffee maker. And although it's not an access feature, the electric fireplace is a nice addition.

The oversized bathroom has a roll-in shower with a hand-held

231

showerhead, grab bars and a fold-down shower seat; and although it has a small lip, it's still doable for most people. Other access features include a roll-under sink and toilet grab bars on the left and back walls (as seated). There's also a separate non-accessible Jacuzzi tub in the bathroom.

The adjacent deck, which features barrier-free access, is the perfect place to enjoy the butterflies and birds that frequent the property.

Candy's Take

This is a pretty low-key property and the cottage is tucked away in the back, so it's very peaceful there. The kitchen is well equipped, in fact with a stop at the local market you can easily prepare all of your meals there. I was also amazed at how many butterflies were around this property, and it was fun to just sit out on the deck and watch them.

Best Fit

Although this room is very spacious and will work for most people, there is a slight lip on the shower, so that may be problematic if you can't roll over it. On the other hand, the day bed can certainly accommodate an attendant if you need some extra assistance. This is a nice property for people who enjoy the outdoors, and because it's so secluded, it also makes a good romantic retreat.

Sink and shower in the Chatsworth Garden Cottage

Toilet and tub in the Chatsworth Garden Cottage

Nearby

The Lyndon B. Johnson National Historic Park (www.nps.gov/lyjo), which is just a short drive away, makes an excellent day trip from the inn. The park is actually located in two separate areas, which are 14 miles apart, but it's a pleasant country drive. The Johnson City part of the park contains the president's boyhood home and the Johnson Settlement, while the Stonewall section features the famed LBJ Ranch.

There's plenty of accessible parking at the Visitor Center in Johnson City, with ramp access to President Johnson's boyhood home, and level access on a hard-packed dirt path to the historic Johnson Settlement. If you can't manage the half-mile walk, you can also park near the barn, off of Highway 290. Just ask the folks at the Visitor Center for directions.

LBJ Ranch, on the other hand, is a bit more luxurious. Also known as the Western White House, this is where the president entertained dignitaries and attended to state business, while he was in Texas.

There's plenty of accessible parking near the hangar, where the guided tour begins. There's ramp access up to the front porch of the house, with room to maneuver a wheelchair on the tour. Afterwards, you're free to wander the grounds and check out LBJ's Air Force One (a Lockheed JetStar which he jokingly referred to as Air Force One-Half), his collection of vintage cars, and daughter Luci's 1965 Corvette. It's an excellent and very nostalgic tour, and a great way to spend the day in the country.

Runnymede Country Inn
184 Fullbrook Lane
Fredericksburg, TX 78624
(830) 990-2449
www.runnymedecountryinn.com

GPS Coordinates
N 30.23111
W 98.90187

President Johnson's childhood home

Cabin on the Lake

Greenleaf State Park, OK

L ocated in Eastern Oklahoma, Greenleaf State Park offers a wide range of family-friendly diversions for day visitors, and includes some historic cabins for overnight stays. And although the historic cabins are not wheelchair-accessible, the purpose-built Cabin on the Lake is a good choice for wheelchair-users and slow walkers. Constructed in 1994 by the Oklahoma Chapter of the Telephone Pioneers of America, it not only boasts every conceivable access feature, but it also comes with a closet filled with medical equipment and assistive devices.

Access Details

There is a paved parking area in front of the cabin, with ramped access to the screened porch that overlooks the lake. The layout is very spacious, with an open great room, an adjacent kitchen and an oversized bedroom furnished with a queen-sized bed and a twin hospital bed.

The bathroom is equipped with a roll-in shower with grab bars, a hand-held showerhead and a fold-down shower seat. Other access features include toilet grab bars on the right and back walls (as seated), and a roll-under sink.

There is also a ceiling track lift in the bedroom and the bathroom. A commode chair, a trapeze and a manual wheelchair are also included. Best of all, there is level access down to a private dock, where you can fish, enjoy the view or even tie up your own boat.

A special reservation policy for this cabin was also implemented, in order to insure that first priority is given to people who have the highest access needs. To that end, a reservation request which includes disability specific questions, must be completed in order to get a place in the reservation queue. Even then, the competition is stiff; but in the rare case that there are any vacancies after the priority reservation period ends, the cabin can then be rented by anyone on a space-available basis.

Candy's Take

I am very impressed by the access features in the cabin, but even more impressed with the reservation policy. Too many times places like these are rented out to able-bodied people, while those that really need the access features are left standing on the sidelines. A discount is also given to disabled guests, making it very affordable. Even better, there's no admission charge to the park!

Best Fit

They thought of everything from a hospital bed to a ceiling track lift in this

Great room in Cabin on the Lake

Bathroom with ceiling track in Cabin on the Lake

cabin, so truthfully it's good for everyone. That said, it's a great choice for a family vacation, and with the lakeside location it's perfect for fishermen. It's also a good choice if you travel with an attendant. Additionally, it offers a large degree of privacy, as it's located at the end of a secluded road, well away from the other cabins. Plan ahead though, as it books up quickly.

Nearby

There are many accessible things to do in the park, but the one-and-a-half-mile Family Fun Trail tops the list. Although this paved trail technically begins near the park office, there are several other access points throughout the park.

Wheelchair access is excellent along this wide level trail, which winds past the campgrounds and through a wooded area. Interpretive signs are located along the way, and it's a great option for wheelers and slow walkers. The trail also passes by the kids fishing pond, where children under 16 and disabled visitors can catch their limit for free.

If you'd like to fish on Greenleaf Lake, then head on down to the accessible floating dock in the marina. Greenleaf Lake is known for its great fishing, with lots of largemouth bass, crappie and catfish to be had. And since the accessible fishing dock is partially covered, it also offers some much-needed protection from the elements. And there's plenty of accessible parking nearby.

There's also a historic side to this park, as the original cabins were constructed in the 1930s by the Civilian Conservation Corps. Although these native stone structures are not wheelchair-accessible, you can check them out on a little driving tour. So as you can see, there are many ways to enjoy this diverse state park.

Cabin on the Lake
Greenleaf State Park
Muskogee, OK 74403
(918) 487-5196
www.travelok.com/listings/view.profile/id.3236

GPS Coordinates
N 35.62045
W 95.17058

A section of the Family Fun Trail in Greenleaf State Park

Lindley House

Duncan, OK

L ocated in a quiet Duncan neighborhood about 80 miles south of Oklahoma City, Lindley House B&B is housed in a landmark property. Built in 1939, this one time home of Dr. E.C and Helen Lindley was completely remodeled and converted to a B&B in 1997. And although the renovation took some 10 years to complete, this historic property now boasts a modern wing with a wheelchair-accessible guestroom.

Access Details

Although steps grace the front of the main house, there is level access to the courtyard rooms in the new wing. Accessible parking is located near the accessible Rose Cottage, which is furnished with a king-sized bed and decorated in a rose motif.

The bathroom features a wide double door and is equipped with a large roll-in shower with grab bars, a hand-held showerhead and a fold-down shower bench. The toilet grab bars are located on the right and back walls (as seated), and there's plenty of room to maneuver a wheelchair in the spacious bathroom. A large vanity with a roll-under sink is located just outside the bathroom.

There's good pathway access to the garden area of the property, with tables to sit and enjoy the view. A full cooked breakfast, which is delivered to the room, is also included.

Candy's Take

I really enjoyed the English garden, and I love the privacy that the cottage offers. You get the best part of staying in a B&B (the breakfast), without feeling like you are staying in someone's spare room. And if the weather is nice, you can even eat breakfast outside, under the arbor. It's a very pleasant way to begin the day.

Best Fit

The large bathroom with a roll-in shower makes this property a great choice for all abilities. It's a good pick for couples, and it would make a nice romantic retreat. You can even add on a package of roses and candles to ramp the romance up a notch. And although kids aren't prohibited there, couples seem to be the main guests.

Nearby

For a little dose of wild west history, save a full day to explore the

Bedroom in the Rose Cottage at Lindley House

Inside the Garis Gallery of the American West

Chisholm Trail Heritage Center (www.onthechisholmtrail.com), located just two miles from Lindley House. You can't miss it — just look for the enormous bronze sculpture of a cattle drive in front.

There's plenty of accessible parking near the entrance and good pathway access throughout the Chisholm Trail Heritage Center. Start your visit with a audio tour of the Garis Gallery of the American West. The rotating exhibits in this gallery include pieces from the museum's large permanent collection of Western art. The works range from sculptures to

Interpretive display at the Chisholm Trail Heritage Center

paintings, and include pieces by Charles Russell, Frederic Remington and Allan Houser.

The rest of the museum is devoted to interactive exhibits for all ages, and includes a branding station, a chuck wagon and even a replica of the old Duncan General Store. And don't miss the Chisholm Trail Experience Theater, where you'll be surrounded by the sights, sounds and smells of the Chisholm Trail.

All in all, it's a fun, accessible and very educational way to spend the day. And in the end, you'll take away a new appreciation for the cowhands that rode the Chisholm Trail.

Lindley House
1211 N. 10th Street
Duncan, OK 73533
(580) 255-6700
www.lindleyhouse.com

GPS Coordinates
N 34.51632
W 97.95814

Shower and toilet in the Rose Cottage

Chateau Avalon

Kansas City, KS

Perched on a hilltop in the upscale Village West shopping district, Chateau Avalon looks more like an English manor house than a hotel. And although it certainly is the latter, the luxurious ambiance and top-drawer service definitely puts it head-and-shoulders above your typical boutique property. And then there are the rooms. Each of the 61 suites are decorated in a different theme — from a Tahitian tree house to Jesse James's hideout, and everything in between.

Access Details

Although steps grace the front entrance to Chateau Avalon, there's a level entrance on the right, near the accessible parking area. From there, it's just a short elevator ride up to the front desk.

The accessible Roman Dynasty Suite is decorated in a rich Roman theme, with walls adorned with murals and a bedroom alcove framed by stately arches. The foyer features a long table, with a red and gold upholstered chair at each end. And of course Caesar's bust looks down on it all from a cozy nook.

There's good pathway access throughout the suite, which is furnished with an oversized jetted tub with grab bars, and a 30-inch high king-sized bed with wheelchair access on one side. The spacious bathroom features a full five-foot turning radius and is equipped with a roll-in shower with grab bars and a hand-held showerhead. The toilet grab bars are on the right and back walls (as seated), and there is also a roll-under sink. It's a very luxurious and accessible room, and to top it off, a made-to-order breakfast is delivered each morning.

There is also good access to the d'Nile wine bar on the first floor, with level access out to the adjacent patio. Additionally, the third-floor spa features barrier-free access; and their hot stone massage will magically melt away your troubles.

Candy's Take

I just love theme rooms, and these ones are very well done. They even leave some rooms open for guests to tour, so you can get an idea of what the other rooms look like. And although they lack accessible bathrooms, there's good pathway access through them, so everyone can take a peak. The d'Nile wine bar is also a favorite spot of mine, and the patio is a very relaxing space to enjoy your favorite libation. Let's not forget the room service breakfast — it's just divine.

Bedroom in the Roman Dynasty Suite at Chateau Avalon

Whirlpool tub in the Roman Dynasty Suite at Chateau Avalon

Best Fit

The access is very well done at this property and the Roman Dynasty Suite will work for wheelchair-users and slow walkers alike. The room is very spacious and it will accommodate even large wheelchairs and scooters. And since it's been dubbed "Kansas City's most romantic luxury hotel" it's the perfect place to spend that special anniversary.

Nearby

NASCAR fans will love the fact that Chateau Avalon is near the Kansas City Speedway (www.kansasspeedway.com). This enormous complex seats over 72,000 people and boasts a one-and-a-half-mile tri-oval suitable for all types of racing, as well as a road course that winds through the infield. Because of this diversity, they are able to host a wide variety or races throughout the year.

The wheelchair seats feature a companion seat next to them, and all wheelchair ticket holders are given a special pass that allows them to park in the accessible parking lot. And since it's quite a hike from the parking lot to the stands, golf carts and trams are available to transport slow walkers. They also have accessible van transportation from the accessible parking area, for wheelchair-users who can't manage the distance.

The Hollywood Casino at the Kansas Speedway (www. hollywoodcasinokansas.com), which features barrier-free access, is located next door. This 10,000-square foot gaming palace offers slots, table games and a live poker room. It's also a good choice for dinner as it has a variety of restaurants, including a steak house, a buffet, a sports bar and a cafe. And let's not forget the live entertainment. There is good access to all areas of the casino and to the restaurants, and a wheelchair is available for loan at the coat check counter. Even if you don't gamble, stop by for a drink or a bite to eat.

If you'd prefer to shop till you drop, you'll be happy to know that Village West has a wide variety of outlets and malls. Nebraska Furniture Mart and Cabela's are just a short drive from Chateau Avalon, and they both feature barrier-free access. The nearby Legends Shopping Center also has a variety of restaurants and shops with wheelchair access. Truth be told, there's really no shortage of shops and outlets in this part of town.

Chateau Avalon
701 Village West Parkway
Kansas City, KS 66111
(913) 596-6000
www.chateauavalonhotel.com

GPS Coordinates
N 39.11127
W 94.81807

Shower and toilet in the Roman Dynasty Suite at Chateau Avalon

246

Southmoreland on the Plaza

Kansas City, MO

Located in the heart of Kansas City's historic arts and entertainment district, Southmoreland on the Plaza has somewhat of a split personality. Although this upscale urban inn is near a gaggle of hip new restaurants and cool shops, the inn itself boasts a definite New England ambiance. From the front facade of the 1913 Colonial Revival mansion, to the cozy fireplace, and the rooms decorated with Chippendale and Shaker pieces, you almost feel like you are in Vermont instead of Missouri. Add in some upscale amenities and top-notch service and you have everything you could possibly want in an inn, and maybe even a bit more.

Access Details

There are steps at the front entrance of the property, but there is a ramp on the side, near the accessible parking area. The accessible August Meyer room is located on the first floor, and it includes wide doorways, good pathway access and wood floors. It's furnished with a 28-inch high king-sized bed with wheelchair access on both sides, and it includes a lowered closet rod and a wheelchair-height full-length mirror.

The spacious bathroom is outfitted with a roll-under sink, toilet grab bars on the back and left walls (as seated), and a two-person Jacuzzi tub with a hand-held showerhead. There are grab bars around the tub, and there is a built-in shower seat in the far corner. A portable shower bench is also included, but because of the size and shape of the tub, most folks will require some transfer assistance.

All of the first-floor public rooms feature level access, with the exception of the solarium, which can be accessed by a portable ramp. Breakfast is generally served in the Harvest Dining Room, which is just around the corner from the August Meyer room. Alternatively, guests can enjoy breakfast on the veranda, which can be also accessed by a portable ramp.

Candy's Take

I totally enjoyed the afternoon wine and hors d'oeuvres, and the after dinner coffee and dessert by the fire. Actually the living room was my favorite room, as it was comfortable and cheery, and a great place to catch up with a friend. I really liked the historic feel of the property, but I'm glad they added some modern features too.

Best Fit

This property is best suited for slow walkers and wheelchair-users who can walk a few steps, because of the tub configuration. Since the built-in bench

Toilet in the August Meyer room at Southmoreland on the Plaza

Sink and tub/shower in the August Meyer room

is located on the far side of the tub, you have to be able to walk a step and pivot to get to it. And if you need a roll-in shower, this property just won't make the cut for you. It's a good choice for a kids-free getaway, or for folks who want to explore the nearby cultural attractions. The people that stay at this property seem to be a chatty bunch at breakfast, which is often served at one large table, so if you'd like a bit more privacy, request a table on the veranda.

Nearby

The inn is located just a few blocks from Country Club Plaza (www. countryclubplaza.com), where you can grab a romantic dinner and enjoy the Spanish architecture. There is good access throughout this 15-block retail and entertainment district, which features buildings patterned after those in Kansas City's sister city, Seville, Spain. Be sure to stroll past the J.C. Nichols fountain before you head back to the inn, as it's quite the sight at night when it's illuminated.

For a cultural treat, head on over to the nearby Nelson Atkins Museum of Art (www.nelson-atkins.org). It features a 22-acre sculpture park that's home to a large collection of Henry Moore's bronze sculptures, as well as some whimsical works by other artists. There are level pathways and barrier-free access to most of the sculptures, so you can roll right up to them for an up-close-and-personal look. Don't miss the iconic, and often photographed, giant shuttlecock sculpture, as it's truly one of a kind.

The museum itself is also a treasure, with works that fill two buildings. There is good wheelchair access throughout the galleries; and best of all, there's no admission charge. And since it's just a short walk from Southmoreland on the Plaza, it's also very convenient.

Southmoreland on the Plaza
116 E. 46th Street
Kansas City, MO 64112
(816) 531-7979
www.southmoreland.com

GPS Coordinates
N 39.04316
W 94.58452

Shuttlecock at the Nelson Atkins Museum of Art

Silver Heart Inn

Independence, MO

B uilt in 1856 by a local businessman, the building that houses the Silver Heart Inn is one of the few Independence structures that survived the Civil War. In post Appomattox times it remained a private residence, until Melanie and Perry Johnson purchased it in 2012 and converted it to a B&B. Today you can get a taste of the past in this stately manor, yet still enjoy the creature comforts of modern times. Additionally, since Melanie's nephew has cerebral palsy, she is acutely aware of the difficulties associated with accessible travel. Says Melanie, "I've not really found a lot of properties that can accommodate an attendant or a family caregiver, so I'm glad we are able to provide this for our guests."

Access Details

There's accessible parking in a paved lot, with level access up to the ramped back entrance. The four guestrooms are located upstairs, with direct elevator access up to the Roy Gamble Room. The Shirley Gamble Room is located next door, and the rooms may be rented together to form a large accessible suite, or individually, if you only need one room. The two rooms share a bathroom, so if only one room is booked, Melanie blocks the other, so guests can be assured of a private bathroom.

The Shirley Gamble Room is the larger of the two guestrooms, and it's furnished with a 33-inch high queen-sized bed with access on both sides. The Roy Gamble Room is much smaller and has a 28-inch high twin bed.

The bathroom is located next to the Roy Gamble Room, and although it's not an adjoining room, it's located in a semi-private hallway, and no other rooms are located in that wing.

The bathroom is equipped with a roll-in shower with a hand-held showerhead and a portable shower chair. Other access features include a roll-under sink, and a large tile floor that makes for easy rolling. The toilet grab bar setup is unique, but it was designed specifically for the previous owner who had a stroke. There are standard grab bars on the back and left walls, (as seated), and a floor mounted grab bar on the other side. The floor mounted grab bar only extends halfway out from the back wall, so there is room for a side transfer, but it may be difficult for some folks.

Candy's Take

I love the fact that there is an elevator in this historic B&B, as you rarely find this feature in small properties like this. It was installed by Roy Gamble, the former owner, after he had a stroke. It's nice to see that this

Courtyard and ramped entry to the Silver Heart Inn

wonderful old property is more accessible because of this addition.

Best Fit

The roll-in shower is nicely done and will accommodate most people, but the toilet grab bars could be problematic for people in large power wheelchairs. The rooms can be rented as a suite, and they will certainly accommodate a caregiver or a child, but the bed in the Shirley Gamble Room is too high for most wheelchair-users (it even comes with a step stool). That said, if you can sleep in the lower bed in the Roy Gamble Room this property may work for you. This is a good choice for slow walkers

The Truman Family Home

and part time wheelchair-users, and it's the perfect home base to explore historic Independence.

Nearby

The Harry S. Truman Library & Museum (www.trumanlibrary.org) is just a mile away from the inn. There's accessible parking near the entrance, with ramp access up to the front door. The museum contains an interesting collection of exhibits that focus on the timeline of Truman's presidency, including the end days of World War II and Truman's decision to use the atomic bomb. There's also information about the Truman family home, lots of family photos and a collection of Truman's cars.

There's level access out to the courtyard, where an eternal flame shines over the Truman graves. There is also level access to the annex which contains the former president's office, which he used from 1957 to 1966.

The Truman family home is also worth a visit. You can buy tickets at the Harry S. Truman National Historic Site Visitor Center (www.nps. gov/hstr), located downtown on the corner of Truman Road and Main Street. There's level access to the building, and accessible seating in the auditorium, where a short film about the home is presented.

The home itself is located about a half-mile away at 219 N. Delaware, but if you decided to walk take Maple Street, as it's the most accessible route. You can also drive to the home, but there's no accessible parking in the street. There is a seven-inch step up to the yard, and although there are four steps up to the front porch, a stair climber is available.

There's level access to the first-floor rooms, including the kitchen, dining room, parlor and living room. The house is left as it was when Bess Truman died in 1982. The tour is very informative and it's almost like stepping into a time capsule. Harry's coat and hat are even still hanging by the door, as if he'll be there to put them on any minute.

Silver Heart Inn
1114 S. Noland Road
Independence, MO 64050
(816) 838-9508
www.silverheartinn.com

GPS Coordinates
N 39.08020
W 94.41424

Shower and toilet for the Gamble suite

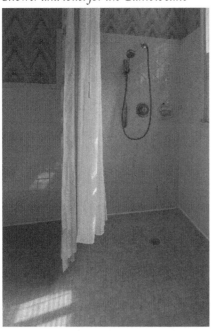

21c Museum Hotel

Bentonville, AR

L ocated in the heart of downtown Bentonville, the 21c Museum Hotel is a far cry from your average cookie-cutter chain property. A very far cry. Although this 104-room boutique hotel includes all the standard hotel amenities, it goes one step further — it also boasts a free contemporary art museum. And the art isn't confined to the inside galleries either; as you'll also find an eye-catching collection of modern sculptures out front. And since the new Crystal Bridges Museum of American Art is located nearby, the 21c Museum Hotel is the perfect place to rest your head in this up-and-coming cultural hotspot.

Access Details

There is level access to the lobby with plenty of room to maneuver a wheelchair inside. The check-in desk is sleek and modern, and the clerks use tablets instead of bulky computers. From there, a barrier-free path leads over to the elevator bank.

The accessible luxury double king room features a wide doorway, with good pathway access throughout the room. It's furnished with two

22-inch high king-sized beds with wheelchair access on both sides. A chair, two tables and a banquette round out the furnishings.

The spacious bathroom has a full five-foot turning radius and is equipped with a roll-in shower with grab bars, a hand-held showerhead and a fold-down shower bench. There are toilet grab bars on the right and back walls (as seated), and there is also a roll-under sink with a lowered mirror in the bathroom. They even remembered the small things like lowered hooks; and then of course there's the rubber ducky, which totally completes the look.

Access is good to all of the public spaces too, including the Hive Restaurant and the first-floor galleries.

Candy's Take

I really like the hip ambiance of this property, and of course the art installations are a lot of fun too. But I totally love the iconic green penguins that were crafted specifically for the property by the Cracking Art Group. You'll find them all over — in the lobby, the restaurant and even on the roof. It's fun to hunt them down — it's kind of like the adult artistic version of "Where's Waldo".

Best Fit

Access is excellent at this newly constructed property so it will work for just about everyone. The accessible rooms are very large, and the

The Raft by Armando Marino at 21c Museum Hotel

256

Crystal Bridges Museum of American Art

bathroom has plenty of room for a large power wheelchair or a scooter. The property is a nice pick for a rural cultural getaway, or even a romantic weekend retreat.

Nearby

The highlight of any Bentonville visit is definitely a trip to the Crystal Bridges Museum of American Art (www.crystalbridges.org). The museum gets its name from a nearby natural spring, and for the bridges incorporated into the design of the building. In fact, the building itself is a work of art; as it features a series of pavilions surrounded by two ponds, as if to unite nature with art.

Access wasn't overlooked in the building design either, as there's a drop-off area in front of the building, with level access to the entrance. Accessible parking is available in the lower garage, with elevator access to the lobby. Access is good on the inside too, with a loaner wheelchair available at the front desk, accessible restrooms and plenty of room to roll around the galleries.

The museum's permanent collection features over 400 American masterworks, from colonial times to the present day. From Charles Wilson Peale's George Washington, to Norman Rockwell's iconic Rosie the Riveter, and Andy Warhol's Dolly Parton, variety is the key word at the museum. There's something for just about every taste from classic to modern art; and since general admission is sponsored by Walmart, you can visit as many times as you want, and it won't cost you a penny.

Outside there is an extensive network of trails and a sculpture garden. The hard-surfaced Orchards Trail is level and winds a half-mile through a grove of pine and cedar trees, from Orchards Park to the main entrance of the museum. The half-mile Art Trail is also wheelchair-accessible, and it features a hard surface with minimal elevation gains. It begins at the south lobby and passes by the amphitheater and a variety of sculptures along the way.

And if you'd like to walk to the museum from the 21c Museum Hotel, you can take the mile-long Crystal Bridges Trail. This paved multi-use trail begins on NE 3rd Street and features a pleasant stroll through Compton Gardens before it connects to the Art Trail. Pack along a picnic lunch and enjoy it on the museum grounds, as there are plenty of accessible public spaces on the campus.

21c Museum Hotel
200 Northeast A Street
Bentonville, AR 72712
(479) 286-6500
www.21cmuseumhotels.com/bentonville

GPS Coordinates
N 36.37410
W 94.20779

Toilet and shower in the bathroom of an accessible luxury double king room at the 21c Museum Hotel

The Peabody
Memphis, TN

The Peabody is an institution in Memphis. This grand old dame is located in a historic building a few blocks from Beale Street, and quite frankly it simply oozes southern charm. And then there are the ducks. In the 1930s The Peabody had duck decoys in the lobby fountain, but today the have been replaced with the real thing. The privileged flock lives in the fountain by day and retreats to their own private penthouse in the evening. Not only is it a tradition, but it's also what makes this property the place to stay in Memphis.

Access Details

There is a ramp access up to this historic property with barrier-free access to the front desk, and elevator access to the upper floors.

Room 527 features wide doorways, good pathway access and a lowered clothing rod in the closet. There is plenty of room to navigate even the largest wheelchair around the two double beds in this spacious room.

The equally spacious bathroom features a full five-foot turning radius and is equipped with a tub/shower combination and grab bars. Other access features include toilet grab bars on the left and back walls (as seated), a lowered sink and mirror, and a lowered clothesline over the tub. A portable shower chair is available upon request.

Bathroom in room 527 at The Peabody

Accessible guestrooms with roll-in showers are also available.

There is good access to the first-floor public spaces too, with ramp access down to the lobby bar and fountain area. Additionally there are accessible public restrooms in the lobby.

Candy's Take

Of course my favorite thing about The Peabody is the famous duck march. Every day at 11 a.m. the ducks march from their overnight digs down to the lobby fountain, and at 5 p.m. they make the return trek upstairs. Throw in a little John Philip Sousa, a red carpet and an official Duckmaster and you have quite the event. Check out the show from the lobby bar, where you can also enjoy the best martini in Memphis.

Best Fit

This is a good property for wheelchair-users and slow walkers alike because of the size of the guest rooms, and because of the choice of bathroom configurations. It's a good romantic retreat, but the kids will like it too because of the duck march. In short if you like music, food and fun, then you'll love both The Peabody and Memphis.

Nearby

Graceland (www.graceland. com) tops the Memphis must-do list. There's plenty of accessible parking near the entrance, with level access to Graceland Plaza, where visitors board a lift-equipped shuttle bus to Elvis Presley's famous mansion. Built in 1939, Graceland features ramp access to the front door and good pathway access on the first floor. The second floor, which was considered Elvis' private sanctuary, is closed to visitors. The basement is only accessible by a flight of stairs, but a video of the area is available. A self-guided audio tour is included in the admission price, so you can tour the site at your own pace.

Duck March at The Peabody

There's much more to see at Graceland besides the mansion, including the beautiful grounds, the Sincerely Elvis Museum, the Automobile Museum (yes the pink Cadillac is there) and Elvis' grave, all of which offer barrier-free access. There are also several places to eat, and of course a gift shop.

On a more somber note, the National Civil Rights Museum (www. civilrightsmuseum.org) is also worth a visit. There is barrier-free access through the museum, which presents a detailed look at the history of the civil rights movement. The museum is constructed in the former Lorraine Motel, where Martin Luther King Jr. was assassinated. In fact the front facade of the hotel and the room where Martin Luther King Jr. spent his last night are both preserved and incorporated into the museum. An excellent audio tour is included with admission.

No trip to Memphis would be complete without a visit to historic Beale Street (www.bealestreet.com). Known as a blues venue for over 50 years, Beale Street experienced a rebirth in the 1980s when the city purchased the property and developed the Beale Street Entertainment District. Today it's a major tourist draw with a multitude of clubs, restaurants, shops and bars.

The street itself is closed to vehicles on the weekends in order to accommodate the influx of pedestrians. Access is good along the street with wide sidewalks and plenty of curb-cuts. Approximately half of the buildings have a level entry, while the rest have one or two steps. It's a good place to people watch, and the place to go if you want to hear some live Memphis music.

The Peabody	**GPS Coordinates**
149 Union Avenue	N 35.14241
Memphis, TN 38103	W 90.05200
(901) 529-4000	
www.peabodymemphis.com	

Elvis Presley's Graceland

Mammoth Cave Hotel

Mammoth Cave, KY

L ocated about a half-hour south of Louisville, Mammoth Cave Hotel is definitely off-the-beaten- path. But as the only hotel in Mammoth Cave National Park, that's also part of its draw. The location couldn't be better, as it's just a short walk from the famous cave and the Visitor Center. Even better, not only does the property offer comfortable and accessible accommodations, but there's also a nice accessible trail just outside the back door.

Access Details

There's plenty of accessible parking near the hotel, with level access to the front lobby. There's also a short level path from the Visitor Center over to the back entrance of the hotel. Inside, there's barrier-free access to the lobby and the front desk.

Accessible Room 403, which is located just a short roll from the lobby, features wide doorways, good pathway access and lowered closet rods. There's plenty of room to navigate a wheelchair through this spacious room, which is furnished with two 24-inch high double beds, with an access aisle between them.

The bathroom has a very ample five-foot turning radius, and it's equipped with a roll-in shower with grab bars and a hand-held showerhead. Other access features include a roll-under sink and a toilet with grab bars on the back and left walls (as seated). A portable shower chair is also included.

There is barrier-free access to the first-floor public areas, including the Travertine Restaurant, the Crystal Lake Coffee Shop and the gift shop.

Candy's Take

Although the hotel room is comfortable enough, I really love the accessible Heritage Trail, which is located next to the hotel. This .3-mile forest trail consists of a level cement pathway and an accessible boardwalk, with several benches strategically placed along the route. There's also a short paved path to the Old Guides Cemetery. And don't miss Sunset Point, where you'll get a great view, even in inclement weather.

Best Fit

Because of the size of the room, and the spacious roll-in shower, this property is a good choice for just about everyone. It's a good home base if you want to explore Mammoth Cave National Park, and people who love the outdoors will feel right at home here.

Boardwalk trail to Sand Cave

Sloan's Crossing Pond Walk

Nearby

Although there are lots of things to do in Mammoth Cave National Park, (www.nps.gov/maca) the caves are not the most accessible option. That said, the most accessible cave tour is the Frozen Niagara Tour, which is touted by park rangers as being suitable for people who use wheelchairs, canes and walkers.

This one-and-a-half-hour tour begins just outside the Visitor Center, and travels by bus to the cave entrance. From there, there are 12 stairs to get into the cave, and another 98 optional stairs along the tour. The elevation gain is only 40 feet, and although it's not barrier-fee it's doable for many people. The bottom line is, you have to be able to negotiate 12 stairs to do this tour.

The good news is, the caves are only part of this 52,000-acre national park. Sloan's Crossing Pond Walk, which is just a short drive away, is definitely worth a visit. There are no marked parking spots at the trailhead, but there's usually plenty of room to parallel park there. This .4-mile boardwalk around the shaded pond is wide and level, and is dotted with accessible viewing platforms, benches and interpretive plaques. There's also a cement pathway to some accessible picnic tables under the trees. It's a very pleasant spot for a midday break.

The trail out to the Sand Cave site is also a good accessible choice. The trailhead is located between the east park entrance and Park Ridge Road, but keep your eyes open, as it's very easy to miss. There's no accessible parking in the paved lot, but there is curb-cut access up to the trail. The .1-mile boardwalk winds through the forest, and because it lacks railings you'll get some nice wildlife views. The trail terminates at an overlook, which has a view of the Sand Cave rescue site; where Floyd Collins was trapped and ultimately died in 1925. Despite Floyd's unfortunate fate, it's actually a pleasant little stroll.

Mammoth Cave Hotel
Mammoth Cave National Park
Mammoth Cave, KY 42259
(270) 758-2225
www.mammothcavehotel.com

GPS Coordinates
N 37.18599
W 86.10147

Toilet and shower in room 403 at the Mammoth Cave Hotel

Cabin in the Woods

Baraboo, WI

Located in Mirror Lake State Park, just three miles south of Wisconsin Dells, the 700-square foot Cabin in the Woods not only boasts good access, but it also includes some extra adaptive equipment. And it's not like it costs an arm and a leg to rent either. Originally constructed by the Telephone Pioneers of America, it was later donated to the Wisconsin Department of Natural Resources. Today that agency rents it out to disabled visitors at a very affordable rate.

Access Details

There's plenty of room to park in front of the cabin, with ramped access up to the screened porch. Out front there is a paved pathway to an accessible picnic table and grill.

The cabin features wide doorways and plenty of room to maneuver a wheelchair on the hardwood floors. The large great room has a full-sized sleeper sofa and a dining table with four chairs. The compact kitchen is furnished with a refrigerator, a microwave, a roll-under sink and a cook top.

The bedroom has an extra wide doorway, with a curtain instead of a door. It's furnished with two twin hospital beds, with an access aisle between them. There are also two single cots, so the cabin can accommodate up to six people.

The bathroom has a wide door, and plenty of room to navigate a wheelchair or scooter. It's equipped with a roll-in shower with a fold-down shower bench. A roll-under sink is also included. As an extra bonus, a sling lift, a rolling shower and commode chair, and a toilet riser with attached grab bars are also available to guests.

Guests have to supply their own cooking utensils, bedding and towels, but it's still a very comfortable cabin. And at just $30 per night, plus a $4 reservation fee, it's also very easy on the wallet.

Candy's Take

This is another great volunteer effort by the Telephone Pioneers of America, and I love the fact that this property is reserved for people with disabilities and their families and friends. Even better, the Wisconsin Department of Natural Resources keeps close tabs on the reservation process to make sure the cabin goes to people who really need the access features.

Best Fit

To be honest, with all the adaptive equipment, spacious layout, and ultra accessible bathroom, I can't think of anyone that this property couldn't

Bedroom in Cabin in the Woods   *Photo credit: Mirror Lake State Park*

Mirror Lake at Mirror Lake State Park

accommodate. It's a great spot for a family getaway, and fisherman will especially love the location.

Nearby

No matter if you just want to relax and enjoy the view, catch some fish for dinner, or take a hike, there are plenty of accessible offerings at Mirror Lake State Park (www.dnr.wi.gov/topic/parks/name/mirrorlake). For starters, there is a paved path out to an accessible fishing pier near the cabin. There's level access to the pier, which has lowered rails to make it easy for wheelchair-users to drop their lines. It's a great option for those who don't have a boat.

Next door, there is a boardwalk down to the accessible boat dock. The boardwalk continues past the dock out to some benches on the water's edge, where you can enjoy the beautiful lake view.

The cabin is also close to the Echo Rock Trail, which is accessible for about a half-mile. The wide paved trail has a slight incline, and features interpretive plaques along the way. It leads out to a nice overlook with benches to enjoy the view, however it loses its access after that point.

If you want to go all the way down to the beach, make a right turn as you exit the Cliffwood Campground, and then take the first right and follow the road until it dead ends in a parking lot. There is an accessible picnic table and shelter in the upper parking lot, but for the best beach access you should park in the lower parking lot. From there, you'll find an accessible asphalt trail that leads down to a grassy area near the shore. Depending on the water level, some wheelchair-users may need a bit of assistance over the grass, but you'll still get a nice view from the path.

Pack along a picnic lunch and enjoy your meal at the accessible picnic table along the path. It has a great view of the lake, and if you have kids in tow, there's also a playground nearby.

Cabin in the Woods
E10320 Fern Dell Road
Baraboo, WI 53913
(608) 254-2333
www.dnr.wi.gov/topic/parks/camping/cabin.html

GPS Coordinates
N 43.56115
W 89.80800

Bathroom in Cabin in the Woods
Photo credit: Mirror Lake State Park

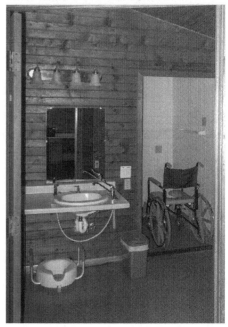

Lake Namakagon Cabin

Cable, WI

Nobody understands access issues better than Sue Overson, which is part of the reason that she and her husband Mark purchased this Lake Namakagon cabin. Says Susan, "My husband has been in a wheelchair for six years, and we really wanted to create a vacation rental for others with mobility issues." The other part of the reason is that the Oversons just love the location. An avid outdoor enthusiast, Mark enjoys kayaking, fishing and snowmobiling, all of which he can do from this Northern Wisconsin lakeside cabin. He's also adapted a number of toys to help him enjoy his favorite activities, many of which are included in the rental rate.

Access Details

There's level access up to the front door, with wide doorways and barrier-free access throughout the cabin. It includes a living room with a fireplace, a gourmet kitchen, a master suite with a bath, two additional bedrooms, another bathroom and a sun porch that doubles as a bedroom. It can accommodate up to 11 people comfortably, but two additional small children can also sleep on the living room sofas, which increases the maximum occupancy to 13.

The master bedroom is furnished with an adjustable Tempur-Pedic queen-sized bed with wheelchair access on both sides. The adjacent bathroom is equipped with a low-step (four-inch) shower with a built in shower seat, and plenty of room for a transfer. The toilet has a grab bar on the right wall (as seated), and the spacious bathroom can accommodate just about any kind of wheelchair or scooter.

One of the other bedrooms has a queen-sized bed, and one is furnished with a full-sized bunk bed with a trundle. Additionally, the sun room has a 22-inch high double bed.

There is level access out to the laundry room, which is equipped with a washer and a dryer. A large garage is also attached to the cabin, and as an added bonus it has a heated floor, which is a great feature for a year-round retreat in this area.

And then there's the lake, which is located down an accessible path from the back door. There is also an accessible fire pit along the way to the dock, and a picnic table near the cabin

Candy's Take

Susan definitely provides her guests with a lot of information about things to do in the area, but I absolutely love the fact that she has a binder filled with access information. And what's not to love about a place that keeps one of my books in its library? She's also spot-on with her

Master bedroom in the Lake Namakagon Cabin

Great Room in the Lake Namakagon Cabin

recommendations, as she steered me to the fun and funky Delta Diner (www.deltadiner.com) for Sunday brunch. This gourmet 50s-style diner was just as accessible as Susan promised, and I would have totally missed it if it hadn't been for her recommendation.

Best Fit

Even though there is a four-inch lip on the shower, the built-in shower bench is close enough for an easy transfer, so this shower setup will work for a lot of people. If however you use a rolling shower chair, and cannot transfer to a bench, this property won't work for you. Fisherman will absolutely love this property, and Mark is quick to point out that the world record Musky was caught on Lake Namakagon. The cabin is also a good choice for a family or multi-family getaway.

Nearby

The big attraction here is the lake, and with Mark's large collection of toys you'll be able to enjoy it to the max.

If you'd like to do a little paddling, there is a selection of kayaks and life vests in the garage. Mark chose ocean kayaks for their stability, and he has a tandem one that will work for people with limited upper body strength.

If you'd like to go fishing, then you can take out Mark's adapted Fish Cat. This single person pontoon boat features a water repellent fabric seat supported by a pontoon on each side. And thanks to Marks adaptation, it's the correct height for a wheelchair transfer.

If you have a larger fishing party, the Oversons also have a standard pontoon boat available for rent. You can just roll on to it from the dock, then take it out and drop anchor and wait for the fish to bite. There are two fishing chairs in the front, or you can fish from your wheelchair.

And if you visit during the winter, then give Mark's accessible ice fishing house a try. It features a back wall that folds down and acts as a ramp, three fishing holes and a propane heater. After you are safe and secure inside, the back ramp can be folded back up so you can fish in heated comfort. Best of all, they have folks who will tow it out on the lake and set it up, supply the bait and the fishing gear, and even clean your catch. It's the easy — and accessible — way to enjoy ice fishing

Lake Namakagon Cabin
21625 Juneks Point Road
Cable WI 54821
(925) 270-3027
www.vrbo.com/430179

GPS Coordinates
N 46.22980
W 91.12047

Shower and toilet in the Lake Namakagon Cabin

Feathered Star B&B

Egg Harbor, WI

L ocated in Egg Harbor Wisconsin, the Feathered Star B&B gets top marks for access, largely because of innkeeper Sandy Chlubnar. As a former occupational therapist, Sandy is well versed in access issues on a professional level; but she's also very familiar with them on a personal level, as her brother was born with Down Syndrome, and her mother had a stroke later in life. "I realized that there was an extreme lack of accessible rooms in Door County, so because of my family and work history I really wanted to do something about that," recalls Sandy. And because of that motivation, she went the extra mile to make sure all of her rooms work for wheelchair-users and slow walkers.

Access Details

There is level access to the front door, with good pathway access inside. Low pile carpet without any padding makes it easy to roll around, and all the beds are open-framed so they can accommodate Hoyer lifts. Named for the popular quilt pattern, the inn also features hand made quilts in all the guest rooms. And for that extra touch of comfort, there is also a fireplace and a refrigerator in every room.

Room 3 and Room 6 each have a roll-in shower with a portable shower bench, grab bars and a hand-held showerhead. Room 3 has toilet grab bars on the back and right walls (as seated), while Room 6 has them on the back and left walls (as seated). Both bathrooms have roll-under sinks. Room 3 is furnished with a 27-inch high queen-sized bed, but if you can't manage that, there is also a recliner in the room. Room 6 has two 26-inch high twin beds.

The other four rooms all have a bathroom with a tub/shower combination with a fold-down shower bench, a hand-held showerhead and grab bars. Other access features include toilet grab bars and a roll-under sink in each bathroom. Room 1, Room 4 and Room 5 have 25-inch high queen-sized beds, while Room 2 is furnished with two 26-inch high twin beds.

There is good access to the public areas of the property, including the dining room, where a "Continental Plus" breakfast is served daily.

Candy's Take

Because of her work history Sandy realizes that different people have different access needs, and I really like that she offers her guests a choice in bed configurations and bathroom access features. Additionally, I agree that the Door Peninsula is sadly lacking in accessible B&Bs, and I'm glad Sandy did something to address the situation in a big way. I just love her attitude.

Room 6 at the Feathered Star B&B

Shower in room 6 at the Feathered Star B&B

Best Fit

Because of the variety of the rooms, this property will work for everyone — whether you need a roll-in shower or a tub/shower combination. Sandy is also happy to work with special access requests. Just let her know what you need, and she'll see if she can make it happen. This property provides a welcome retreat from city life, and it's a good choice for a road trip stopover or a romantic getaway.

Nearby

The Door Peninsula is packed with orchards, country markets and even wineries, so make sure and get out and taste the local products while you're in the area. Harbor Ridge Winery (www.HarborRidgeWinery.com), which is located just north of the Feathered Star B&B on Highway 42, offers grape and fruit wine tasting. There's an accessible entrance through the patio, and plenty of space to navigate a wheelchair in the tasting room. They are well known for their cherry crush wine, but they also have a nice selection of grape wines — from dry to sweet.

Wisconsin Cheese Masters (www.wisconsincheesemasters.com), which is located next door, offers over 65 varieties of Wisconsin cheese. There is level access to the front door, so stop by and have a sample or two. There's also level access to a nice patio area, if you'd like to stay a spell and nosh on some cheese and crackers.

Top off your tasting tour with a stop at Lautenbach's Orchard

Country Winery and Market (www.orchardcountry.com), located on Highway 42, about a half-mile past Fish Creek. There is level access to the store, which boasts a bountiful collection of local goodies; from cheese and freshly baked goods, to cherry preserves and wines. Not only do they offer a selection of traditional grape wines, but they also have fruit wines, sparkling wines and fruit and grape blends. Stop buy and have taste, then pick up some goodies to take back home with you. It's a tasty way to remember your Door County visit.

Feathered Star B&B
6202 Highway 42
Egg Harbor, WI 54209
(920) 743-4066
www.featheredstar.com

GPS Coordinates
N 44.96987
W 87.33591

Sink and toilet in room 6 at the Feathered Star B&B

Douglas Lodge
Park Rapids, MN

B uilt in 1903, historic Douglas Lodge is surrounded by a stand of virgin pine forest in the heart of Itasca State Park. With finger-like Lake Itasca dominating the landscape, this Minnesota park is known for its scenic beauty. It's also the place where the mighty Mississippi begins its 2,552-mile journey to the Gulf of Mexico. And although the original lodge wasn't built to be accessible, access upgrades have been added over the years. Today, thanks to the addition of the Itasca Suites, wheelchair-users and slow walkers have a very accessible place to rest their head while exploring one of Minnesota's oldest state parks.

Access Details

There's plenty of accessible parking near the main lodge, with level access to the lobby, registration desk and dining room. From there it's just a short drive to Itasca Suite 61, an accessible two-room suite that's furnished with rustic pine furniture. There's accessible parking in front, with a barrier-free path over to the six-plex unit. The screened porch is furnished with a table and four chairs, and there's a wide doorway into the suite.

The living room is furnished with a double futon and a television, and the adjacent kitchen is equipped with a microwave, refrigerator, stove top and a dishwasher. A bar with high stools separates the two areas, and the kitchen also has a good selection of dishes and cooking utensils.

The bedroom includes a 25-inch high queen-sized bed with an access aisle on both sides, an easy chair, a chest of drawers and some TV trays. There is also a roll-under sink and a mirror in a small alcove.

The bathroom features a wide doorway with a full five-foot turning radius. It's equipped with a roll-in shower with a hand-held showerhead, grab bars and a fold-down bench. Toilet grab bars are located on the right and back walls (as seated), and there's also a small table for toiletries.

This suite can also be combined with one next door, as the screened porch has a removable divider and there's a connecting door in the living room.

Candy's Take

My favorite part of the suite the screened porch. Not only does it do a good job of keeping the mosquitoes away, but it's also a very pleasant and accessible place to eat. I also like the fact that the suite has a real woodsy feel to it. As an added bonus, the suites are open all year, which is not the case with the rooms in the main lodge.

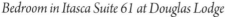

Bedroom in Itasca Suite 61 at Douglas Lodge

Kitchen and living room in Itasca Suite 61 at Douglas Lodge

Best Fit

Because of the large bathroom with a roll-in shower this property is a good fit for all abilities. There's plenty of room throughout the suite for a large wheelchair or scooter; however you may have to move the bedroom chair for better access. This is a good choice for anyone who loves the outdoors, but doesn't want to pitch a tent.

Nearby

There are a number of accessible trails in Itasca State Park (www.dnr.state. mn.us/state_parks/itasca/index.html), beginning with the Doc Roberts Trail. The trailhead is located just a short drive from the main lodge parking area — just follow the sign to the boat pier.

There's usually plenty of parking available in the dirt parking lot, which has accessible toilets on the far end. From there a hard-packed dirt trail winds through the woods to the Old Timer Cabin. There is ramp access to this Civilian Conservation Corps cabin, but it's only open for ranger programs. After that the trail gets bumpy, and there are a lot of ruts and roots along the way, so you'll have to double back.

Another nice trail is located over at the Brower Visitor Center. There's accessible parking in the lot with level access to the building, which houses a variety of interpretive exhibits. The accessible Maadaadizi Trail begins to the left of the Visitor Center. The half-mile hard-packed dirt trail is covered with crushed granite, and makes for a nice roll through the surrounding forest.

If you'd prefer a driving tour instead, then take Wilderness Drive from the Visitor Center to the headwaters. Along the way you'll be treated to a number of great windshield views, as the trees form a canopy over the road, and squirrels and deer scamper around in the underbrush.

Up at the Mary Gibbs Mississippi Headwaters Center, there is accessible parking near the visitor pavilion, which houses a number of interpretive exhibits and an accessible restroom. There is also level access to the gift shop and restaurant inside. A 600-foot paved trail leads out to a viewing platform, where you can see the headwaters of the Mississippi River. After that a hard-packed dirt trail winds out to the water. From there the Headwaters Loop Trail continues as a boardwalk, then changes to a hard-pack dirt trial before it loops back to the visitor pavilion. It's a very pleasant walk in the woods, and a rare opportunity to check out the source of a major river.

Douglas Lodge   **GPS Coordinates**
Itasca State Park   N 47.16497
Park Rapids, MN 56470   W 95.19670
(866) 857-2757
www.dnr.state.mn.us/state_parks/itasca/index.html

Toilet and shower in Itasca Suite 61 at Douglas Lodge

Eastern States

Hotel Viking

Newport, RI

The Hotel Viking opened its doors on May 25, 1926, with two lavish parties to celebrate the occasion. Over the years this historic Newport property has gone through a number of renovations. In 1999 a $3 million refurbishment project brought this grand old dame back to her original splendor, and in 2003 an additional $5 million was invested in her lavish public spaces. Finally in 2007 the original guest rooms were renovated to the tune of $6.8 million. Today this landmark property boasts modern accessible rooms, yet retains a historic ambiance. From the front desk clock embellished with ancient Nordic runes, to the original 1926 brass letter box in the lobby, there's definitely a taste of yesteryear in this stately old gem.

Access Details

Accessible parking is located near the front entrance, and valet parking is also available. The entrance (which is on the second floor) is up a flight of stairs, but there is ramp access on the left side. Inside, there's plenty of room to navigate a wheelchair in the spacious lobby.

There is elevator access to accessible Room 1022, which is located down one floor, at street level. The room features wide doorways, good pathway access and lowered closet rods. It's furnished with a 26-inch high king-sized bed with wheelchair access on both sides. Other furnishings include a wing back chair, a desk with a chair, and an armoire.

The spacious bathroom features a full five-foot turning radius and is equipped with a roll-in shower with a fold-down shower bench, grab bars and a hand-held showerhead. Toilet grab bars are located on the back and right walls (as seated), and there is also a roll-under sink in the bathroom.

There is good access to all the public spaces at the Hotel Viking, including the two dining rooms and all-day lounge at One Bellevue, the restaurant. Additionally, both the pool and spa have lifts.

Candy's Take

It's a beautifully restored property with excellent access. I also really enjoyed my breakfast in the garden room at One Bellevue. It's such a light airy room, and the service is top notch. I almost felt regal, and I savored every last bite of my leisurely meal. It's a great way to start the day in historic Newport.

Best Fit

Because of the spacious guestroom and the nicely done roll-in shower, this property will work for wheelchair-users and slow walkers. It's a good place to base yourself if you'd like to tour the historic mansions, as the period

Room 1022 at Hotel Viking

Doris Dukes' Rough Point

furnishings and historic architecture of the property really set that gilded age mood. It would also make a nice romantic getaway.

Nearby

No visit to Newport is complete without touring a few mansions, some of which are now accessible. At the top of the list is Doris Dukes' Rough Point (www.newportrestoration.org/visit/rough_point), which is an excellent example of the opulence that marked the gilded age. There is accessible parking in front of the mansion, with level access to the building. Inside, there's ample room to maneuver a wheelchair on the guided tour. Out of all the Newport mansions, this one has the most valuable antiques, because unlike the other summer residents, the Dukes never fell on hard times, so they never had to sell off their treasures.

Another must-see mansion is Rosecliff (www.newportmansions. org/explore/rosecliff), where the Great Gatsby was filmed. This French Renaissance mansion was built for the express purpose of hosting the most elaborate summer party; and from the photos on display inside, it appears that goal was continually achieved. There is accessible parking near the entrance with level access into the foyer. There are four steps to the main house, but a stair lift is also available. You can tour the property at your own pace with the excellent audio tour. And if you get tired there are chairs to sit and rest along the way. Stairs lead up to the second floor, but directions to the elevator are given on the audio tour. And if you have any questions, the docents are happy to assist.

Last but not least, don't miss The Breakers (www.newportmansions.org/explore/the-breakers), the stunning Vanderbilt family home. There is accessible parking near the front gate, and a level walkway up to the mansion. If you don't have an obvious disability and can't do stairs, let the gate attendant know, and he will direct you to the accessible entrance. This Italian Renaissance mansion is the largest mansion in Newport, and the excellent audio tour offers visitors a glimpse into its past. Although there are steps along the main tour route, there is an accessible route that uses the elevator. Directions to the accessible route are detailed on the audio tour, which also includes some fun family stories, and a brief history of the mansion.

Hotel Viking
1 Bellevue Avenue
Newport, RI 02840
(401) 847-3300
www.hotelviking.com

GPS Coordinates
N 41.48746
W 71.31003

Shower and toilet in room 1022 at Hotel Viking

Noble View Outdoor Center
Russell, MA

This hilltop Berkshire retreat is operated by the Appalachian Mountain Club; and although the lodges were built over 100 years ago, modern access features have been added. The quiet mountain top location features over 385 acres of woodlands, abandoned farm fields, small brooks and diverse habitats. It's a good place to get away from the city and enjoy a slice of nature. And thanks to the continued efforts of the Appalachian Mountain Club, Noble View Outdoor Center is far more accessible today than it was 10 years ago.

Access Details

There's accessible parking near the two lodges — Double Cottage which was built in 1903, and North Cottage which was built in 1907. There is ramp access up to both buildings, which have large front decks. Double Cottage is located next to the parking area and North Cottage is next door, and there's an accessible path between the two.

North Cottage has a large common area that's furnished with two sofas, a love seat and an easy chair, and a wood stove for heat. It also includes a large dining room table and a nice commercial kitchen with a stove and a refrigerator, and a good selection of pots, pans, dishes and utensils.

The cottage can accommodate up to 10 guests in four bedrooms, and it includes an accessible ground floor bedroom. The accessible bedroom (Room 1) is furnished with two 17-inch high twin beds. If a wheelchair-user books the room, one bed is turned on its side, which creates a full five-foot turning radius. The other bedrooms are located on the second floor, and can be only be accessed by stairs.

Double Cottage has the same features as North Cottage, except that it has two wings with a double commercial kitchen between them. The ground floor accessible bedrooms (Room 1 and Room 5) have the same access features as the one in North Cottage. One accessible bedroom is located in each wing, and the cottage can accommodate up to 18 people.

The bathhouse is behind North Cottage, at the end of an accessible path. A unisex accessible shower room is located between the men's and women's showers. There is level access to the shower room, which has a roll-in shower with a fold-down shower seat, grab bars and a hand-held showerhead. An accessible toilet with grab bars on the right and back walls (as seated) is located at one end of the room, and there is a large roll-under sink in the center. There's more than ample room for even the largest wheelchair or scooter in the spacious room. Additionally, there's a sink for washing dishes right outside the unisex shower room.

Room 1 in North Cottage

Great room in North Cottage

Because the camp is so remote guests must carry out all of their garbage, so keep that in mind when you pack your supplies. Bedding and towels are also not provided.

Candy's Take

The location of these cabins couldn't be better, as it's totally away from the city, and it's a great place to just kick back and take in all that Mother Nature has to offer. I'm happy that the Appalachian Mountain Club included access in their renovations, so now everyone can overnight there.

Best Fit

This property will work for most wheelchair-users and slow walkers, however it's not a good choice for two wheelchair-users who want to share the same room. Also, if you have to have an ensuite bathroom, this place won't work for you. It's a good choice for family reunions, as you can rent out the whole cottage and do your own cooking. It would also be a fun place to have a girlfriends getaway.

Nearby

To be honest, there aren't really any nearby attractions, but then again, that's part of the charm of this property. It's a good place to get away from the city, do a little star gazing and get reacquainted with family and friends.

The large covered front deck is a great place to even enjoy a cup of coffee in the morning or a glass of wine in the evening. Additionally, there is a large grassy area in front of North Cabin which has a nice view. It's an excellent place to enjoy the sunset, and although there isn't a path across the grass, it's level and easy to navigate in a wheelchair.

Although there aren't any accessible trails at Noble View, the Appalachian Mountain Club hopes to change that. They plan to secure grant funding to construct a one-to-two mile wheelchair-accessible trail in the near future. So hopefully one day wheelers will be able to also enjoy the surrounding hemlock forest.

On your way back home be sure and stop at the Russell Inn. It's located about five miles from Noble View, and they serve up a very tasty breakfast on the weekends. It's a cute little joint, and the owners are friendly. It has one step up at the front, so although it's not an option for most wheelchair-users, it's a good choice for slow walkers.

Noble View Outdoor Center	**GPS Coordinates**
635 South Quarter Road	N 42.13319
Russell, MA 01071	W 72.86042
(413) 572-4501	
www.nobleviewoutdoorcenter.org	

Toilet and shower in the bathhouse

Brook Farm Inn

Lenox, MA

Built in 1882, Brook Farm Inn simply oozes Victorian charm. It served as a private residence until 1949, when Lena and Max Rosenberg welcomed their first guests to — as it was called then — the Shadowood Inn. The name was subsequently changed to Brook Farm Inn, and over the years the property went through a number of innkeepers. Finally in 2001 Linda and Phil Halpern purchased it, and set out to refurbish and enlarge this historic gem. As fate would have it, Phil was very familiar with access issues as both of his parents used wheelchairs; so when it came time to build the carriage house he was very motivated to add a wheelchair-accessible room. As a result, today the property boasts not one — but two — very accessible and elegant guestrooms.

Access Details
There's accessible parking near the entrance, and although there are steps up to the main inn building, the Halperns are happy to make accommodations if you can't access the lobby.

The Carriage House, which contains the Green Room (Shadowood 1) and the Burgundy Room (Shadowood 2), is located directly behind the main inn. There is a barrier-free pathway from the adjacent parking area to both rooms.

The Burgundy Room, which is decorated in tones of cream, pink and burgundy, features a level threshold, wide doorways and plenty of room to maneuver a wheelchair or scooter. It's furnished with a 25-inch high queen-sized bed with wheelchair access on both sides, a love seat, a small coffee table, a chest of drawers and a writing desk with a chair. And even with all that furniture, there's still good pathway access throughout the room. Round out the furnishings with a fireplace and a refrigerator and you have a very comfortable space. There is also level access out to a shared deck that overlooks the garden.

The large bathroom has a standard two-person Jacuzzi tub and a roll-in shower with a fold-down shower seat, grab bars and a hand-held showerhead. The toilet grab bars are located on the back and left walls (as seated) and there is also a roll-under sink in the bathroom.

The Green Room has the same access features, except it's decorated in tones of green.

Breakfast can be delivered your room if you can't manage the steps up into the main inn. Just let Linda know, and she's happy to make it happen. She can also accommodate gluten-free diets — just let her know in advance.

The Burgundy Room at Brook Farm Inn

All Persons Trail at the Pleasant Valley Wildlife Sanctuary

Candy's Take

The gardens are very pleasant, but to be honest the thing I like best about the inn is that the accessible rooms are private, luxurious and very roomy. Phil even added extra insulation on the common wall, so you don't get any noise from the adjacent room. Linda also knows the local food scene, and her suggestion of Jae's Asian Bistro (www.jaeslenox.com) was perfect. Not only is the restaurant very accessible, but they serve up a tasty offering of sushi, Thai and Korean specialties.

Best Fit

The access is great in the bathrooms, and this property will work for most wheelchair-users. It makes a nice road trip stopover, and it's the perfect choice for a romantic getaway or even an anniversary.

Nearby

If you want to explore the outdoors, then make sure and stop by Pleasant Valley Wildlife Sanctuary (www.massaudubon.org/get-outdoors/wildlife-sanctuaries/pleasant-valley) while you're in town. This thousand-acre preserve features some nice trails — including a wheelchair-accessible one — through a forest, meadow and wetlands habitat.

There's accessible parking near the trailhead, however there are three steps up to the office where admission fees are collected. There is a chain across the accessible path to the trailhead — presumably to prevent cars from driving on it — but it's not locked and the chain is very easy to unhook.

The third-mile All Persons Trail is wide, level and covered in crushed granite. It winds through a hemlock grove and crosses a field of wildflowers, before it gives way to a boardwalk around Pikes Pond. There are interpretive plaques along the way, and there's also a bench at the pond. The beavers are very active, and you'll also spot red-winged black birds, great blue herons and belted kingfishers there. It's a short but pleasant walk, and a nice find in the middle of a city.

The Norman Rockwell Museum (www.nrm.org) is also located nearby, in the village of Stockbridge. There's level access to the main building, which houses the world's largest collection of Norman Rockwell's work. The artist's former studio, which stands today much as it did in Rockwell's lifetime, is also accessible. And if you have problems with distances, there is a wheelchair available for loan.

Brook Farm Inn
15 Hawthorne Street
Lenox, MA 01240
(800) 285-7638
www.brookfarm.com

GPS Coordinates
N 42.35256812
W 73.28851

Shower and toilet in the Burgundy Room bathroom

Red Hook Country Inn

Red Hook, NY

L ocated in the middle of a charming upstate New York village, the
Red Hook Country Inn transports guests back to a kinder and
gentler era. The 1841 Federal Colonial building is just two hours
from New York City, yet it's a world away from the hustle and bustle of
city life. Innkeeper Pat Holden did an excellent job of decorating and
furnishing this historic property with period furniture. And although this
10-room inn wasn't at all accessible back in the 1800s, today it's a good
choice for some wheelchair-users and slow walkers.

Access Details

Accessible parking is available in a paved lot behind the inn, near a barrier-
free path to the accessible front porch. The front entrance has a wide
double door that will accommodate wheelchairs and scooters, and there is
good pathway access to the registration desk.

Room 9 — also known as the Taproom — is located just behind the
front desk. There is level access to the room, which is furnished with a 38-
inch high king-sized bed with wheelchair-access on one side. The room

is also adorned with a large art deco mahogany bar complete with an old cash register, hence the name "Taproom". Top it off with a gas fireplace and you have a very cozy room.

There is a wide pocket door into the bathroom, which is equipped with a roll-in shower with a fold-down shower seat and grab bars. There is no hand-held showerhead in the 37-inch wide shower, but there is a large rain showerhead with controls located near the shower bench. There is one small vertical grab bar in front of the toilet (on the right side as seated), and the bathroom also has a roll-under sink. The bathroom has a full five-foot turning radius, but you may have to move the small portable towel rack for optimum access.

There is also level access to the first-floor public rooms, including the front parlor which has a large fireplace and is furnished with turn-of-the-century pieces.

Candy's Take

I really love the front porch, as it's a great place to relax, with it's rocking chairs and comfy sofas. It's a wonderful old house — just like grandma's — filled with period furnishings. It's also close to several restaurants, so you can just park your car for the evening and enjoy a pleasant stroll to dinner.

Springwood — the Roosevelt family home

Best Fit

Because of the type and placement of the toilet grab bar, and the height of the bed, independent transfers may be difficult or impossible for full time wheelchair-users. That said, if you have someone to assist you, it's a good choice for slow walkers and wheelchair-users who can walk a step or two. It's important to note that it is an old house, not a reproduction, so if you are expecting something modern, then this place isn't for you. It's the perfect place for folks who appreciate history and a good home base for a Hyde Park visit.

Bronze of a young FDR in the Roosevelt family home

Nearby

The Franklin D. Roosevelt Presidential Library and Museum (www.fdrlibrary.marist.edu) is located in nearby Hyde Park, just 15 miles from the inn. There are two attractions at the site; the museum itself and Springwood, the Roosevelt family home.

Accessible parking is available in a paved parking lot, with barrier-free access over to the Wallace Visitor Center. Inside you can buy tour tickets, see a film about the former president, and browse through a few interpretive exhibits. There is level access to the auditorium, where the film is shown, and there is wheelchair-seating with adjacent companion seats inside. A loaner wheelchair is also available at the front desk.

The presidential library and museum is located behind the visitor center. It features level access and plenty of room to maneuver a wheelchair in the galleries. The first floor features a chronology of the events during Roosevelt's presidency, including the depression, The New Deal, World War II and even the president's famous fireside chats.

The lower level, which is accessible by elevator, includes the former president's collections of model ships, furniture and sculptures, as well as his 1936 Ford Phaeton with hand controls. It also houses a large collection of family photos and the First Lady's Gallery.

Springwood (www.nps.gov/hofr/index.htm) is located about 400 yards from the visitor center, along a level pathway; however if you can't manage the distance, a shuttle with ramp access is available. Although there are steps up to the front door of the house, there is also ramp access on the right.

There is a guided tour of the first-floor, which includes the library, parlor, quilting room and smoking room. There is good pathway access throughout the home, which features a Chinese temple bell that was used as a dinner gong, Roosevelt's homemade wheelchair and his large taxidermy collection. There is elevator access to the second floor where visitors can have a gander at the bedrooms and the servants wing. The third floor is not open to visitors.

Save some time to stroll around the accessible trails on the beautiful campus, and to visit the rose garden and the Roosevelt graves. It's a very pleasant place to just sit back and relax.

Red Hook Country Inn
7460 S. Broadway
Red Hook, NY 12571
(845) 758-8445
www.theredhookinn.com

GPS Coordinates
N 41.99379
W 73.87626

Bathroom in room 9 at the Red Hook Country Inn

The Pearl of Seneca Lake

Dundee, NY

Peter and Mary Muller are living their retirement dream at The Pearl of Seneca Lake, in the heart of New York's Finger Lakes Region. It all began in 1982 when they purchased 14 acres of land on the shore of Lake Seneca. Over the years they camped on it, and in 2005 they finally built their four-room inn. And because of some inclusive thinking they included an accessible guestroom in their plans. Today they enjoy welcoming guests from around the world, and sharing their little piece of heaven with them.

Access Details

Parking is located in a gravel area across from the inn, and since it's gravel it's not striped. That said, there are only four rooms at the inn, so there's plenty of room for a ramped van to park. It's a bit uphill to the front door from the parking lot, but there is a paved drop-off area next to the garage with level access over to the front door. There is a slight lip at the front door, with barrier-free access to the living room, kitchen and dining room.

The accessible Merlot Room is located at the end of the hallway, and it features wide doorways and ample room for a wheelchair. It's furnished with a 25-inch high queen-sized bed with wheelchair-access on one side, a dresser, and a table with two chairs. There is also a refrigerator and a microwave in the room.

There is level access to the bathroom which is equipped with a roll-in shower with a fold-down shower bench, grab bars and a hand-held showerhead. There is a slight lip on the shower, and the shower bench is positioned so that a direct transfer from outside the shower is not possible, so some assistance may be required. The toilet grab bars are located on the back and right walls (as seated), and the bathroom has a roll-under sink.

There is also a slight lip on the threshold to the back deck, but there is level access on the deck and ramp access down into the yard.

Candy's Take

The back deck is my favorite place at this property, as it has a great lake view and it's very quiet. I even nodded off there one afternoon while I was waiting for a friend to pick me up for dinner. Mary is also quite the baker, and if you let her know in advance she can even whip up some gluten-free goodies for you.

The Merlot Room at The Pearl of Seneca Lake

The back porch which offers a good view of Seneca Lake

Best Fit

Because the roll-in shower has a slight lip, most folks will need a little assistance. The same holds true for the lips on the door thresholds. That said, it will definitely work for slow walkers, part time wheelchair-users and people who have assistance. It's a nice place for a romantic retreat because of the location, but since the breakfast is served family style, you may want to take it back to your room for more privacy. As Mary said, "One of our greatest pleasures is visiting with our guests at breakfast time and sharing their experiences," and that may not be very conducive to romance.

Nearby

Although you can certainly just sit back on the deck and enjoy the lake, you may want to check out some of the Finger Lakes wineries along Highway 14.

At the top of the list is Hickory Hollow Wine Cellars (www.hickoryhollowwine.net). There is level access from the parking lot to the tasting room, and good access inside. This winery offers a variety of sweet and dry red and white wines.

Next on the list is Fulkerson Winery (www.fulkersonwinery.com) which also has an accessible tasting room. They offer over 25 varieties of wine, including a large selection of Rieslings. And for the home winemaker they have 33 varieties of fresh grape juice in the fall. They also have a full line of home winemaking supplies.

Rock Stream Vineyards (www.rockstreamvineyards.com) is also a must-do. There is level access to their tasting room which has a nice selection of red and white wines and ports. Plus it's the only winery in the area that sells grappa and grape brandy.

Last but not least, be sure and stop in at the Fruit Yard Winery (www.fruityardwinery.com), which offers both fruit and grape wines. There is level access to the tasting room, with barrier-free access inside. Their fruit wine selections include cherry, cranberry, plum, strawberry and blueberry. And if you're more of a traditionalist, try their rich Merlot or their no-oak Chardonnay. Truly they have something for just about every taste.

The Pearl of Seneca Lake
4827 Red Cedar Lane
Dundee, NY 14837
(607) 243-5227
www.thepearlofsenecalake.com

GPS Coordinates
N 42.53215
W 76.91594

Toilet and shower in the Merlot Room at The Pearl of Seneca Lake

John Dillon Park Lean-Tos

Long Lake, NY

Located 15 miles from Tupper Lake in upstate New York, John Dillon Park is a fully accessible Adirondack wilderness facility. The result of a partnership between International Paper and Paul Smith's College, this unique park features lean-tos, trails and other recreational opportunities, all of which are wheelchair-accessible. The first facility of its kind, it allows everyone to explore the wilderness, sleep out under the stars and enjoy Mother Nature. Best of all, since it's about two miles off the main road, it offers campers a real chance to get away from the maddening crowds.

Access Details

Accessible parking is located near the Welcome Center, with barrier-free access over to the front door and good pathway access inside.

All of the lean-tos are either ramped or built at the appropriate wheelchair-transfer height; and they come equipped with a fold-down bed, a fire ring and a picnic table. Composting toilets and potable water are available at each lean-to and the Welcome Center has a flush toilet and a refrigerator for medication storage.

The only lean-to you can drive to is Bear Cub, as it's the closest one to the Welcome Center. The others are built in pairs along the accessible trail; with the farthest one located one-and-a-half miles from the Welcome Center. A golf cart is available to help folks get their gear to the more remote lean-tos.

There is no charge to use John Dillon Park, but it's only open to people with disabilities and their companions. Proof of disability, such as a America the Beautiful Access Pass or a doctor's note, is required at registration.

The maximum stay at John Dillon Park is 10 days and reservations are recommended, although walk-ins can be accommodated on a space available basis. The park is open daily in the summer and on weekends after Labor Day. It's also available for day use during those times.

Candy's Take

I really love it when people get creative and think outside the box, and that's exactly what they did when they designed John Dillon Park. My favorite innovation is the solar powered battery charger that can be wheeled from site to site, as it allows folks with power wheelchairs and scooters to more fully enjoy the wilderness. I also really like that the facility is rustic, but accessible. And hey, the price is right too!

The Wild Center at Tupper Lake

Trail at John Dillon Park

Best Fit

Access wise the park will work for everyone, as it was designed and built to be accessible. That said, you will be sleeping on a platform which has three sides and an open front, so if that's too Robinson Crusoe for you, then this park isn't a good choice. On the other hand, if you crave a real Adirondack wilderness adventure, then John Dillon Park is just what the doctor ordered.

Nearby

You can certainly have a great time without ever leaving the park, as there are many accessible recreational opportunities to occupy your time. There are over three miles of trails and a number of picnic areas, if you'd like to set out on a hike and check out the local wildlife. There is also an accessible fishing pier, so you can certainly have some fresh fish for dinner. And if you'd like to enjoy some accessible fun on Grampus Lake, you can launch your own canoe or kayak from the accessible dock, or hop aboard the accessible pontoon boat.

For a good primer on Adirondack wildlife, head on over to the Wild Center (www.wildcenter.org) in Tupper Lake. This natural history museum of the Adirondacks features interpretive exhibits, live animals and educational programs about the flora and fauna of the region. There is excellent access throughout the museum with a level entry, barrier-free access to all exhibits and accessible restrooms.

Highlights of the permanent collection include an authentic Adirondack lean-to, a glacial wall and a gaggle of playful otters in the Living River Trail exhibit. Visitors are exposed to the full range of Adirondack habitats as they travel from the lean-to through bogs, streams, lakes and forests, and up to the summit of a high peak.

Outside there's a half-mile barrier-free trail that winds around Greenleaf Pond. The hard-packed trail is covered in crushed granite, and there's plenty of interpretive signs and benches along the way. It's a great way to end your Wild Center visit, as you can pause and reflect on peaceful Rainbow Bridge, before you follow the trail out to the parking lot.

John Dillon Park
2150 Tupper Road
Long Lake, NY 12847
(518) 524-6226
www.johndillonpark.org

GPS Coordinates
N 43.98566
W 74.45854

Composting toilet at John Dillon Park

Admiral Fell Inn

Baltimore, MD

F ells Point is one of the most historic neighborhoods in Baltimore, and there's just no better place to get a sense of this history than at the Admiral Fell Inn. Located on the waterfront, the property exudes a subtle ambiance of yesteryear, and comes complete with a gaggle of resident ghosts. And even though this European-style hotel dates back to the 1700s, modern access features have been added over the years, so today everyone can enjoy this grand old inn.

Access Details

Although four steps grace the front entrance of the property, an accessible side entrance is located just around the corner on Shakespeare Street. It's easy to find, and it has a key controlled door for security. Valet parking is also available at the front entrance; which is the preferred option if you can't snag one of the street spaces in front of the property.

Room 193, which is located on the first floor near the accessible entrance, is the most accessible guest room. It features wide doorways, a lowered peephole and good pathway access; and it's furnished with a very comfortable double bed with wheelchair-access on both sides. Other furnishings include a wing back chair, an armoire and a desk with a chair.

The bathroom is equipped with a spacious roll-in shower with grab bars and a hand-held showerhead. Other access features include toilet grab bars on the left and back walls (as seated) and a roll-under sink. A portable shower chair with a back is also included. There is also a roll-under sink in an alcove outside the bathroom.

There is good access to all of the first-floor public spaces including the lobby, which is furnished with period furnishings. And if you should want for anything, the employees at this luxurious inn are very accommodating.

Candy's Take

I think it's great that they were able to add access features to this property, yet still retain its historic feel. Room 193 is one of the historic rooms, so that's an added bonus. I also like the lobby, especially the fireplace. It's a comfy place to enjoy a book or even answer some e-mail.

Best Fit

The spacious bathroom in Room 193 will work for just about everyone, and if you'd prefer an accessible room with a tub/shower combination,

Bathroom in room 193 at the Admiral Fell Inn

they have those too. So this property gets high marks for variety and accessibility. It's a fun place for a weekend getaway or a romantic retreat, and it would be great to spend Halloween there.

Nearby

Since the Admiral Fell Inn is considered one of the top ten haunted places in Baltimore, the Admiral's Ghost Tour is a must. The tour cost is included in the nightly rate, and the tour guides regale guests with lively ghost tales as they tour the seven historic buildings which make up the Admiral Fell Inn.

You'll likely hear the tale of the man who died in Room 413. Although the official reports are somewhat lacking in details, many folks suspect foul play was involved. What is evident is the apparent chill in the room, sometimes followed by a light breeze (even though the windows are closed). And then of course there are reports from housekeeper Frances Gale, of having the sensation of someone placing a hand on her shoulder, even though she was alone in the room.

Outside sink in room 193 at the Admiral Fell Inn

And if you happen to hear some thumping or bumping along the way, it's probably the work of Bitsy and Grady. Bitsy tends to visit the rooms on the second floor while Grady reportedly prefers the third-floor rooms. And when guests call to complain about the noise, it mysteriously stops.

Last but not least, there's the tale of the 2003 Hurricane Isabel "party", when several employees heard loud party noises coming from the second-floor rooms. One front desk employee even saw the ceiling vibrate above him. The reason this was so strange was that the hotel was deserted. And in all cases, when the employees went to investigate, they found empty rooms. Some folks surmised that the ghosts liked having the hotel to themselves, so they decided to throw a party. But then again, I guess the howling wind can often be mistaken for clinking champagne glasses.

In any case, the ghost tour is fun, fascinating and very educational. And although there are a few steps here and there throughout the property, the tour steers clear of those areas, so it's nicely accessible to everyone.

Admiral Fell Inn
888 South Broadway
Baltimore, MD 21231
(410) 522-7380
www.admiralfell.com

GPS Coordinates
N 39.28187
W 76.59368

The Columbia Inn at Peralynna — Columbia, MD

L ocated on Route 108 just outside Columbia, Maryland, this European-style manor home gets high marks for luxury. And the good news is, access hasn't been overlooked either; in fact it was factored into the equation from the beginning. "Our house was originally built as a multigenerational home, so we've always been aware of access issues," recalls innkeeper Cynthia Lynn. "Of course accessibility was brought to the forefront at our wedding," she continues, "as the reception was held here; and we needed to make sure it was accessible to everyone, especially our parents." Today guests continue to benefit from the accessible features that were incorporated in the original design.

Access Details

There is accessible parking in the rear, with ramp access to the back deck and level access to the lobby. Inside, there's plenty of room to maneuver a wheelchair, with wide doorways and barrier-free access to the first-floor public areas.

Suite A (also called the Peacock Suite) is located across the driveway, next to the accessible parking area. There is ramp access to the bedroom terrace and good pathway access throughout the suite. The bedroom boasts a 26-inch high Tempur-Pedic bed with wheelchair access on both sides, a gas fireplace and a standard Jacuzzi tub. A roll-under sink is located near the tub, and a separate toilet room features grab bars on the side and back walls.

The full bathroom is much more luxurious, with a roll-in grotto shower with a built-in shower bench, two hand-held showerheads and five stationary showerheads. Other access features include shower and toilet grab bars, an easy-access shower curtain and a roll-under sink.

The living area is outfitted with a sofa and chairs, a gas fireplace, a plasma screen TV, a wet bar and an espresso maker. There is also a small dining table and plenty of closet space. The private terrace has a table and chairs, and it's a nice place to enjoy a glass of wine at sunset.

Breakfast is a luxurious affair at the inn. It's made-to-order, and there's no menu. You just tell them what you want and it's all custom made for you. And with advance arrangements, breakfast can also be served in your suite. Evening hors d'oeuvres, wine and beer are served in the lobby; and coffee and cookies are available all day.

Sitting room in the Peacock Suite

Savage Mill Mall

Candy's Take

I love the bathroom as it has a gorgeous stained glass peacock window — that's how the suite got its nickname. It's also a very comfortable and spacious suite and the Tempur-Pedic bed is dreamy. It's almost like staying in your own home, and it's very private as it's away from the main house.

Best Fit

The suite is large enough for everyone, and the nice roll-in shower will work for wheelchair-users and slow walkers alike. It's a great choice for a romantic weekend, or that special anniversary. It's also a beautiful wedding venue.

Nearby

The Iron Bridge Wine Company (www.ironbridgewines.com), which is located next door, makes a good dinner choice. Although it's certainly within walking distance, it's much safer to drive as the pathway sometimes extends into the busy road. The restaurant features accessible parking and ramped access, and it's a great place for wine and beer tasting, lunch and dinner.

And if you fancy a spot of antique shopping, then head over to Savage Mill (www.savagemill.com). This huge antique mall is just a short drive away, and it features accessible parking and elevator access to all levels. It's a fun place to browse, and if you happen to work up an appetite, there are also a few restaurants on the premises.

Additionally, since Columbia is just 30 minutes from Baltimore, and 45 minutes from Washington DC, you could explore those cities during the day and retreat back to this peaceful country inn at night. It's the best of both worlds.

The Columbia Inn at Peralynna
10605 State Route 108
Columbia, MD 21044
(410) 715-4600
www.mycolumbiainn.com

GPS Coordinates
N 39.23497
W 76.87921

Toilet and shower in the Peacock Suite

Graceland Inn & Conference Center — *Elkins, West Virginia*

L ocated on the Davis & Elkins College campus, the Graceland Inn is the former summer home of U.S. Senator Henry Gassaway. Named after Gassaway's daughter Grace, the castle-like mansion is a picture perfect example of Victorian elegance. This National Historic Landmark boasts hardwood floors and rich paneling, and is furnished with period pieces and reproductions. It's staffed by the college's hospitality and tourism students, and although it's not fully accessible, some access upgrades have been added, so today it's a good choice for many slow walkers and part time wheelchair-users.

Access Details

Although steps grace the front of this historic building, the accessible entrance is located just to the left, near the accessible parking space. There is a level pathway to the accessible entrance, however the door is not marked. Once inside, the corridor on the right will take you past the elevator and around to the front desk.

The accessible Nanny's Room is located on the third floor. The elevator is a very old model (remember you are in a historic building), and it measures just two feet deep and five feet wide. The door is on the front in the lobby and on the side on the third floor, so it might be a pretty tight fit for some folks.

The Nanny's Room features a wide doorway and good pathway access. It's furnished with a 30-inch high queen-sized bed with wheelchair access on one side, an armoire and two side chairs.

The bathroom has a full five-foot turning radius and it is equipped with a low-step shower (five inches high) with grab bars and a hand-held showerhead. The shower door is 28 inches wide, and the shower itself measures 41 inches wide by 34 inches deep. The toilet is located in an alcove with grab bars on the right and back walls (as seated), and the bathroom also has a roll-under sink.

There is barrier-free access to the first floor public areas, including the spacious lobby.

Candy's Take

I just love this beautiful old building, and I'm glad they were able to at least add a few access upgrades so more people can enjoy it. The billiards room, which is right across from the Nanny's Room, is my favorite place on the property. It's furnished with an antique billiards table and other furnishings, and it's like taking a step back in time.

The Nanny's Room at Graceland Inn and Conference Center

Trail a the West Virginia State Wildlife Center

Best Fit

Because of the small elevator and the high bed this property won't work for power wheelchair-users. Additionally, if you have to do a lateral transfer, the toilet placement in the alcove may prove problematic. Still it's a good choice for a slow walker or a part time manual wheelchair-user, or anybody who can walk a few steps and has assistance available. It's a good road trip stopover and it is also a good meeting venue, as the adjacent Robert C. Byrd Center for Hospitality & Tourism has a large accessible conference area.

Nearby

The country around Elkins is beautiful, and the West Virginia State Wildlife Center (www.wvdnr.gov/wildlife/wildlifecenter.shtm), which is located about 40 miles away in French Creek, is definitely worth a visit. Operated by the West Virginia Division of Natural Resources, the center presents native wildlife in a natural setting.

There's level access to the gift shop, where you pay the very reasonable $3 entrance fee. From there, a mile-and-a-quarter trail runs through the facility, with interpretive signs along the route. The trail is paved and wide, and although people with power wheelchairs and scooters may be able to manage the first hill, it's best for manual wheelchair-users to take the trail in reverse.

If the first part of the trail is too steep for you, then head back to the gift shop parking lot and pick up the trail at the other end. Along the way you'll see lots of native wildlife including wolves, eagles, skunks, boars and coyotes. Once you reach the cougars you may have to turn around if you can't manage the last hill.

Still for the most part the trail is accessible, and although it splits off in places, the accessible routes are well marked. It's a pleasant stroll along a shaded path through the forest.

There is also a separate elk viewing area which you can reach by car. From the gift shop parking lot take a left, go through the second parking area and take the first left. The short road leads down to the picnic area, but the elk are usually down by the water, so the best way to see them is to just stop along the way. There is accessible parking at the end of the drive, and there's level access to the covered picnic area. Even if the elk are a little shy, it's a pleasant place for a picnic lunch.

Graceland Inn & Conference Center
Davis & Elkins College
Elkins, WV 26241
(304) 637-1600
www.gracelandinn.com

GPS Coordinates
N 38.93072
W 79.84783

Toilet and shower in the Nanny's Room at Graceland Inn and Conference Center

Northshore Lake House

Raleigh, NC

L ocated just 10 minutes from downtown Raleigh, the Northshore Lake House is Christine Harrison's private oasis. If you're craving the creature comforts of home, then this property will really appeal to you. And there's a reason that this two story duplex is so homey — it *is* Christine's home. Christine lives upstairs and previously her mother (who used a manual wheelchair) occupied the downstairs space. Today that section — which is blocked off for privacy — is reserved for guests, so it's almost like having your own little lakeside apartment.

Access Details

There's ramp access to the three-bedroom unit which features a large living room that's furnished with a sofa, chairs and a fireplace. The adjacent dining room is equally spacious and it has a table and chairs, plus a bookshelf full of games, books and other diversions.

Lakeview is the largest bedroom, and it's furnished with a 26-inch high queen-sized bed. Seagrass (the next largest bedroom) has a 22-inch high queen-sized bed and Cottage (the smallest bedroom) has a 23-inch high twin bed. Christine is also happy to move or remove furniture, so speak up if something is in the way.

The hallway is 26-inches wide and the bathroom has a wide door and includes a tub/shower combination with grab bars and a hand-held showerhead. It's a tight fit for a wheelchair with the door closed, but you can close off the hallway and leave the bathroom door open for a little more space.

The kitchenette and bar area is not large enough for a wheelchair, but Christine is happy to move the small refrigerator and microwave to another area if requested. Although no breakfast is served, guests will find a breakfast basket upon arrival, which includes cereal, fruit, bread and other goodies.

With advance notice, Christine can also provide a wheelchair or walker.

There's also a grill out back, and of course a comfortable porch with a nice view of the lake. And if you're lucky — and come at the right time of the year — you'll also share the backyard with the resident geese.

Candy's Take

Christine is very helpful and she has lots of tips for things to see and do in Raleigh. Staying at the Northshore Lakehouse is like staying with relatives, except there's no emotional baggage. It's a welcome place to come home to after a long day of sightseeing.

The Seagrass Room at the Northshore Lake House

The North Carolina State Capitol

Best Fit

The bathroom and the hallway are too small for a power wheelchair or scooter, and this property won't work if you absolutely need a roll-in shower. That said, it's a good choice for slow walkers as well as some manual wheelchair-users. It's a great choice for a family as it can sleep five, and you can cook your own meals and save a few bucks. And at $150 a night, it's pretty easy on the wallet.

Nearby

Founded in 1587 by Sir Walter Raleigh, the capital city boasts a long and colorful history. And there's no better way to immerse yourself in it than by visiting Raleigh's historic trifecta — three downtown sites that trace the roots of the city and offer a good overview of key historic events from a local, regional and national perspective.

The best place to begin your journey through history is at the City Museum of Raleigh (www.cityofraleighmuseum.org), located in the Briggs Building, on Fayetteville near Hargett Street. Once home to the Briggs Hardware Store, the building dates back to 1874. Access is good throughout the building with a level entrance, power doors and barrier-free access to the first-floor museum. The museum features rotating exhibits that highlight Raleigh's history, but the building is a treasure by itself.

From there, head north on Fayetteville for a block, until the street dead ends at the North Carolina State Capitol (www.nchistoricsites.org/

capitol). There is good pathway access through Capitol Park, to the visitors entrance on the east side of the building. Although stairs lead up to the door, there is ramp access on the right. Inside, there is elevator access to all floors of this well preserved Greek Revival building that originally housed the governor's office, cabinet offices, state library and the state geologist's office. Today, many of the rooms are restored to their former glory and decorated as they were in the 1850s.

Wrap up your history stroll with a visit to the North Carolina Museum of History (www.ncmuseumofhistory.org), located across the street from the capitol building. There is ramp access to the entrance, barrier-free access through the galleries, and a free loaner wheelchair available at the information desk. The Story of North Carolina, which is located on the first-floor, draws on the museum's permanent collection as it traces life in North Carolina, from its earliest inhabitants through the 20th century. The museum also has an impressive collection of Civil War artifacts, and it features a variety of rotating exhibits throughout the year.

Northshore Lake House
Waterbury Road
Raleigh, NC 27604
(919) 665-6700
www.northshorelakehouse.com

GPS Coordinates
N 35.83913
W 78.58508

Bathroom at the Northshore Lake House

Red Horse Inn

Landrum, SC

L ocated in rural South Carolina, just off the Cherokee Foothills National Scenic Byway, the Red Horse Inn is the perfect place to get away from it all. Surrounded by pastures and woodlands, this Landrum property is run by two savvy innkeepers who know how to provide those extra little touches. As an added bonus, they also give their guests a heaping helping of privacy, which makes this a very relaxing and low key property.

Access Details

Access is good at this 12-room country inn, with barrier-free access through the Gathering Room to the accessible East Bedroom. This first-floor room features wide doorways, plenty of room to maneuver a wheelchair, and nearby accessible parking.

The room is furnished with a 30-inch high king-sized bed, and a sofa with a 16-inch high fold-out bed. There is also a large fireplace and a private terrace with a great view of the adjacent pasture. The terrace has wide French doors and a small step, but it can be easily accessed from the outside. It's a great place to sip a glass of wine and enjoy a romantic sunset.

The bathroom is equipped with a whirlpool tub with a built-in bench, grab bars and a hand-held showerhead. The toilet grab bars are located on the left and back walls (as seated), and the spacious bathroom also has a roll-under sink.

Breakfast is a very private affair at the Red Horse Inn, with all the makings provided in built-in kitchen closets in each room. The menu includes coffee, a fruit parfait, an egg casserole, juice, oatmeal and some very yummy muffins. A microwave and a refrigerator are also included in each kitchen closet; and when you're done with breakfast, everything folds up neatly out of the way.

Candy's Take

The terrace is very pleasant, and it offers a great view of the horses in the pasture. You really get the feeling of being out in the country, and it's just so quiet and peaceful there.

Best Fit

This property will work for many people, but if you absolutely have to have a roll-in shower it's not for you. On the plus side, because of the sofa bed, you do have a choice of bed heights. Romance is in the air here, and there's lots of privacy. Innkeeper Mary Wolters can also make arrangements for

Bed in the East Bedroom at the Red Horse Inn

Bathroom in the East Bedroom at the Red Horse Inn

a romantic in-room dinner or other special romantic touches. It's a great pick for a special anniversary.

Nearby

This is covered bridge country and Mary is happy to map out a scenic drive along the Cherokee Foothills National Scenic Byway for you.

Located on Highway 414, Campbell's Covered Bridge is the closest one to the inn. There's one accessible parking place on a cement slab near the bridge, with a paved pathway down to the bridge. Built in 1909, this 35-foot bridge that crosses Beaverdam Creek was named for Alexander Lafayette Campbell, who owned the local grist mill. Although there are two steps up to the bridge itself, you can still get a good view of it all from the end of the pathway.

To continue along on your historic bridge tour, backtrack on Highway 414, go north on Highway 14 to Gowensville, then take Highway 11 west. A few miles down the road you'll find the Klickety-Klack Covered Bridge, at the entrance to Look Away Farm. Named for the sounds the timbers make when vehicles drive over them, this refurbished bridge is level and easy to walk across. There's no real parking area, so just pull over close to the bridge and check it out.

The last bridge — Pointsett's Bridge — dates back to the 19th century. From the Klickety-Klack Bridge, continue west on Highway 11, take a right on State Road H912, then travel a few miles and turn right on Calahan Mountain Road. The bridge is located on the right, just past the Boy Scout camp, but the parking area is located across the street. This stone bridge crosses Little Gap Creek at the beginning of the old toll road to Charleston. You can't drive over the bridge any more, but you can get a great view it from Calahan Mountain Road.

If all this driving has worked up your appetite, then continue along Highway 11 to Cleveland for a romantic lunch at Victoria Valley Vineyards (www.victoriavalleyvineyards.com). Styled after a French chateau, the tasting room features level access and an accessible restroom. They also have an intimate cafe that serves a light lunch menu of appetizers, salads, sandwiches and desserts. And if you're not hungry, then enjoy a little wine on the terrace that overlooks the vineyard.

Red Horse Inn	**GPS Coordinates**
45 Winstons Chase Court	N 35.09816
Landrum, SC 29356	W 82.25773
(864) 909-1574	
www.theredhorseinn.com	

Campbell's Covered Bridge

Lee House

Pensacola, Florida

At first glance this Pensacola Bay property seems an unlikely choice for wheelers and slow walkers, as steps grace the front facade. The good news is, Lee House is a modern re-creation of the home that stood on the same spot in 1886. Even better, access features were factored into the building plans from day one. As a result, today this charming inn features the best of both worlds, as it combines the charm of the historic south with modern day accessibility.

Access Details

There's accessible parking available across the street in the public lot, with a level path of travel to the accessible entrance on Alcanz Street. Just look for the gate to the Alcanz Courtyard, where you'll find ramp access up to the wrap around front porch, and a level threshold at the front door.

Inside, the spacious Gathering Room, is adorned with artifacts that were unearthed during the construction of the inn. It's a very comfy place to relax and read, with barrier-free access throughout the room, and an accessible public restroom nearby.

The most accessible suite in this eight-room property is the Chipley Suite, which is located on the ground floor. It's decorated with photos and mementos honoring William Dudley Chipley, who devoted himself to the Pensacola and Atlantic Railroad that linked the Atlantic Coast and the Gulf Coast for the first time.

Access features include wide doorways and barrier-free access throughout the suite. It's furnished with a 25-inch high king-sized bed, with wheelchair-access on both sides; and includes level access to the wrap around porch through wide French doors.

The bathroom features a roll-in tiled shower with a hand-held showerhead. The toilet is located in a separate toilet closet, with good pathway access but no grab bars. The public restroom does however have toilet grab bars on the left and back walls (as seated). The Chipley Suite bathroom also includes a roll-under sink.

There is barrier-free access to all the ground floor public areas, as well as the wrap around porch.

Candy's Take

The wrap around porch is wonderful, as since the property is right across the street from the ocean, there's a good view from the porch. It was nice to be lulled to sleep by the sound of the ocean too. This property is a great reproduction of an old house tucked into a historic neighborhood.

Old Christ Church in Historic Pensacola Village

Some of the buildings in Historic Pensacola Village have access upgrades

Best Fit

The Chipley Suite is very spacious and has a large roll-in shower, but since it lacks grab bars it won't work for everyone. This is a great property for history buffs, as there are lots of historic homes and sites in the neighborhood. It also makes a nice romantic retreat.

Nearby

The property is right across the street from Seville Square and Fountain Park. It's fun to just wander the neighborhood and enjoy the historic homes, some of which date back to the 1700s.

It's also within easy rolling distance of Historic Pensacola Village (www.historicpensacola.org), which features properties in the Pensacola National Register Historic District.

Although many of the historic buildings have steps up into them, there are level brick pathways throughout the neighborhood, so it's pretty easy to wheel around. Additionally, access features are added to buildings as they are renovated. And although there's an admission charge to the site, wheelchair-users and their companions are admitted free, because it's not 100% accessible.

The best place to start your visit is at Tivoli house, where you can get a map and an admission ticket. There's a two-inch step up into this 1805 boarding house, but the staff is happy to bring your ticket out to you.

Next door, there's level access to the Museum of Commerce, which is filled with an 1890s streetscape, and includes a print shop, a hardware store and a music shop. There's also a nice collection of horse-drawn buggies in this old warehouse building. Across the street, you'll find equally good access to the Museum of Industry, which contains photographs, tools and equipment from Pensacola's 19th century industrial boom.

Although the guided tours of Historic Pensacola Village are not technically accessible, because they include three structures with steps; you can still tag along for the excellent interpretation. Additionally, you'll get a peek inside Old Christ Church, which has an accessible entrance. All in all, it's a pleasant place to wander, talk with the costumed interpreters and soak up a little history.

Lee House
400 Bayfront Parkway
Pensacola, FL 32502
(850) 912-8770
www.leehousepensacola.com

GPS Coordinates
N 30.40871
W 87.20879

Toilet and shower in the Chipley Suite

Heron Cay Lakeview B&B

Mount Dora, FL

T he Heron Cay Lakeview B&B is appropriately named, as it sits
on two beautifully landscaped acres that overlook Lake Dora.
This Queen Anne manor was built in 1995, yet it exudes a charm
of yesteryear, thanks to the period furnishings and distinctly Victorian
decor. And because the property is a re-creation, it also has a bevy of access
features that weren't available in the 1890s. Innkeeper Margie Salyer is
proud of that accessibility too, and she's quick to point out that wheelchair-
users have been very pleased with her inn.

Access Details

There's ramped access up to the front porch of the inn, and wide doorways
and barrier-free pathways throughout the home. This intimate property
features six guest rooms, including the accessible Zoi Garden Room.

The accessible room features barrier-free access through a private
entrance, which is located near the accessible parking space. There is also
an entrance through the house. It's furnished with a 29-inch high queen-
sized bed with wheelchair access on both sides. A step stool is available

if needed, and if the bed is too high a lower twin bed can be set up in the room. There is also level access to a large private deck through a set of French Doors.

The bathroom is equipped with a roll-in shower with a built-in shower bench, grab bars and a hand-held showerhead. There is a toilet grab bar on the back wall, and the bathroom also has a roll-under sink.

The public areas of the inn, including the breakfast room and the back porch, all feature barrier-free access. Margie serves up a full hot breakfast every morning, and snacks and soft drinks are available around the clock. And if you want to pack your dinner leftovers back to the inn, don't worry, as every room also has a refrigerator.

Candy's Take

I like the private entrance, and the private deck out back is very nice. It's a very quiet and peaceful property. I especially like how the inn is decorated with period furnishings, which makes it feel like a historic home.

Best Fit

The roll-in shower is nicely done, and the spacious bathroom will work for most people. The lack of a side toilet grab bar may be problematic for some people, however there is a counter on the right side (as seated) to steady or brace yourself. The choice of bed heights makes it an attractive option for

The Zoi Garden Room at Heron Cay Lakeview B&B

The parlor at Heron Cay Lakeview B&B

many people. This property is a good pick for a romantic getaway, and it's also a great place to decompress after a hectic Orlando visit. And since it's off-the-beaten-path, it's also a nice road trip stopover.

Nearby

Mount Dora is one those places that seems to be stuck in a time wrap — and that's a very good thing. It's almost like going back to the 1950s, when the pace was slower and the whole atmosphere was just more relaxed. There are lots of specialty and antique shops around town, and although some have a step or two, many have level access. It's a nice place to stroll and window shop.

There are also several accessible eateries in town. Pisces Rising (www.piscesrisingdining.com) is located on the edge of the downtown area, and overlooks Lake Dora. There is level access to the modern addition of the restaurant, which wraps around a 1920s bungalow. The food is equally creative, and they serve up a nice selection of steaks and seafood entrees with fresh vegetables and a definite local flair.

Cecile's French Corner also has level access to the outdoor patio area. They offer a decidedly French menu with everything from escargot and crepes, to a sumptuous cheese plate and a wide selection of breads.

And don't miss the Windsor Rose Tearoom (www.windsorrose-tearoom.com) which serves breakfast, lunch and high tea. There is level access to the quaint restaurant where the servers don Victorian aprons. And if you'd like to take home a taste of Britain, they also have a large selection of British groceries and imported teas for sale.

Heron Cay Lakeview B&B
495 West Old Highway 441
Mount Dora, FL 32757
(352) 383-4050
www.heroncay.com

GPS Coordinates
N 28.80325
W 81.64874

Bathroom in the Zoi Garden Room

My Mountain Hideaway

Morgantown, GA

Necessity is the mother of invention. And when your mother is in a wheelchair, you do your best to make sure everything is as accessible as possible, including your vacation home. That's exactly why Charlie Roberts built My Mountain Hideaway to be wheelchair-accessible. Located about 90 miles south of Atlanta in the scenic Blue Ridge Mountains, this rural retreat is the perfect place to get away from city life.

Access Details

There is ramp access up to the deck from the parking area, with level access to the four-bedroom cabin. Inside, you'll find wood floors for easy rolling, lowered counters and wide doorways. The great room and kitchen features good pathway access, with plenty of room to maneuver a wheelchair. There is also level access out to the wrap around deck, which is outfitted with a collection of porch swings and rocking chairs.

The accessible bedroom is furnished with a 27-inch king-sized bed, with wheelchair access on both sides. The adjacent bathroom is equipped with a roll-in shower with a built-in shower bench, grab bars and a hand-held showerhead. Round it out with a toilet with a grab bar on the left side (as seated), and you have a very accessible suite.

Although there are stairs down to the lower level game room, there is also level access to it from outside. If you'd prefer to linger upstairs, there's level access to the screened porch, which has a hot tub and a fireplace.

Candy's Take

This place has everything you could possibly want in a cabin. I love the huge great room and the wrap around porch. It's very quiet there, and to be honest it's difficult to find an accessible cabin in this area. The folks at the property management company are also very helpful and well versed in the access features of the property.

Best Fit

The nice roll-in shower and the spacious floor plan makes this property a good fit for just about any wheelchair-user or slow walker. This large cabin is perfect for a family reunion or a multigenerational getaway.

Nearby

Of course you could just spend your time relaxing on the wrap around porch and enjoying the mountain scenery, but save at least one day

Accessible bedroom at My Mountain Hideaway

The Great Room at My Mountain Hideaway

for an excursion on the Blue Ridge Scenic Railway (www.brscenic.com). The train departs from the Blue Ridge Depot, which is just seven miles from the cabin, and travels along the Toccoa River to McCaysville.

Accessible street parking is available near the depot, with level access over to the boarding area. Coach 405, which was modified for access in 2008, includes a lift on both sides, and wheelchair tie-downs on board. This open-air car features benches that face the windows, with wheelchair spaces at the end. The lift has a 750 pound limit, and once you are aboard the train you can transfer to a bench or stay in your own wheelchair. You have to be seated to use the lift, but a loaner wheelchair is available for slow walkers.

There is also an accessible restroom in Coach 405, which has a roll-under sink and toilet grab bars on the right and back walls (as seated). It's very roomy, with space enough for a power wheelchair and an attendant.

The train travels at a very leisurely pace, so the 26-mile journey takes about an hour. It pulls into McCaysville around noon, and departs for Blue Ridge two hours later. Passengers have plenty of time to explore the town, and even walk up the street to the twin border town of Copperhill, Tennessee.

There is ramp access from the McCaysville Depot, down to a covered picnic area, and level access out to the street. An accessible restroom is also located near the picnic pavilion. The town is fairly level, with wide sidewalks and curb-cuts at most corners. Most of the shops and galleries are also accessible, and it's a pleasant place to browse before the return trip to Blue Ridge.

My Mountain Hideaway
Morgantown, GA
(877) 374-2057
www.abovetherestcabins.com/mymountainhideaway.htm

GPS Coordinates
N 34.87667
W 84.24556

Bathroom in the accessible room at My Mountain Hideaway

Seventy-Four Ranch

Jasper, GA

L ocated just an hour north of Atlanta in rural Jasper, the Seventy-Four Ranch is a nostalgic slice of the old west. Situated on 50 acres of beautiful pastureland, this working ranch also welcomes overnight lodging guests. But it didn't start out that way; in fact co-owner Pam Butler describes herself as an "accidental innkeeper". "Our friends and family who visited us just loved the place, so the B&B part of the ranch just seemed a natural expansion," she recalls. Today, thanks to some access upgrades, many wheelchair-users and slow walker can also enjoy this ranch stay experience.

Access Details

There's plenty of parking in a level grass area just outside the front gate, with a barrier-free path over to the Butler Cape House. Built in the mid-1800s, this historic house now serves as the lobby and dining room for the ranch. Although there are steps at the front entrance, there's ramp access to the back porch and good pathway access inside.

The accessible suite is located in the building just behind the Butler Cape House. It's composed of two bedrooms with a bathroom in between

341

them. The Porch Cabin features a 26-inch high queen-sized bed; while the Saddle House is furnished with four bunk beds, a dining table, a wood stove and lots of cowboy art and saddles. The Saddle Room sleeps four-to-eight people, and the whole suite can accommodate up to 10 people. You can also rent each room separately, but if you do that you may have to share a bathroom with strangers.

The bathroom features a low-step shower (five inch) with grab bars and a hand-held showerhead. The toilet grab bars are located on the left and back walls (as seated), and the bathroom also includes a free standing sink.

There's level access to a private porch from the Porch Cabin, and plenty of space to roll around outside. There is also level access over to the cabana, which has a fan, lights and a swing. It's a pleasant place to relax in the evening, and it features level access on one side.

A full country breakfast is served each morning in the Butler Cape House.

Candy's Take

If you love animals, this is the place for you, as you can enjoy the horses in the nearby pasture or laugh at the antics of Pam and Larry's very animated Jack Russell Terriers. And if you'd like to explore more of the pasture, Pam and Larry are happy to give you a golf cart tour.

Porch Cabin at Seventy-Four Ranch

Shared accessible bathroom at Seventy-Four Ranch

Best Fit

Since the shower has a lip, it won't work for everybody, but if you can bump over it you'll be good to go. It's a beautiful country space, and it's a great choice for a family reunion or multigenerational getaway. It's also a good wedding venue.

Nearby

After you've poked around the ranch, save some time for a drive along nearby Apple Orchard Alley. Billed as one of the most scenic drives in the state, this two-lane country road runs between Highway 183 and Ellijay on Highway 52.

Fall is prime time for the apple houses that dot Apple Orchard Alley, however Mack Aaron's Apple House opens in mid-July. It features a level entrance and plenty of room to roll around on the cement floor inside. They have a wide variety of apples for sale, and they're also known for their fried fruit pies. And if you're watching your diet, they even have some sugar-free fruit pies.

Make plans for a lunch stop in Ellijay, which is located at the western end of Apple Orchard Alley. Accessible street parking is available at the end of River Street, and there are several accessible restaurants within rolling distance.

The Cantaberry Restaurant (www.cantaberry.com) and River Street Tavern (www.riverstreettavern.com) are located on River Street, and they both feature level access. Each of the eateries offers sandwiches, salads and lunch specials at very reasonable prices.

After you've had your fill of food, save some time for a little stroll around town. The sidewalks are level and there are curb-cuts at most corners; but if you run into an access obstacle you can always roll in the street, as there's not much traffic in this small town.

Seventy Four Ranch
9205 Highway 53 West
Jasper, GA 30143
(706) 692-0123
www.seventyfourranch.com

GPS Coordinates
N 34.48028
W 84.58417

Shower in the accessible bathroom

Still Meadows Cabins

Thomaston, GA

Located in sleepy little Thomaston, Georgia, these two log cabins sit on 40 acres of beautiful country land. The rustic structures were originally built in 1885, at a time when access wasn't exactly all the rage. But that didn't stop Mary Pat Jones from adding modifications to one of the cabins, so her wheeler son could use it. And he loved it dearly. So much so, that Mary Pat decided to add it to her rental inventory, so that more people can enjoy life down home on the farm.

Access Details

Loaded with chicken bric-a-brac, rustic accents and lots of natural wood, accessible Cabin 2 has a definite country feel to it. There's barrier-free access from the parking area to a level boardwalk which leads to the front door of the cabin.

There's good pathway access throughout the first floor, which features a large kitchen, a comfy living room and a spacious bedroom. The downstairs bedroom is furnished with a queen-sized bed with wheelchair access on both sides.

The bathroom includes one room with the original claw foot tub and a standard sink; plus an addition with access modifications. The addition has a Continental style shower with grab bars and a hand-held showerhead. The toilet has grab bars on the back and right walls (as seated) and the bathroom also has a roll-under sink. Best of all there are no shower rails, rods or curtains; and because of the full five-foot turning radius there's plenty of room to maneuver even a large wheelchair in the bathroom.

There is a second bedroom located upstairs that has two twin beds and a rope bed. All in all, it's a very comfortable place, with a fireplace in the living room and a barbeque on the back porch. Additionally, the living room futon can sleep two people.

Outside, there's an accessible boardwalk down to the lake, so don't forget to bring your fishing pole. And if you like animals, you're in luck, as there's a resident donkey, some goats, a flock of chickens and one very vocal turkey to keep you amused. And thanks to the chickens, you'll always have fresh eggs for breakfast

Candy's Take

This place has chickens — how could you not love it? Seriously, it's a very low key place with lots of farm animals. And the boardwalk down to the lake is well done. It's just a pleasant and pristine place.

First-floor bedroom in Cabin 2 at Still Meadows Cabins

Living room in Cabin 2

Best Fit

The large Continental shower will work for most people, but be sure to pack along your own shower chair. It's a good choice for a family getaway, as the kids will just love the animals. It's also perfect for a romantic retreat, as it's very private and secluded.

Nearby

If you're up for a little sightseeing while you're in the area, then head on down to Warm Springs, Georgia to have a look at Roosevelt's Little White House (www.nps.gov/nr/travel/presidents/roosevelts_little_white_house.html) It's just a half-hour drive from the cabin, and it offers a very personal look at America's 32nd president.

There's plenty of accessible parking near the entrance to this historic site, with manual wheelchairs and scooters for loan inside the museum. There's barrier-free access through the museum, which includes some personal possessions, a few pieces from the original house and even a set of hand-controls designed by President Roosevelt. It's somewhat reminiscent of a presidential museum, only on a smaller scale; as it includes information on family members, events that occurred during Roosevelt's presidency and gifts sent to him by an adoring public. There's also an excellent film in the adjacent theater that gives a good overview of the Roosevelt presidency.

Outside there are paved pathways, with level access to most areas.

The one exception is the Walk of Flags, which may be a bit steep for manual wheelchairs.

The Little White House — where the president stayed and conducted business while he was in town — is accessible to manual wheelchairs, but because of a weight restriction on the walkway, power wheelchairs and scooters are prohibited. Still, there is a loaner manual wheelchair available for self-guided tours of the house; so as long as you can transfer, you're good to go. Outside, there's also level access to the carriage house.

President Roosevelt originally sought out the healing waters of Warm Springs as a cure for his polio, and admission to the historic pools is also included with your Little White House ticket. The pools are just a short drive away, and there is level access to the pool building from the accessible parking area, and a barrier-free pathway through the small museum. Outside there's even ramp access down into the main pool, which is kept empty most of the year. Still it's an interesting site, and definitely worth a visit.

Still Meadows Cabins
150 Roland Road
Thomaston, GA 30286
(706) 741-5012
www.stillmeadowscabins.com

GPS Coordinates
N 32.90088
W 84.45327

Toilet and shower in Cabin 2 (**grab bars were added after photos were taken**)

Kelleys Island Yurts

Kelleys Island, OH

L ocated in the middle of Lake Erie, Kelleys Island boasts an interesting collection of geological, ecological and archaeological treasures. Known as Lake Erie's Emerald Island, it can only be reached by ferry from Marblehead, Ohio. Although it's just a 20 minute ferry ride from the mainland, because of its location the island is pretty remote, so it's a very inviting and relaxing retreat. And as luck would have it, there are two nicely accessible yurts in the 677-acre state park which graces the north shore of the island.

Access Details

Although Kelleys Island State Park Campground only has two yurts, both of them are wheelchair-accessible. They also occupy a prime piece of real estate with an excellent lake view. The round canvas structures are pretty upscale for yurts, as they have wood floors, electricity and even running water.

Accessible parking is located near the yurts, with ramp access up to their large decks. Inside, there is good pathway access in the yurts and

349

they each can sleep six, on two futons and a bunk bed. The kitchens are equipped with a stove, microwave and a refrigerator, and there's also a gas grill on each deck.

These yurts also have bathrooms, which is definitely an upscale feature. There is barrier-free access to the large bathrooms which are equipped with a roll-in shower with grab bars and a hand-held showerhead. There is also a roll-under sink in each bathroom.

And for a little more luxury, there's even a TV and a DVD player in each yurt.

Each yurt also has a fire ring, a large deck, and an excellent Lake Erie view. Best of all, the yurts are a bargain, at only $100 per night or $600 per week.

Additionally, the Kelleys Island Ferry (www.kelleysislandferry. com), features ramp access at both stops, however there is one step up to the passenger cabin. On the other hand, it's a short ride, and you can also enjoy the view from the open deck.

Candy's Take

By far the best feature of the yurts is the great Lake Erie view. Even though you are in the middle of a campground it's really quite peaceful. The yurts also get bonus points for having ensuite bathrooms, so there are no long walks to the campground restrooms.

Lake Erie view from the deck

Best Fit

The yurts are very roomy and with the good pathway access and roll-in showers they will work for just about everybody. It's very outdoorsy, but because of all the creature comforts you never feel like you're roughing it, so even non-campers will enjoy the yurts. This is a good family vacation spot, but be sure and book early as the yurts are very popular.

Nearby

Of course you can just sit and enjoy the lake view from your yurt, but save some time to explore the rest of the island.

The best place to begin your island tour is in the downtown area, which has a few restaurants, shops and many old homes. There are some curb-cuts in the area, but to be honest there's not that much traffic, so it's pretty safe to walk or roll in the street.

This is a good place to stock up on supplies, grab a beer or get a bite to eat. Accessible restaurants include The Village Pump (www.villagepumpki.com) and The Casino (www.kelleysislandcasino.com). It's also a great place to drive around and look at some of the old historic homes.

After you've had your fill of downtown, head back up to the north side of the island to have a look at the glacial grooves. The groves were cut into the rock over 18,000 years ago when a giant sheet of ice covered North America. Today there is a massive 400-foot long trough, which is surrounded by a viewing platform. Although there are steps up to the viewing platform, you can get a glimpse at the groves near the front steps.

Unfortunately there aren't any accessible trails on the island. Although some people claim that the North Shore Loop Trail is accessible, in reality it's filled with rocks, ruts, mud and hills. Even my friend who uses a power wheelchair couldn't do it without a lot of assistance — and at one point we almost didn't make it.

As an alternative you might want to try a modified driving tour — just drive around, find a place to park and explore as much as you can. It really is a beautiful island, with a lot of secluded nooks and crannies. Even though there are some access obstacles, it's still very much worth a visit, especially if you are a nature lover.

Kelleys Island Yurts
920 Division Street
Kelleys Island, OH 43438
(866) 644-6727
parks.ohiodnr.gov/kelleysisland

GPS Coordinates
N 41.61520
W 82.70621

Cabin in the Woods

Wakeman, OH

L ocated in Wakeman, Ohio, this family-run B&B is an eclectic cross between a rustic lodge and an upscale inn. Prior to building the B&B, Innkeeper Peggy Pleban worked for Invacare, so professionally she understands the importance of access. She also understands access on a personal level, as one of her friends is a C-4 quadriplegic. So when Peggy and her husband Walt built the property they designed it to be accessible — not because they had to, but because it was something they wanted to do. "I think everyone should have the opportunity to enjoy this beautiful country setting," says Peggy. And thanks to the Pleban's proactive efforts, now they can.

Access Details

There's ramp access from the parking area up to the large wrap around porch; and level access to the B&B through the wide front door. The most accessible room in the house is Rosie's Room — named for Peggy's friend — but it's also called the USA Room.

Access features include wide doorways, barrier-free pathways and wood floors. It's furnished with a 25-inch high double bed and a twin hospital bed. A wide double door leads out to the wrap around porch, so you can access the room without going through the front entrance.

The bathroom is equipped with a roll-in shower with a fold-down shower bench, grab bars and a hand-held showerhead. The shower also has wheelchair-height soap and shampoo dispensers. The toilet grab bars are located on the left side (as seated), and there is a roll-under sink in the bathroom. A portable shower chair is also available.

The Luxury Suite — located across the hall — may also work for some slow walkers. This room features a 35-inch high bed with a step stool, grab bars on the right side of the toilet (as seated), a low-step shower and sliding door access out to the wrap around porch. It's ideal for someone who needs a little more room, and can't do stairs.

There is barrier-free access to the ground-floor great room, where a full breakfast is served daily. Peggy can also accommodate dietary restrictions, and she's got a good collection of gluten-free recipes.

Candy's Take

I really like the fact that Walt and Peggy genuinely enjoy their work, and you can't really say that of all innkeepers. They make their guests feel welcome, not merely accommodated. I also love the location, as the property is set back off the road in a rural subdivision, so you get a real feeling of privacy.

Rosie's Room at Cabin in the Woods

The Great Room at Cabin in the Woods

Best Fit

Peggy and Walt really thought of everything access wise, so this property will work for everyone. It has a nice roll-in shower and a lower bed for wheelchair-users, and low-step shower and a higher bed for slow walkers. It's great to have choices. The property is a good pick for a road trip stopover, or even a family retreat. There is a third bedroom upstairs, and you can rent the whole property out for a family get together and do your own cooking.

Nearby

Cedar Point (www.cedarpoint.com) amusement park, which is located 20 miles away in Sandusky, is one of the most popular attractions in the area. There is good access at the park entrance, and barrier-free pathways through the shops and food stands in the park.

Guests with mobility disabilities are given a Ride Boarding Pass, which allows them to access a specific ride at specific time through the exit ramp. On most rides wheelchair-users have to transfer, but the wheelchair can be left at the ride entrance. On the plus side, it's easy to plan your day with the Ride Boarding Pass, as you won't spend unnecessary time standing in line, because you'll have an appointment for each ride.

Peggy also recommends a visit to Schoepfle Garden in nearby Birmingham. This 70-acre botanical garden features a number of level garden paths through the beds filled with rhododendrons, roses, cannas, hostas and trees. They also have a very nice children's garden.

And if you're in the area the late June, don't miss the Ohio Scottish Games (www.ohioscottishgames.com), held at the Lorain County Fairground in nearby Wellington. This festive event highlights the traditional dance, music and athletics of the ancient Highland Games. It's great fun for the whole family, in a very accessible venue.

Cabin in the Woods
13719 Garfield Road
Wakeman, OH 44889
(440) 965-5525
www.cabininthewoods.net

GPS Coordinates
N 41.31899
W 82.38116

Shower in Rosie's Room

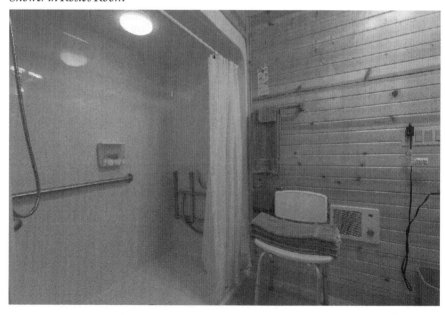

Maumee Bay Lodge

Oregon, OH

L ocated in northern Ohio, Maumee Bay State Park is a nature
lovers dream; but that doesn't mean you have to rough it when
you overnight there. Quite the contrary, as access upgrades have
been added to the very comfortable Maumee Bay Lodge. Billed as Ohio's
premier resort, this family friendly lakeside property features 12 accessible
lodge rooms, as well as five accessible family cottages. Truly there really is
something for everybody at Maumee Bay Lodge.

Access Details

There's plenty of accessible parking in the lodge lot, with a barrier-free path
to the main lobby. Additionally, there's a large drop-off area directly outside
the lobby entrance. Inside, there's wheelchair access to all the public areas,
including the Water's Edge dining room and the Icebreaker Lounge.

The accessible guest rooms, which are just a short walk from the lobby,
all have wide doorways, level thresholds and barrier-free pathway access. Six
of the rooms are furnished with one king bed, while the other six have one
double bed and one twin bed. Each accessible bathroom is outfitted with

a tub/shower combination, a hand-held showerhead, a roll-under sink and shower and toilet grab bars. A portable shower bench is available upon request.

The cottages, which are equally spacious, are located just a short drive from the main lodge. The largest accessible cottage (Cottage 17) is midway down the mile-long road, and it overlooks the adjacent marsh.

Accessible parking is available in a paved area in front of the cottage, with a wide level walkway up to the front porch. Although there's a small lip at the transition from the walkway to the porch, it's doable for most folks with a little assistance. The four-bedroom cottage features wide doorways and excellent pathway access to all the first-floor rooms, with stairway access to the two upstairs bedrooms.

One downstairs bedroom is furnished with a bunk bed, a twin bed and a rollaway, while the other bedroom has a 24-inch high king bed. Upstairs, one bedroom has a bunk bed and a twin bed, and the other bedroom has a double bed. Throw in the sleeper sofa in the living room, and the cottage can comfortably sleep 13 people.

The ground floor bathroom is equipped with a roll-in shower with a fold-down shower bench, grab bars and hand-held showerhead. Other access features include a roll-under sink and toilet grab bars on the back and right walls (as seated). The second-floor bathroom has a low-step shower, but it lacks grab bars or the space to maneuver a wheelchair.

Downstairs you'll also find a gas fireplace, a washer and dryer, a

Bathroom in Cottage 17

Accessible guestroom at Maumee Bay Lodge

spacious deck and a hot tub. And although there's a barrier-free pathway to the hot tub, you have to be able to climb up two steps to get into it.

Two-bedroom accessible cottages are also available. These smaller cottages have comparable access features, but they have tub/shower combinations instead of roll-in showers. They also don't include a washer, dryer or hot tub.

Candy's Take

My favorite thing about Cottage 17 is the large kitchen. I love to cook when I'm on the road and this kitchen has just about everything you could imagine. I also totally enjoyed the privacy that the cottage affords.

Best Fit

Whether you use a large power wheelchair, or just get around a little slower, there's something at Maumee Bay Lodge that will meet your access needs. The large family cottages are great for family reunions, and the smaller cottages are a good choice for a romantic getaway.

Nearby

There's certainly no shortage of recreational activities at Maumee Bay Lodge, many of which are accessible and can be enjoyed by the whole family. There is barrier-free access to the indoor splash area, which includes seven splash features, as well as a waterfall that spills into the pool. There is also an accessible locker room nearby, which is equipped with roll-in showers.

If you'd prefer to keep your little ones active but dry, then check out the soft play area, which includes pirate-themed climbing features on a cushioned floor. There is level access to this brightly colored indoor area, and plenty of room to roll around the climbing features.

Outside, there are a number of accessible options, including bicycling or hiking on one of the many bicycle trails throughout the park. Although the trails weren't specifically designed to be accessible, most of them are level and very doable for wheelers and slow walkers.

Finally, if you want to learn a little about the native flora and fauna, head over to the Trautman Nature Center, located next to the lodge. There is barrier-free access to the building, which houses a number of interpretive exhibits detailing the nature and history of the area.

Afterwards, save some time for a first-hand look at the local inhabitants on the two-mile boardwalk, just east of the lodge. There is barrier-free access to this excellent loop trail, and interpretive signs along the way. Best of all, one side of the boardwalk is pleasantly devoid of railings, so wheelers can enjoy unobstructed views of the surrounding wetlands.

Maumee Bay Lodge
1400 State Park Road
Oregon, OH 43616
(800) 282-7275
www.maumeebaystateparklodge.com

GPS Coordinates
N 41.68577
W 83.36860

Bathroom in an accessible guestroom at Maumee Bay Lodge

Watersong Woods

Logan, OH

The Watersong Woods cabins are located on 75 acres of woodland in scenic Hocking County. Owner Joy Upton lives nearby on her farm, and the two cabins — one of which is accessible — are about a quarter-mile away. And although Joy is happy to welcome guests to her farm and introduce them to the animals, she's just as happy to give you some privacy if that's what you want. Add in a scenic little creek and you have all the makings for a secluded and accessible country retreat.

Access Details

Parking is available in front of the accessible Melody cabin on a combination dirt and gravel pad. From there, it's just a short level roll to the small front porch which offers level access to the cabin. Inside, there is good pathway access throughout the great room which includes a kitchen, bedroom and living area.

The kitchen is equipped with a stove, microwave and a refrigerator; and the living area is furnished with two rocking chairs. The queen-sized bed is 22-inches high and has wheelchair access on one side. There is also a small dining table and two chairs in the unit.

There is a 41-inch wide doorway into the spacious bathroom, which is equipped with a roll-in shower with a fold down shower bench, grab bars and a hand-held showerhead. The toilet is located in a 30-inch wide alcove and it has grab bars on both sides. The bathroom has a full five-foot turning radius, and it also includes a roll-under sink.

There is level access out to the back deck which is furnished with two chairs, a table, an electric grill and a hot tub. There's plenty of room to navigate a wheelchair on the deck, but you have to be able to climb up the steps to access the 35-inch high hot tub.

Candy's Take

The property is appropriately named as you can hear the running water from the creek when you sit out on the deck. It's very peaceful and quiet there, and I really enjoyed sipping my morning cup of coffee on the deck. I also liked the bird life.

Best Fit

This property has a nice roll-in shower but if you have to do a lateral toilet transfer, that may be problematic because of the toilet placement in an alcove. Additionally, if you have a large wheelchair or scooter, you may need to move some of the furniture. It's a very private cabin, so it's a great

Inside the Melody Cabin at Watersong Woods

Kitchen in the Melody Cabin

choice for a romantic getaway. You never have to see the owner if that's your druthers. She leaves the key under the mat with phone number. After that, the choice is up to you.

Nearby

Hocking Hills State Park (parks.ohiodnr.gov/hockinghills), one of the state's most scenic areas, is located about 11 miles away from the cabin.

Although the drive through the park is very scenic, there are a number of accessible sites along the route. At the top of the list is Ash Cave, a 700-foot wide horseshoe cave located at the end of a narrow gorge.

Accessible parking is available near the trail to the cave, and there is an accessible pit toilet just over the bridge. The quarter-mile paved trail to the cave runs through a hemlock grove along Ash Creek. At the end of the trail you can roll under the cave's overhang, but after that it's pretty sandy. Still, the view of what's billed as the most impressive recess cave in the state is great.

There is another accessible trail over at Conkles Hollow. Although there is accessible parking in front of the porta-potty and near the picnic area, it's best to park at the far end of the parking lot, as it's closer to the trailhead. The half-mile Gorge Trail starts with an accessible boardwalk, and then transitions into an accessible trail that winds along the bottom of the gorge.

The paved trail goes past several recess caves including haunted Horsehead Grotto and crosses a number of bridges, before it ends when a narrow passage through the rocks blocks wheelchair access. That said, it's worth the walk, as it's a very pleasant shaded trail that wanders past fern lined cliffs and through the surrounding hemlock forest.

And when you're through, head over to the picnic area for a lunch break. There's an accessible picnic table on the grass, and it's a nice place for a midday meal.

Watersong Woods
9180 Bauer Road
Logan, Ohio
(877) 966-3788
www.watersongwoods.com

GPS Coordinates
N 39.59814
W 82.45549

Bathroom in the Melody Cabin

Cornerstone Inn

Nashville, IN

Nashville, Indiana is simply brimming with small town charm. From the quaint shops along the main drag, to the white picket fences that adorn the well-kept homes, it brings to mind the grace and elegance of a bygone era. And so does the 37-room Cornerstone Inn. Although this grand old property was built in 1933, it's seen its fair share of improvements over the years. Today the historic inn gets high marks for both accessibility and ambiance. And since the property is just a short stroll from an impressive assortment of charming shops, unique galleries and eclectic eateries, it's the perfect choice for a Brown County getaway.

Access Details

Although steps grace the front façade of the main building, an accessible entrance is located on the side. Inside, there's elevator access to the dining area, which also serves as a day lobby

The most accessible room — Goshen 1 — is located behind the main building in one of the four-plex cottage units that were added in 2009. Accessible parking is located directly in front of the building, with level access to the front door.

The accessible room features a level threshold, wide doorways and barrier-free pathway access. It's furnished with a king-sized bed with wheelchair access on both sides, a dresser and a dual reclining love seat. Other amenities include a remote controlled gas fireplace and a small refrigerator. There is also level access to a very private screened porch which offers a nice view of the gazebo.

The bathroom has a roll-in shower with a fold-down shower bench, grab bars and a hand-held showerhead. The toilet grab bars are located on the back and left walls (as seated); and the bathroom is also outfitted with a roll-under sink and a standard Jacuzzi tub.

A breakfast buffet is offered in the dining area every morning, and complimentary snacks are available the rest of the day. Guests are also invited to play games, read, watch TV or just visit in this spacious and accessible public area.

Candy's Take

I really like that Goshen 1 lacks the institutional feel that you find in many other accessible rooms. It's very tastefully decorated and that is what really stands out. I also like that it's set back from the main house, as it gives you more privacy. And you just can't beat the location, as it's just a block from Van Buren Street, which is the main drag.

Goshen 1 at the Cornerstone Inn

The Henry Wolfe Covered Bridge at the north entrance to Brown County State Park

Best Fit

The very spacious accessible room has a nice roll-in shower, so it will work for both wheelchair-users and slow walkers. It's a great choice for a girlfriend's getaway (rent out the whole four-plex), but it also makes a good romantic retreat.

Nearby

The number one thing to do in the area is to explore Nashville on foot. Van Buren Street has wide level sidewalks with curb-cuts at every corner, and most of the shops and restaurants have a level entrance.

Make sure and stop in at the Brown County Visitors Center (www.browncounty.com/visitors-center) located on the corner of Main and Van Buren Streets. They have detailed maps of the area, a very helpful staff and free wifi access. And if you find that walking is a bit more tiring than you anticipated, they also rent wheelchairs.

For a real treat, make dinner plans at the Artists Colony Inn (www.artistscolonyinn.com), which features level access from the side courtyard. This local favorite is known for crafting creative dishes from fresh ingredients. Jack's Chicken is a good choice if you're watching calories, while Lucie's Pot Pie is the way to go if you just want to throw caution to the wind.

Save at least one day to explore Brown County State Park (www.browncountystatepark.com), located just south of Nashville. The Friends

Trail, which is located in the middle of the park, is a good choice for wheelers and slow walkers. Constructed by the Friends of Brown County State Park, this barrier-free trail winds though a hardwood forest and features a wide paved pathway, with a short boardwalk section. There are plenty of benches along the way, and an accessible viewing platform at the end of the line.

It's also a good park to see by car, as there are a lot of great windshield views along the way. Don't miss the Henry Wolfe Covered Bridge, which is located at the north entrance. Built in 1838, it was moved to this site from Putnam County in 1932. It's a great photo op, and it's especially scenic when the leaves change colors in the fall.

Cornerstone Inn	**GPS Coordinates**
54 E. Franklin Street	N 39.20603
Nashville, IN 47448	W 86.24617
(812) 988-0300	
www.cornerstoneinn.com	

Toilet and shower in Goshen 1

West Baden Springs Hotel

French Lick, IN

Located about two hours south of Indianapolis, French Lick has long been know for its healing therapeutic waters. So much so, that back in 1855 Lee W. Sinclair opened the Mile Lick Hotel, and people came from all over to enjoy the healing waters. Unfortunately a fire destroyed the hotel in 1901, but Sinclair rebuilt it in a grand fashion in 1902. Over the years that property saw times of boom and bust until it fell into disrepair. Finally in 1994 it was purchased by an investment group, and shortly thereafter it underwent a multimillion dollar renovation. And the good news is, not only was this gem restored to her former glory, but updated access features were also added.

Access Details

This 234-room National Historic Landmark features level access to the front entrance, barrier-free access throughout the atrium, and elevator access to all floors. Room 4231 is a typical accessible room, which boasts lever handles, a lowered peephole, wide doorways and good pathway access. It's furnished with a 27-inch high queen-sized bed with wheelchair access on both sides.

Access features in the bathroom include a low-step shower with a fold-down shower seat, grab bars and a hand-held showerhead. Although there is a six-inch lip on the shower, it's possible to transfer directly to the shower bench without rolling into the shower. It's actually a good design, as the lip prevents the bathroom from flooding, yet the placement of the bench makes for an easy transfer. Other bathroom access features include a toilet with grab bars on the back and left walls (as seated) and a roll-under sink.

The public areas of the hotel are equally accessible, including the spa and pools. There is barrier-free access to the spa which features locker rooms with roll-in showers, and accessible toilets with grab bars. Additionally, the massage tables can be lowered for easier transfers. The sauna has a small one-inch lip, but that's about the biggest access obstacle. There is also barrier-free access to the indoor and outdoor pools, and lift access to both.

There's level access to all the public areas, including Sinclair's restaurant, which is located just off the atrium.

Candy's Take

By far my favorite place at this property is the atrium, as it's an architectural treasure. Patterned after the grand spas of Europe, it features a magnificent 200-foot dome, with six tiers of guest rooms towering over the lobby. Elegantly decorated, it simply exudes bliss; so much so, that I actually felt my heart rate lower as I crossed the threshold. You just can't help but relax there.

Room 4231 at West Baden Springs Hotel

Entrance to West Baden Springs Hotel

Best Fit

The access is excellent at this property and it will work for almost everyone. The one exception is that if you absolutely have to use a rolling shower chair and can't transfer to the shower bench, it just won't work for you. This is a great choice for a romantic getaway or a spa weekend. Additionally, folks who love historic architecture will love it too.

Nearby

For a little stroll down memory lane, be sure and stop in at the old barber shop, just off the atrium. There's level access to this small museum and plenty of room to check out the antique barber chair and shoeshine stand, photos, china and other historic artifacts. And you might even learn a little about the lithium-filled water at French Lick — which was actually bottled and sold as Pluto Water well into the seventies.

Guided tours of the property are also available on Wednesday through Sunday at 10 a.m., 2 p.m. and 4 p.m. The hour-long tour is wheelchair-accessible and includes a good historic overview of the property and allows guests a peek at the lavish interior and stunning gardens. Tickets are available at the Indiana Landmarks museum shop just off the atrium. And if you miss the tour, be sure and take a stroll through the gardens, which are also accessible

Save some time for a look at the sister property, French Lick Springs Hotel, which is located just down the road. Although it's completely different from the West Baden Springs Hotel, the front lobby is equally impressive. It's hard to believe that the mosaic floor was covered with linoleum and the gold leaf wall embellishments were painted over, prior to the renovation. Today, it is returned to its former glory and quite frankly, it's stunning.

There's also barrier-free access to the public areas of the hotel including 1875: The Steakhouse, one of the more formal dining options. And if that's not your cup of tea, there are also several family restaurants, a pizzeria, a deli and even an ice cream parlor on the premises — all of which have good wheelchair access. And if you'd like to try your hand at lady luck, there is good wheelchair access to the adjacent casino.

West Baden Springs Hotel
8670 W State Road 56
French Lick, IN 47432
(812) 936-2100
www.frenchlick.com/hotels/westbaden

GPS Coordinates
N 38.55213
W 86.62057

Bathroom in room 4231 at West Baden Springs Hotel

Coenen Cabin

Two Rivers, WI

Located about an hour-and-a-half north of Milwaukee, the Coenen Cabin sits on the western shore of Lake Michigan, in the middle of Point Beach State Forest. At first glance I didn't really expect much from this "rustic cabin", as it's described as an indoor group camp, and the facilities seemed pretty basic. I was pleasantly surprised, as although the cabin amenities are somewhat standard, the location is excellent. It's far removed from the main campground, with just one other cabin nearby. And if the other cabin happens to be vacant (as it was on our visit) you'll have this lovely piece of real estate all to yourself.

Access Details

There's plenty of room to park on a level dirt space in front of the cabin, with level access up to the front door. It's furnished with eight bunk beds, and can accommodate 16 people. The bottom bunk is just 18 inches high, so it's a good transfer height for wheelers. The cabin also has a large table, a kitchen counter with food cabinets, and a wood burning stove for heat. There are no lights in the cabin, but there is one electrical outlet, and plenty of spots to hang lanterns.

The cabin doesn't have any running water, but fresh water is available from the pump outside the pit toilets, The pit toilets are located next to the cabin, and they feature accessible stalls with grab bars on both sides.

It's also good to note that towels and bedding are not provided.

Additionally, there's a deck out back, and a wheelchair-accessible boardwalk that leads out to a Lake Michigan overlook. It's the perfect place to enjoy the sunset. A large covered picnic shelter, with a charcoal grill and accessible picnic tables, sits next to the cabin; and there is an accessible fire ring at the end of the road.

There are no showers in the cabin (remember it's rustic), but some are located down the road in the main campground. The most accessible choice is the private accessible shower room near campsite 31. You will need to get a key from the camp office to access it, but it has a full five-foot turning radius and is equipped with a 36-inch wide roll-in shower with grab bars, a fold-down shower bench and a hand-held showerhead. There is also a toilet in the shower room, with grab bars on the left and back walls (as seated), as well as a roll-under sink.

Another accessible shower room is located next to campsite 119. This one does not require a key, and it has all the features of the other shower room, except that the shower is 29-inches wide.

Wood burning stove and bunks in the Coenen Cabin

Dining area in the Coenen Cabin

Candy's Take

The boardwalk out to the lake is beautiful, and there is a bench on the overlook where you can sit and enjoy it all. It's very peaceful out there, and the surrounding pine and hemlock forest provides the perfect backdrop to enjoy nature, de-stress and unwind.

Best Fit

The cabin and campground showers will work for wheelchair-users and slow walkers alike. That said, if you absolutely have to have an ensuite bathroom, and don't like campground showers, this property probably isn't a good choice for you. Even though this is an indoor group camp, it's perfect for a small family, and it's very affordable at $60 per night. Both cabins are usually booked in the summer, so try visiting in Fall or Spring for better availability, and if you're lucky, more privacy.

Nearby

There are lots of things to do at Point Beach State Forest. While you're in the main campground, be sure and stop by the Nature Center. There's accessible parking in front, with level access to the front door. Inside, there are a number of interpretive exhibits; and naturalist programs are presented there from Memorial Day to Labor Day. There is also an accessible lakeside picnic area outside.

Don't miss the Rawley Point Lighthouse on your way out. Billed as one of the largest and brightest lighthouses on the Great Lakes, the light sits on a tower that rises 113 feet above the lake surface. Before it was erected, some 26 ships were stranded on the point. A picnic area with two accessible tables and an accessible pit toilet is located nearby. It's a nice place for a picnic lunch, with a good view of the lighthouse, and a perfect addition to a rustic Lake Michigan getaway.

Coenen Cabin
Point Beach State Forest
Two Rivers, WI 54241
(920) 794-7480
dnr.wi.gov/topic/parks/name/pointbeach

GPS Coordinates
N 44.19336
W 87.52637

Pit toilet adjacent to the Coenen Cabin

Wildlife Refuge Cabins
South Range, MI

The brainchild of avid snowmobilers David and Lori Sleeman, the Wildlife Refuge Cabins are located on Highway 26, five miles south of Houghton on Michigan's Upper Peninsula. A lot of thought was put into the design of the six-cabin complex, as Lori really wanted to make one cabin wheelchair-accessible, because she's encountered more than a few disabled snowmobilers in her travels. So the property was built from the ground up to be accessible; and even if you aren't a snowmobiler, you can still enjoy it from spring to fall.

Access Details

There's plenty of room to park a ramped van in front of accessible Cabin 1; however, there's no striped parking. Still the parking area is reserved for that cabin, so there shouldn't be any problem. Cabin 1 features ramp access up to the front porch, and it has a wide doorway and a level threshold.

Inside, there's plenty of room to maneuver a wheelchair around the great room and the adjacent kitchenette. There is a gas fireplace near the sofa, and the kitchenette is equipped with a microwave, refrigerator, sink,

377

and a table with chairs. And if you'd like to cook outside, there's a gas BBQ on the front porch. The bedroom is furnished with an 18-inch high double bed with wheelchair-access on one side, and a bunk bed.

There is level access to the bathroom, which is equipped with a roll-in shower with a fold-down shower bench, grab bars and a hand-held showerhead. The shower has a one-inch lip, but because of the location of the shower bench it's quite doable for most people. The toilet grab bars are located on the back and left walls (as seated) and the bathroom also has a roll-under sink.

There's also barrier-free access to all the public spaces, including the office, the common room and the sauna.

Candy's Take

You don't often find a property with a wheelchair-accessible sauna, so I love that the Sleeman's made sure everyone can access theirs. I also like the mural work by Lori, and the taxidermy and rustic log furnishings in the cabin. It's just a beautiful place to base yourself while you explore Michigan's Upper Peninsula.

Best Fit

The roomy roll-in shower will work for most everyone, and there's plenty of room in the bathroom to maneuver a large power wheelchair or scooter.

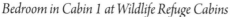

Bedroom in Cabin 1 at Wildlife Refuge Cabins

Shower in Cabin 1 at Wildlife Refuge Cabins

This private cabin is a good choice for a romantic getaway, but if you want to bring along the kids, the bunk bed makes that possible too.

Nearby

Snowmobiling is the big activity in South Range in the winter, but during the rest of the year Pictured Rocks National Lakeshore (www. nps.gov/piro) makes a good day trip. The lakeshore is located about two hours from South Range, and it extends for 42 miles, from Munising to Grand Marais. Along the way you'll be treated to a diverse and beautiful landscape — from sandstone cliffs and rugged beaches, to mountain waterfalls, arid sand dunes and secluded marshes.

Munising Falls, which is just two miles from the western terminus of the route, makes a good first stop. Here you'll find a wide paved 800-foot trail that winds through the forest along a creek before it ends at Munising Falls. There is level access to the viewing platform, and although there are steps to the top of the falls, you can get a great view from the platform.

Sand Point, which is just a mile up the road, offers a completely different look at the natural environment. The half-mile Sand Point Marsh Trail travels through the forest and features interpretive panels and benches along the way. It was constructed by the Youth Conservation Corps in 1989, and allows everyone to get a look at this wetlands habit filled with squirrels, pileated woodpeckers and noble spruce trees.

No trip to Lake Superior is complete without a good look at the famous pictured rocks, and the best vantage point for that is at the Miners Castle Overlook. A paved trail leads from the parking area out to the lower overlook, where you'll get a good look at the mineral stained pictured rocks and a nice view of the Miners Castle formation.

Last but not least, don't miss Lake Superior Overlook and Log Slide Overlook, located just down the road. There's barrier-free access out to both overlooks, which offer good views of Lake Superior and the Au Sable Light Station.

If you continue along Highway 58, you'll exit the park just after you pass the Grand Sable Visitor Center. From there, head over to Grand Marias, then take Highway 77 south to Seney, and loop back to Munising through the Seney National Wildlife Refuge. And don't forget to pack along a picnic lunch, as there are many scenic picnic sites along the route.

Wildlife Refuge Cabins
101 Wildlife Lane
South Range, MI 49963
(906) 482-1001
www.wildliferefugecabins.com

GPS Coordinates
N 47.06993
W 88.64318

Sink and toilet in Cabin 1 at Wildlife Refuge Cabins

22 Accessible Road Trips Driving Vacations
for Wheelers and Slow Walkers

By Candy B. Harrington

Billed as the world's first inclusive road trip book, this detailed resource features 22 driving routes across the United States, with information about wheelchair-accessible sites, lodging options, trails, attractions and restaurants along the way. A great read for anyone who wants to hit the road—disabled or able-bodied—*22 Accessible Road Trips* captures the diversity of America, with off-the-beaten-path finds and unique roadside attractions, as well as must-see metropolitan sights in the gateway cities. www.22accessibleroadtrips. com

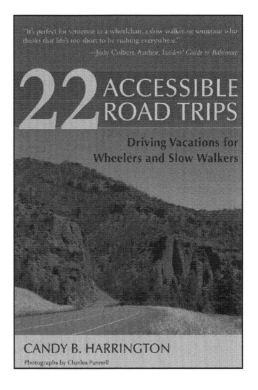

"It's perfect for someone in a wheelchair, a slow walker, or someone who thinks that life's too short to be rushing everywhere."
—Judy Colbert, Author, *Insiders' Guide to Baltimore*

22 ACCESSIBLE ROAD TRIPS
Driving Vacations for Wheelers and Slow Walkers

CANDY B. HARRINGTON
Photographs by Charles Pannell

Made in the USA
San Bernardino, CA
12 June 2015